A Short Time

From Here to Eternity
An Ellen G. White Devotional

Compiled By Doug Baker

TEACH Services, Inc.
PUBLISHING
www.TEACHServices.com • (800) 367-1844

World rights reserved. This book or any portion thereof may not be copied or reproduced in any form or manner whatever, except as provided by law, without the written permission of the publisher, except by a reviewer who may quote brief passages in a review.

The author assumes full responsibility for the accuracy of all facts and quotations as cited in this book. The opinions expressed in this book are the author's personal views and interpretations, and do not necessarily reflect those of the publisher.

This book is provided with the understanding that the publisher is not engaged in giving spiritual, legal, medical, or other professional advice. If authoritative advice is needed, the reader should seek the counsel of a competent professional.

Copyright © 2016 TEACH Services, Inc.
ISBN-13: 978-1-4796-0632-0 (Paperback)
ISBN-13: 978-1-4796-0633-7 (ePub)
ISBN-13: 978-1-4796-0634-4 (Mobi)
Library of Congress Control Number: 2015917331

Published by

TEACH Services, Inc.
PUBLISHING
www.TEACHServices.com • (800) 367-1844

Table of Contents

January 7
February 26
March 43
April 62
May 81
June 100
July 119
August 139
September 159
October 178
November 199
December 219

Here, where the Son of God tabernacled in humanity; where the King of glory lived and suffered and died, — here, when He shall make all things new, the tabernacle of God shall be with men, "and He shall dwell with them, and they shall be His people, and God Himself, shall be with them, and be their God." And through endless ages as the redeemed walk in the light of the Lord, they will praise Him for His unspeakable Gift, Immanuel, "God with us." – E. G. White, Review and Herald, February 25, 1915

Introduction

Seek ye first the kingdom of God, and his righteousness; and all these things shall be added unto you. Matthew 6:33. This is the first great object—the kingdom of heaven, the righteousness of Christ. Other objects to be attained should be secondary to these.

Satan will present the path of holiness as difficult while the paths of worldly pleasure are strewed with flowers. In false and flattering colors will the tempter array the world with its pleasures before you? Vanity is one of the strongest traits of our depraved natures, and he knows that he can appeal to it successfully. He will flatter you through his agents. You may receive praise which will gratify your vanity and foster in you pride and self-esteem, and you may think that with such advantages and attractions it really is a great pity for you to come out from the world and be separate, and become a Christian. … But consider that the pleasures of earth will have an end, and that which you sow you must also reap. Are personal attractions, ability, or talents too valuable to devote to God, the Author of your being, He who watches over you every moment? Are your qualifications too precious to devote to God?

The young urge that they need something to enliven and divert the mind. I saw that there is pleasure in industry, a satisfaction in pursuing a life of usefulness. Some still urge that they must have something … to which the mind can turn for relief and refreshment amid cares and wearing labor. The Christian's hope is just what is needed. Religion will prove to the believer a comforter, a sure guide to the Fountain of true happiness. The young should study the word of God and give themselves to meditation and prayer, and they will find that their spare moments cannot be better employed.

Young friends, you should take time to prove your own selves, whether you are in the love of God. Be diligent to make your calling and election sure.

Seek first the kingdom of God and His righteousness. Make this first and last. Seek most earnestly to know Him whom to know aright is life eternal. Christ and His righteousness is the salvation of the soul.[1]

January 1

In His Image

And God said, Let us make man in our image, after our likeness: … So God created man in his own image, in the image of God created he him; male and female created he them. Genesis 1:26, 27

When Adam came from the Creator's hand, he bore, in his physical, mental, and spiritual nature, a likeness to his Maker. "God created man in His own image" (Genesis 1:27), and it was His purpose that the longer man lived the more fully he should reveal this image—the more fully reflect the glory of the Creator. All his faculties were capable of development; their capacity and vigor were continually to increase. Vast was the scope offered for their exercise, glorious the field opened to their research. The mysteries of the visible universe—the "wondrous works of Him which is perfect in knowledge" (Job 37:16)—invited man's study. Face-to-face, heart-to-heart communion with his Maker was his high privilege. Had he remained loyal to God, all this would have been his forever. Throughout eternal ages he would have continued to gain new treasures of knowledge, to discover fresh springs of happiness, and to obtain clearer and yet clearer conceptions of the wisdom, the power, and the love of God. More and more fully would he have fulfilled the object of his creation, more and more fully have reflected the Creator's glory.[1]

January 2

To Reveal His Glory

Be ye therefore perfect, even as your Father which is in heaven is perfect.
Matthew 5:48

In the creation of man was manifest the agency of a personal God. When God had made man in His image, the human form was perfect in all its arrangements, but it was without life. Then a personal, self-existing God breathed into that form the breath of life, and man became a living, breathing, intelligent being. All parts of the human organism were put in action. The heart, the arteries, the veins, the tongue, the hands, the feet, the senses, the perceptions of the mind—all began their work, and all were placed under law. Man became a living soul. Through Jesus Christ a personal God created man and endowed him with intelligence and power.

Our substance was not hid from Him when we were made in secret. His eyes saw our substance, yet being imperfect; and in His book all our members were written, when as yet there were none of them.

Above all lower orders of being, God designed that man, the crowning work of His creation, should express His thought and reveal His glory.[2]

Man was originally endowed with noble powers and a well-balanced mind. He was perfect in his being, and in harmony with God. His thoughts were pure, his aims holy.[3]

January 3

Greater Works than These

Verily, verily, I say unto you, He that believeth on me, the works that I do shall he do also; and greater works than these shall he do; because I go unto my Father.
John 14:12

Man was the crowning act of the creation of God, made in the image of God, and designed to be a counterpart of God; … Man is very dear to God, because he was formed in his own image.

In order to understand the value which God places upon man, we need to comprehend the plan of redemption, the costly sacrifice which our Saviour made to save the human race from eternal ruin. … The Lord gave his only begotten Son to ransom us from sin. … Our character is to be modeled after the divine similitude, and to be reformed by that faith that works by love and purifies the soul. The grace of God will beautify, ennoble, and sanctify the character. The servant of the Lord who works intelligently will be successful. Our Saviour said, "Greater works than these shall ye do; because I go unto my Father." What are these "greater works"? If our lips are touched with the living coal from off the altar, we shall reveal to the world the wonderful love manifested by God in giving Jesus, his only begotten Son, to the world, "that whosoever believeth in him should not perish, but have everlasting life."[4]

January 4

Manifested in Him

Believe me that I am in the Father, and the Father in me: or else believe me for the very works' sake. John 14:11

"Believe Me that I am in the Father, and the Father in Me: or else believe Me for the very works' sake." ... Christ's work testified to His divinity. Through Him the Father had been revealed. ...

Christ was seeking to lead them from their low condition of faith to the experience they might receive if they truly realized what He was, — God in human flesh. He desired them to see that their faith must lead up to God, and be anchored there. ...

"Verily, verily, I say unto you," Christ continued, "He that believeth on Me, the works that I do shall he do also." The Saviour was deeply anxious for His disciples to understand for what purpose His divinity was united to humanity. He came to the world to display the glory of God, that man might be uplifted by its restoring power. God was manifested in Him that He might be manifested in them. Jesus revealed no qualities, and exercised no powers, that men may not have through faith in Him. His perfect humanity is that which all His followers may possess, if they will be in subjection to God as He was.[5]

January 5

One in Him

That they all may be one; as thou, Father, art in me, and I in thee, that they also may be one in us: that the world may believe that thou hast sent me. John 17:21

What an argument of power is the prayer, "That they all may be one; as Thou, Father, art in Me, and I in Thee, that they also may be one in Us: that the world may believe that Thou hast sent me."

I have repeated this wonderful statement; for it contains the very evidence that we are to present to the world, — the perfection of unity in the followers of Christ. The members of the church of God must reach this perfection. ... The Saviour has presented before us how much will be gained in working out the unity that will join one believer to another in the perfection of Christian love. ...

Those who enter heaven must be one with Christ. ... Here we are to be stamped with the image and superscription of God. The virtue of the grace of Christ will perfect the character of every believer who truly accepts Him. All true disciples are made members of the royal family. All have the new heart, and all blend in perfect harmony. ... Their manner of expression may not be the same, but their one desire is for the highest end in this life, — the sanctification of the same Spirit. They love as brethren.[6]

January 6

More than Recovery

But he was wounded for our transgressions, he was bruised for our iniquities: the chastisement of our peace was upon him; and with his stripes we are healed.
Isaiah 53:5

Christ was treated as we deserve, that we might be treated as He deserves. He was condemned for our sins, in which He had no share, that we might be justified by His righteousness, in which we had no share. He suffered the death which was ours, that we might receive the life which was His. "With His stripes we are healed."

By His life and His death, Christ has achieved even more than recovery from the ruin wrought through sin. It was Satan's purpose to bring about an eternal separation between God and man; but in Christ we become more closely united to God than if we had never fallen. In taking our nature, the Saviour has bound Himself to humanity by a tie that is never to be broken. Through the eternal ages He is linked with us. ... God has adopted human nature in the person of His Son, and has carried the same into the highest heaven. It is the "Son of man" who shares the throne of the universe. ... He who is "holy, harmless, undefiled, separate from sinners," is not ashamed to call us brethren. Heb. 7:26; 2:11. In Christ the family of earth and the family of heaven are bound together. Christ glorified is our brother. Heaven is enshrined in humanity, and humanity is enfolded in the bosom of Infinite Love.[7]

January 7

To Know Him

And this is life eternal, that they might know thee the only true God, and Jesus Christ, whom thou hast sent. John 17:3

In order to understand what is comprehended in the work of education, we need to consider both the nature of man and the purpose of God in creating him. We need to consider also the change in man's condition through the coming in of a knowledge of evil, and God's plan for still fulfilling His glorious purpose in the education of the human race.

When Adam came from the Creator's hand, he bore, in his physical, mental, and spiritual nature, a likeness to his Maker. "God created man in His own image" (Genesis 1:27), and it was His purpose that the longer man lived the more fully he should reveal this image —the more fully reflect the glory of the Creator. ... More and more fully would he have fulfilled the object of his creation, more and more fully have reflected the Creator's glory. ...

By infinite love and mercy the plan of salvation had been devised, and a life of probation was granted. To restore in man the image of his Maker, to bring him back to the perfection in which he was created, to promote the development of body, mind, and soul, that the divine purpose in his creation might be realized — this was to be the work of redemption. This is the object of education, the great object of life.[8]

January 8

Fellowship with Christ

And I have declared unto them thy name, and will declare it: that the love wherewith thou hast loved me may be in them, and I in them. John 17:26

"The light of the knowledge of the glory of God" is seen "in the face of Jesus Christ." From the days of eternity the Lord Jesus Christ was one with the Father; He was "the image of God," the image of His greatness and majesty, "the outshining of His glory." It was to manifest this glory that He came to our world. To this sin-darkened earth He came to reveal the light of God's love, — to be "God with us." Therefore it was prophesied of Him, "His name shall be called Immanuel."

By coming to dwell with us, Jesus was to reveal God both to men and to angels. ... In His prayer for His disciples He says, "I have declared unto them Thy name ... that the love wherewith Thou hast loved Me may be in them, and I in them." ... It will be seen that the glory shining in the face of Jesus is the glory of self-sacrificing love. ...

Heavenly beings woo the hearts of men; they bring to this dark world light from the courts above; by gentle and patient ministry they move upon the human spirit, to bring the lost into a fellowship with Christ which is even closer than they themselves can know.[9]

January 9

The Word Made Flesh

And the Word was made flesh, and dwelt among us, (and we beheld his glory, the glory as of the only begotten of the Father,) full of grace and truth. John 1:14

When Adam's sin plunged the race into hopeless misery, God might have cut Himself loose from fallen beings. ... But He did not do this. Instead of banishing them from His presence, He came still nearer to the fallen race. He gave His Son to become bone of our bone, and flesh of our flesh. "The Word was made flesh, and dwelt among us (and we beheld His glory, the glory as of the only begotten of the Father), full of grace and truth." Christ by His human relationship to men drew them close to God. He clothed His divine nature with the garb of humanity, and demonstrated before the heavenly universe, before the unfallen worlds, how much God loves the children of men.

The gift of God to man is beyond computation. Nothing was withheld. ... In the gift of Christ He gave all heaven.

Thus it is that God desires to fulfil for us His purpose of grace. By the power of His love, through obedience, fallen man, a worm of the dust, is to be transformed, fitted to be a member of the heavenly family, a companion, through eternal ages, of God and Christ and the holy angels.[11]

January 10

He Must Increase

He must increase, but I must decrease. John 3:30

Looking in faith to the Redeemer, John had risen to the height of self-abnegation. He sought not to attract men to himself, but to lift their thoughts higher and still higher, until they should rest upon the Lamb of God. ...

Love for self will be swallowed up in love for Christ. No rivalry will mar the precious cause of the gospel. [Christ's disciples] will recognize that it is their work to proclaim, as did John the Baptist, "Behold the Lamb of God, which taketh away the sin of the world." John 1:29. ...

Christ could say, "I seek not Mine own will, but the will of the Father which hath sent Me." John 5:30. ...

So [it is] with the followers of Christ. We can receive of heaven's light only as we are willing to be emptied of self. We cannot discern the character of God, or accept Christ by faith, unless we consent to the bringing into captivity of every thought to the obedience of Christ. To all who do this the Holy Spirit is given without measure. In Christ "dwelleth all the fullness of the Godhead bodily, and in Him ye are made full." Col. 2:9, 10, R. V.[10]

January 11

Shortly Come to Pass

The Revelation of Jesus Christ ... to shew unto his servants things which must shortly come to pass ... Rev. 1:1

The risen Saviour made His presence known to John; and the testimony then given him is given also to us. God would have us search the Scriptures, that we may know what will be in the last days of this earth's history. ...

Grace be unto you, and peace ... from Jesus Christ, who is the faithful witness, and the first begotten of the dead, and the prince of the kings of the earth. Unto him that loved us, and washed us from our sins in his own blood, And hath made us kings and priests unto God and his Father; to him be glory and dominion for ever and ever. Amen. Behold ... every eye shall see him ... and all kindreds of the earth shall wail because of him. Even so, Amen.

I was in the Spirit on the Lord's day, and heard ... a great voice, ... Saying, I am Alpha and Omega, ... What thou seest, write in a book, ... And ... I saw ... one like unto the Son of man, ... And when I saw him, I fell at his feet as dead. And he laid his right hand upon me, saying unto me, Fear not; I am the first and the last: I am he that liveth, and was dead; and, behold, I am alive for evermore, Amen; and have the keys of hell and of death.

This is a most powerful testimony, but its true significance is but dimly discerned. Let the student of Scripture carefully ponder every word in the first chapter of Revelation, for every sentence and every word is of weight and consequence.[12]

January 12

Revealing Christ

And he said unto me, These sayings are faithful and true: and the Lord God of the holy prophets sent his angel to shew unto his servants the things which must shortly be done. Revelation 22:6

The Father in heaven desires that the world shall see Christ in his followers. Life and immortality are to be brought to light through those who are one with God in Christ. ... Constantly we are to behold him who lived among men a life of perfect obedience. And the more closely we study him, the more nearly shall we resemble him in character, and the greater will be our efficiency in working for others. ...

In order to do intelligently the solemn work committed to us, we must hide self in Christ. We have a short time in which to accomplish the work that is essential. ... I am instructed to say to all our people, Let your light so shine in words and deeds, that you will reveal that truth is cherished in the heart. ...

Those who labor for souls need to remember that they are pledged to co-operate with Christ, to obey his directions, to follow his guidance. Every hour they are to ask for and to receive power from on high. ... They will go forth clothed with holy zeal, and their efforts will be accompanied by a power proportionate to the importance of the message they proclaim.[13]

January 13

His Work In You

[H]e which hath begun a good work in you will perform it until the day of Jesus Christ: Philippians 1:6

As Christ draws [men] to look upon his cross, to look upon him whom their sins have pierced, the commandment comes home to the conscience. The wickedness of their life, the deep-seated sin of the soul, is revealed to them. They begin to comprehend something of the righteousness of Christ, and exclaim, "Was all this love, all this suffering, all this humiliation demanded that we might not perish, but have everlasting life?" They then understand that it is the goodness of God that leadeth to repentance. A repentance such as this lies beyond the reach of our own powers to accomplish; it is obtained only from Christ, who ascended up on high, and has given gifts unto men. Christ is the source of every right impulse. He is the only one who can arouse in the natural heart enmity against sin. He is the source of our power if we would be saved. No soul can repent without the grace of Christ. The sinner may pray that he may know how to repent. God reveals Christ to the sinner, and when he sees the purity of the Son of God, he is not ignorant of the character of sin. By faith in the work and power of Christ, enmity against sin and Satan is created in his heart. Those whom God pardons are first made penitent.

The pleasing fable that all there is to do is to believe, has destroyed thousands and tens of thousands, because many have called that faith which is not faith, but simply a dogma.[14]

January 14

Not One In One Hundred

Go ye therefore, and teach all nations, baptizing them in the name of the Father, and of the Son, and of the Holy Ghost: Teaching them to observe all things whatsoever I have commanded you: ... Matthew 28:19, 20

The Word of God must not be kept apart from our life. It must be entertained in the mind, welcomed in the heart, and be cherished, loved, and obeyed. We need also much more knowledge; we need to be enlightened in regard to the plan of salvation. There is not one in one hundred who understands for himself the Bible truth on this subject that is so necessary to our present and eternal welfare. When light begins to shine forth to make clear the plan of redemption to the people, the enemy works with all diligence that the light may be shut away from the hearts of men. If we come to the Word of God with a teachable, humble spirit, the rubbish of error will be swept away, and gems of truth, long hidden from our eyes, will be discovered. [15]

We should work as did Jesus, departing from our own pleasure, turning away from Satan's bribes, despising ease, and abhorring selfishness, that we may seek and save that which is lost, bringing souls from darkness into light, into the sunshine of God's love. We have been commissioned to go forth and preach the gospel to every creature. We are to bring to the lost the tidings that Christ can forgive sin, can renew the nature, can clothe the soul in the garments of his righteousness, bring the sinner to his right mind, and teach him and fit him up to be a laborer together with God.[16]

January 15

Arise Shine

Arise, shine; for thy light is come, and the glory of the LORD is risen upon thee.
Isaiah 60:1

The Lord in compassion is seeking to enlighten the understanding of those who are now groping in the darkness of error. He is delaying his judgments upon an impenitent world, in order that his light-bearers may seek and save that which is lost. He is now calling upon his church on the earth to awake from the lethargy that Satan has sought to bring upon them, and fulfil their heaven-appointed work of enlightening the world. His message to his church at this time is, "Arise, shine; for thy light is come, and the glory of the Lord is risen upon thee." To meet the conditions existing at the time when darkness covers the earth, and gross darkness the people, the church of God has been commissioned to co-operate with God in shedding abroad the light of Bible truth. To those who seek to do their part faithfully as bearers of precious light, is given the assurance: "The Lord shall arise upon thee, and his glory shall be seen upon thee. And the Gentiles shall come to thy light, and kings to the brightness of thy rising."

The world today is in crying need of a revelation of Christ Jesus in the person of his saints. … the lives of [church] members, sanctified by the Spirit of truth, are to bear witness to the verity of the messages proclaimed. [17]

January 16

Stand as Lights

He hath shewed thee, O man, what is good; and what doth the LORD require of thee, but to do justly, and to love mercy, and to walk humbly with thy God?
Micah 6:8

Every one is to keep himself separate from the world, which is full of iniquity. We are not to walk with God for a time, and then part from his company, and walk in the sparks of our own kindling. There must be a firm continuance, a perseverance in acts of faith. We are to praise God, to show forth his glory in a righteous character. …

It is time we were more intense in our devotion. To us is committed the arduous, but happy, glorious work of revealing Christ to those who are in darkness. We are called to proclaim the special truths for this time. For all this the outpouring of the Spirit is essential.

God desires his people to place themselves in right relation to him … to reveal to every struggling soul in the world what it means "to do justly, and to love mercy, and to walk humbly" with their God. …

In order to stand as lights in the world, they need to have the clear light of the Sun of Righteousness constantly shining upon them. Ever are they to remember that all about them is a world lying in darkness, and perishing for lack of knowledge.[18]

January 17

Study Daniel and Revelation

I saw another mighty angel come down from heaven… And he had in his hand a little book open: Revelation 10:1, 2

The Lord … desires us to enlist our interests in his cause, as Daniel did. We should receive great benefits from a study of the book of Daniel in connection with the Revelation. Daniel studied the prophecies. He earnestly sought to know their meaning. He prayed and fasted for heavenly light. And the glory of God was revealed to him in even greater measure than he could endure. We are in equal need of divine illumination. God has called us to give the last message of warning to the world. There will be voices heard on every side to divert the attention of God's people with new theories. We need to give the trumpet a certain sound. We do not half realize what is before us. If the books of Daniel and the Revelation were studied with earnest prayer, we should have a better knowledge of the perils of the last days, and would be better prepared for the work before us — we should be prepared to unite with Christ and to work in his lines.[19]

These books should be published together in pamphlet form, with a few explanations added, and they should be circulated everywhere. The words of inspiration will do their appointed work; for the Holy Spirit will impress hearts in regard to the prophecies given.[20]

January 18

Daniel Revealed

[T]here is a God in heaven that revealeth secrets, and maketh known ... what shall be in the latter days. Daniel 2:28

I tried to present to the people the short time we have in which to work. I tried to present before them the necessity of prayer, earnest, heart-felt prayer. ...

The things revealed to Daniel were afterward complemented by the revelation made to John on the isle of Patmos. These two books should be carefully perused. Twice Daniel inquired, How long shall it be to the end of time? ...

Daniel stood in his lot to bear his testimony, which was sealed until the time of the end, when the first angel's message should be proclaimed to our world. These matters are of infinite importance in these last days, but while "many shall be purified, and made white, and tried," "the wicked shall do wickedly: and none of the wicked shall understand."

How true this is. Sin is the transgression of the law of God, and those in the denominational churches who will not accept the light in regard to the law of God will not understand the proclamation of the first, second, and third angel's messages. The book of Daniel is unsealed in the revelation to John, and carries us forward to the last scenes of this earth's history.[21]

January 19

Blessed is He...

Behold, I come quickly: blessed is he that keepeth the sayings of the prophecy of this book. Revelation 22:7

Daniel and Revelation must be studied, as well as the other prophecies of the Old and New Testaments. ... The Holy Spirit, shining upon the sacred page, will open our understanding that we may know what is truth.[22]

Rich blessings will come to him who reads and hears the words of this prophecy, [Revelation] and keeps those things which are written therein. ...

When the books of Daniel and Revelation are better understood, believers will have an entirely different religious experience. They will be given such glimpses of the open gates of heaven that heart and mind will be impressed in regard to the character all must develop in order to realize the blessedness which is to be the reward of the pure in heart. The Lord will bless all who will seek humbly and meekly to understand that which is revealed in the Revelation. This book contains so much that is large with immortality and full of glory that all who read and search it earnestly receive the blessing to those "that hear the words of this prophecy, and keep those things which are written therein."

One thing will certainly be understood from the study of Revelation – that the connection between God and His people is close and decided.[23]

January 20

The Sanctuary

I will meditate also of all thy work, and talk of thy doings. Thy way, O God, is in the sanctuary... Psalm 77:12, 13

The significance of the Jewish economy is not yet fully comprehended. Truths vast and profound are shadowed forth in its rites and symbols. The gospel is the key that unlocks its mysteries. Through a knowledge of the plan of redemption, its truths are opened to the understanding. Far more than we do, it is our privilege to understand these wonderful themes. We are to comprehend the deep things of God. Angels desire to look into the truths that are revealed to the people who with contrite hearts are searching the word of God, and praying for greater lengths and breadths and depths and heights of the knowledge which He alone can give. [24]

As we near the close of this world's history, the prophecies relating to the last days especially demand our study. The last book of the New Testament scriptures is full of truth that we need to understand.

The subject of the sanctuary and the investigative judgment should be clearly understood by the people of God. All need a knowledge for themselves of the position and work of their great High Priest. Otherwise it will be impossible for them to exercise the faith which is essential at this time or to occupy the position which God designs them to fill.[25]

January 21

Within the Veil

Which hope we have as an anchor of the soul, both sure and stedfast, and which entereth into that within the veil; Hebrews 6:19

The sanctuary in heaven is the very center of Christ's work in behalf of men. ... It opens to view the plan of redemption, bringing us down to the very close of time and revealing the triumphant issue of the contest between righteousness and sin. It is of the utmost importance that all should thoroughly investigate these subjects and be able to give an answer to everyone that asketh them a reason of the hope that is in them.

The intercession of Christ in man's behalf in the sanctuary above is as essential to the plan of salvation as was His death upon the cross. ... We must by faith enter within the veil, "whither the forerunner is for us entered." Hebrews 6:20. There the light from the cross of Calvary is reflected. There we may gain a clearer insight into the mysteries of redemption.[26]

The correct understanding of the ministration in the heavenly sanctuary is the foundation of our faith.[27]

The mediatorial work of Christ, the grand and holy mysteries of redemption, are not studied or comprehended by the people who claim to have light in advance of every other people on the face of the earth.[28]

January 22

Open the Door

... I stand at the door, and knock: if any man hear my voice, and open the door, I will come in to him ... Revelation 3:20

When the books of Daniel and Revelation are better understood, believers will have an entirely different religious experience. They will be given such glimpses of the open gates of heaven that heart and mind will be impressed in regard to the character all must develop in order to realize the blessedness which is to be the reward of the pure in heart. The Lord will bless all who will seek humbly and meekly to understand that which is revealed in the Revelation. This book contains so much that is large with immortality and full of glory that all who read and search it earnestly receive the blessing to those "that hear the words of this prophecy, and keep those things which are written therein."[29]

The Laodicean message has been sounding. Take this message in all its phases and sound it forth to the people wherever Providence opens the way. Justification by faith and the righteousness of Christ are the themes to be presented to a perishing world. Oh, that you may open the door of your heart to Jesus! The voice of Jesus, the great vendor of heavenly treasures, is calling to you, "I counsel thee to buy of Me gold tried in the fire, that thou mayest be rich; and white raiment, that thou mayest be clothed."[30]

January 23

Oil for the Lamp

And the foolish said unto the wise, Give us of your oil; for our lamps are gone out. Matthew 25:8

In the parable, all the ten virgins went out to meet the bridegroom. All had lamps and vessels for oil. For a time there was seen no difference between them. So with the church that lives just before Christ's second coming. All have a knowledge of the Scriptures. All have heard the message of Christ's near approach, and confidently expect His appearing. But as in the parable, so it is now. A time of waiting intervenes, faith is tried; and when the cry is heard, "Behold, the Bridegroom cometh; go ye out to meet Him," many are unready. They have no oil in their vessels with their lamps. They are destitute of the Holy Spirit.

Without the Spirit of God a knowledge of His word is of no avail. … One may be familiar with the commands and promises of the Bible; but unless the Spirit of God sets the truth home, the character will not be transformed. Without the enlightenment of the Spirit, men will not be able to distinguish truth from error, and they will fall under the masterful temptations of Satan.[31]

The class represented by the foolish virgins are not hypocrites. They have a regard for the truth … but they have not yielded themselves to the Holy Spirit's working.[32]

January 24

Cold or Hot?

So then because thou art lukewarm, and neither cold nor hot, I will spue thee out of my mouth. Revelation 3:16

Many of the young have not a fixed principle to serve God. They do not exercise faith. They sink under every cloud. They have no power of endurance. They do not grow in grace. They appear to keep the commandments of God. They make now and then a formal prayer and are called Christians. Their parents are so anxious for them that they accept anything which appears favorable, and do not labor with them, and teach them that the carnal mind must die. They encourage them to come along and act a part; but they fail to lead them to search their own hearts diligently, to examine themselves, and to count the cost of what it is to be a Christian. The result is, the young profess to be Christians without sufficiently trying their motives.

Says the True Witness: "I would thou wert cold or hot. So then because thou art lukewarm, and neither cold nor hot, I will spew thee out of My mouth." Satan is willing that you should be Christians in name, for you can suit his purpose better. If you have a form and not true godliness, he can use you to decoy others into the same self-deceived way. Some poor souls will look to you, instead of looking to the Bible standard, and will come up no higher. They are as good as you, and are satisfied.[33]

January 25

Be Not Deceived

... lovers of pleasures more than lovers of God; having a form of godliness, but denying the power thereof... 2 Timothy 3:4, 5

People will show what power affects their hearts and controls their actions. If it is the power of divine truth, it will lead to good works. It will elevate the receiver, and make him noblehearted and generous, like his divine Lord. But if evil angels control the heart, it will be seen in various ways. The fruit will be selfishness, covetousness, pride, and evil passions.

The heart is deceitful above all things, and desperately wicked. ... Some ... seem to think that a profession of the truth will save them. When they subdue those sins which God hates, Jesus will come in and sup with them and they with Him. They will then draw divine strength from Jesus, and will grow up in Him...

Many, I saw, were flattering themselves that they were good Christians, who have not a single ray of light from Jesus. They know not what it is to be renewed by the grace of God. They have no living experience for themselves in the things of God. And I saw that the Lord was whetting His sword in heaven to cut them down. Oh, that every lukewarm professor could realize the clean work that God is about to make among His professed people![34]

January 26

The Easy Way

For we wrestle not against flesh and blood, but against principalities, against powers, against the rulers of the darkness of this world, against spiritual wickedness in high places. Ephesians 6:4

Some — yes, a large number — have a theoretical knowledge of religious truth, but have never felt the renewing power of divine grace upon their own hearts. These persons are ever slow to heed the testimonies of warning, reproof, and instruction indicted by the Holy Spirit. …

They may read the Bible, but its threatenings do not alarm or its promises win them. They approve things that are excellent, yet they follow the way in which God has forbidden them to go. ….

To become a disciple of Christ is to deny self and follow Jesus through evil as well as good report. Few are doing this now. …

The Christian life is a warfare. The apostle Paul speaks of wrestling against principalities and powers as he fought the good fight of faith. … A religious life once presented difficulties, and demanded self-denial. All is made very easy now. And why is this? — The professed people of God have compromised with the powers of darkness.[35]

January 27

A Lack of Knowledge

My people are destroyed for lack of knowledge: because thou hast rejected knowledge, I will also reject thee, that thou shalt be no priest to me: seeing thou hast forgotten the law of thy God, I will also forget thy children. Hosea 4:6

Young Sabbathkeepers are given to pleasure seeking. I saw that there is not one in twenty who knows what experimental religion is. They are constantly grasping after something to satisfy their desire for change, for amusement; and unless they are undeceived and their sensibilities aroused so that they can say from the heart, "I count all things but loss for the excellency of the knowledge of Christ Jesus my Lord," they are not worthy of Him and will come short of everlasting life. The young, generally, are in a terrible deception, and yet they profess godliness. Their unconsecrated lives are a reproach to the Christian name; their example is a snare to others. They hinder the sinner, for in nearly every respect they are no better than unbelievers. They have the word of God, but its warnings, admonitions, reproofs, and corrections are unheeded, as are also the encouragements and promises to the obedient and faithful. ... Their minds are filled with nonsense. Their conversation is only empty, vain talk. They have a keen ear for music, and Satan knows what organs to excite to animate, engross, and charm the mind so that Christ is not desired. The spiritual longings of the soul for divine knowledge, for a growth in grace, are wanting.[36]

January 28

Overcoming

He that overcometh shall inherit all things; and I will be his God, and he shall be my son. Revelation 21:7

I make an appeal to the youthful disciples of Christ to arouse, no longer to indulge in pleasure-seeking, in self-love and ease; no longer be controlled by inclination, and by the lusts of the carnal heart. Do not settle down in Satan's easy chair, and say that there is no use, you cannot cease to sin, that there is no power in you to overcome. There is no power in you apart from Christ, but it is your privilege to have Christ abiding in your heart by faith, and he can overcome sin in you, when you cooperate with his efforts, putting your will on the side of God's will. He says, "I have overcome the world." In him you lift up the banner as one who conquers. "We are more than conquerors through him that loved us." You may have a constant testimony in your life to the power of the grace of Christ, and may understand what are the operations of the Spirit of God. You may be living epistles, known and read of all men. You are not to be a dead letter, but a living one, testifying to the world that Jesus is able to save.

My prayer to God is that the converting power of his Holy Spirit may come upon our youth, that they may become working agents to win scores of youth to Jesus Christ, that they may be among the number who shall be accounted wise, who shall "shine as the brightness of the firmament," and "as the stars forever and ever."[37]

January 29

Write Unto the Church

... These things saith the Amen, the faithful and true witness, the beginning of the creation of God; Revelation 3:8

I saw that the testimony to the Laodiceans applied to God's people at the present time, and the reason it has not accomplished a greater work, is because of the hardness of their hearts. But God has given the message time to do its work. The heart must be purified from sins which have so long shut Jesus out. … When it was first presented, it led to close examination of heart. Sins were confessed, and the people of God were stirred everywhere. Nearly all believed that this message would end in the loud cry of the third angel. But as they failed to see the powerful work accomplished in a short time, many lost the effect of the message. I saw that this message would not accomplish its work in a few short months. It was designed to arouse the people of God, to discover to them their backslidings, and lead to zealous repentance, that they might be favored with the presence of Jesus, and be fitted for the loud cry of the third angel. …

If the counsel of the True Witness had been fully heeded, God would have wrought for his people in greater power. … I saw that God would prove his people. Patiently Jesus bears with them, and does not spue them out of his mouth in a moment. Said the angel, "God is weighing his people." If the message had been of as short duration as many of us supposed, there would have been no time for God's people to develop character.[38]

January 30

A Religion of Vanity

Wherefore the Lord said, Forasmuch as this people draw near me with their mouth, and with their lips do honour me, but have removed their heart far from me… Isaiah 29:13

The church at this time should have the faith once delivered to the saints, which will enable them to say boldly: "God is mine helper;" "I can do all things through Christ which strengtheneth me." The Lord bids us arise and go forward. Whenever the church at any period have forsaken their sins, and believed and walked in the truth, they have been honored of God. There is in faith and humble obedience a power that the world cannot withstand. The order of God's providence in relation to His people is progression—continual advancement in the perfection of Christian character, in the way of holiness, rising higher and higher in the clear light and knowledge and love of God, to the very close of time. Oh! why are we ever learning only the first principles of the doctrine of Christ?

The Lord has rich blessings for the church if its members will seek earnestly to arouse from this perilous lukewarmness. A religion of vanity, words devoid of vitality, a character destitute of moral strength,—these are pointed out in the solemn message addressed by the True Witness to the churches, warning them against pride, worldliness, formalism, and self-sufficiency. To him that says, "I am rich, and increased with goods, and have need of nothing," the Lord of heaven declares, Thou "knowest not that thou art wretched, and miserable, and poor, and blind, and naked."[39]

January 31

Be Not Deceived

Take heed to yourselves, that your heart be not deceived, and ye turn aside, and serve other gods, and worship them; Deuteronomy 11:16

What greater deception can come upon human minds than a confidence that they are right, when they are all wrong? The message of the True Witness finds the people of God in a sad deception, yet honest in that deception. ... While those addressed are flattering themselves that they are in an exalted spiritual condition, the message of the True Witness breaks their security by the startling denunciation of their true situation of spiritual blindness, poverty, and wretchedness. ...

It is difficult for those who feel secure in their attainments, who are believing themselves to be rich in spiritual knowledge, to receive the message which declares that they are deceived and in need of every spiritual grace. ...

We are, as a people ... very much wanting in Bible humility, patience, faith, love, self-denial, watchfulness, and a spirit of sacrifice. ... The plain message of rebuke to the Laodiceans is not received. Many cling to their doubts and their darling sins, while they are in so great a deception as to talk and feel that they are in need of nothing. ... They lack almost every essential qualification necessary to perfect Christian character. They have not a practical knowledge of Bible truth, which leads to lowliness of life, and a conformity of their will to the will of Christ.[40]

February 1

Self Exhaltation

For if a man think himself to be something, when he is nothing, he deceiveth himself. Galatians 6:3

How many have altogether too high an opinion of their own ability! lifting up themselves, extolling self, while they censure and condemn their brethren, … They feel sufficient to dictate, look upon themselves as wise, and capable of accomplishing great things, able to tell others what to do, full of confidence in their own ways and wisdom, when the genuine truth is, they are not acquainted with themselves, and do not know half as much as they should know or as they think they know. They are really elevating themselves. While such deceive others by exalting their acquirements and their self-sufficiency, they deceive their own souls, and will meet with the greatest loss themselves. They are not free from blunders or mistakes, and fall under temptations while they self-confidently think themselves standing securely.

The exhortation of the apostle (Phil. 2:3) is, "Let nothing be done through strife or vainglory; but in lowliness of mind let each esteem other better than themselves. … Let this mind be in you, which was also in Christ Jesus." … If the gospel of Christ has indeed benefited you, then reveal this in striving for harmony and love. Do nothing through strife or vainglory. Do not do anything that will create feelings of discord and strife.¹

February 2

Return to Me

*Return, ye backsliding children, and I will heal your backslidings. …
Jeremiah 3:22*

Oh, how precious was this promise, as it was shown to me in vision! "I will come in to him, and will sup with him, and he with Me." Oh, the love, the wondrous love of God! After all our lukewarmness and sins He says: "Return unto Me, and I will return unto thee, and will heal all thy backslidings." This was repeated by the angel a number of times. "Return unto Me, and I will return unto thee, and will heal all thy backslidings." …

"To him that overcometh will I grant to sit with Me in My throne, even as I also overcame, and am set down with My Father in His throne." We can overcome. Yes; fully, entirely. Jesus died to make a way of escape for us, that we might overcome every evil temper, every sin, every temptation, and sit down at last with Him.

It is our privilege to have faith and salvation. The power of God has not decreased. His power, I saw, would be just as freely bestowed now as formerly. It is the church of God that have lost their faith to claim, their energy to wrestle, as did Jacob, crying: "I will not let Thee go, except Thou bless me." Enduring faith has been dying away. It must be revived in the hearts of God's people. There must be a claiming of the blessing of God. Faith, living faith, always bears upward to God and glory; unbelief, downward to darkness and death.[2]

February 3

Help Mine Unbelief

... if thou canst do any thing, have compassion on us, and help us. Mark 9:22

By sin we have been severed from the life of God. Our souls are palsied. Of ourselves we are no more capable of living a holy life than was the impotent man capable of walking. There are many who realize their helplessness, and who long for that spiritual life which will bring them into harmony with God; they are vainly striving to obtain it. In despair they cry, "O wretched man that I am! who shall deliver me from this body of death?" Romans 7:24, margin. Let these desponding, struggling ones look up. The Saviour is bending over the purchase of His blood, saying with inexpressible tenderness and pity, "Wilt thou be made whole?" ... Whatever may be the evil practice, the master passion which through long indulgence binds both soul and body, Christ is able and longs to deliver. He will impart life to the soul that is "dead in trespasses." Ephesians 2:1. ...[3]

It is faith that connects us with heaven, and brings us strength for coping with the powers of darkness. ... But many feel that they lack faith, and therefore they remain away from Christ. Let these souls, in their helpless unworthiness, cast themselves upon the mercy of their compassionate Saviour. ... He who healed the sick and cast out demons when He walked among men, is the same mighty redeemer today. Faith comes by the Word of God. ... Cast yourself at His feet with the cry, "Lord, I believe; help Thou mine unbelief."[4]

February 4

Buy of Me

I counsel thee to buy of me gold tried in the fire, that thou mayest be rich; and white raiment, that thou mayest be clothed, and that the shame of thy nakedness do not appear; and anoint thine eyes with eyesalve, that thou mayest see.
Revelation 3:18

Faith and love are the true riches, the pure gold which the True Witness counsels the lukewarm to buy. However rich we may be in earthly treasure, all our wealth will not enable us to buy the precious remedies that cure the disease of the soul called lukewarmness. Intellect and earthly riches were powerless to remove the defects of the Laodicean church, or to remedy their deplorable condition. …

The gold here recommended as having been tried in the fire is faith and love. It makes the heart rich; for it has been purged until it is pure, and the more it is tested the more brilliant is its luster. The white raiment is purity of character, the righteousness of Christ imparted to the sinner. This is indeed a garment of heavenly texture that can be bought only of Christ for a life of willing obedience. The eyesalve is that wisdom and grace which enables us to discern between the evil and the good, and to detect sin under any guise. God has given His church eyes which He requires them to anoint with wisdom, that they may see clearly; but many would put out the eyes of the church if they could; for they would not have their deeds come to the light, lest they should be reproved. The divine eyesalve will impart clearness to the understanding. Christ is the depositary of all graces. He says: "Buy of Me."[5]

February 5

At the Door

Behold, I stand at the door, and knock: if any man hear my voice, and open the door, I will come in to him, and will sup with him, and he with me.
Revelation 3:20

The reason why we are not rejoicing in the freedom of the sons of God, is because we have piled up rubbish and barred the door of our hearts. Let us sweep it away, open the door, and let the Saviour in.

We cannot afford to keep Jesus outside. We cannot afford to let him pass by. We cannot afford to be without the knowledge of Christ. Says Jesus, "This is life eternal, that they might know thee the only true God, and Jesus Christ, whom thou hast sent." We want Jesus to abide in our families and in our churches. We should give ourselves, soul and body, to his work, and submit ourselves to the training process that is to fit us for Heaven.

Many of us have idols in our hearts. But you will fail to find satisfaction in the things of this life. Jesus says, "Whosoever drinketh of this water shall thirst again; but whosoever drinketh of the water that I shall give him shall never thirst; but the water that I shall give him shall be in him a well of water springing up into everlasting life." What is the meaning of these words? They mean that when your mind is attracted by heavenly things, when you dwell upon Christ, then your idols are crucified, and you are satisfied with the love of God. But how little are thoughts of Christ brought into our lives! How few talk of Jesus! How little he is lifted up![6]

February 6

Eye-salve to See

Who is blind, but my servant? or deaf, as my messenger that I sent? who is blind as he that is perfect, and blind as the LORD's servant? Isaiah 42:19

The Laodiceans boasted of a deep knowledge of Bible truth, a deep insight into the Scriptures. They were not entirely blind, else the eye-salve would have done nothing to restore their sight, and enable them to discern the true attributes of Christ. Says Christ, By renouncing your own self-sufficiency, giving up all things, however dear to you, you may buy the gold, the raiment, and the eye-salve that you may see.

The Lord sees the necessities and the peril of the soul. He came to our world in the garb of humanity, that his humanity might meet our humanity. While we were in sin, he pledged his life for us. He loves the sinner, but hates the sin. Therefore he does not leave his tempted ones with eyes that are nearly blind to their own imperfections. The man who uses the eye-salve is enabled to see himself as he is. His wretchedness is discovered; he feels his imperfections, his spiritual poverty, and his need of being healed of his spiritual malady.[7]

The greatest anxiety should be to have clear eyesight to discern our own shortcomings, and a quick ear to catch all needed reproof and instruction, lest by our inattention and carelessness we let them slip and become forgetful hearers and not doers of the work.[8]

February 7

Full of Light

The light of the body is the eye: therefore when thine eye is single, thy whole body also is full of light; but when thine eye is evil, thy body also is full of darkness. Luke 11:34

The Lord would have everyone that receives Him by faith perfect a Christian character during probationary time. ... The work of the Spirit of God embraces the whole man, soul, body, and spirit.

[Man's] undivided powers, even his thoughts, are brought into captivity to Christ. This is true sanctification. ... He does not keep part to himself, to do with just as he pleases. ...

Thus it was with Enoch. He walked with God. His mind was not defiled by an impure, defective eyesight. Those who are determined to make the will of God their own must serve and please God in everything. Then the character will be harmonious and well balanced, consistent, cheerful, and true.

"But if thine eye be evil" [Matt. 6:23], if you study selfish purposes, and work only to that end, the whole character is defective, the whole body is full of darkness. Such do not look to Jesus. They do not behold His character, and they are not changed into His image. The spiritual vision is defective, and the way from earth to heaven is darkened by the hellish shadow of Satan. ...

"If therefore the light that is in thee be darkness, how great is that darkness." The conscience is the regulative faculty, and if a man allows his conscience to become perverted, he cannot serve God aright.⁹

February 8

To See Jesus

And Jesus said, For judgment I am come into this world, that they which see not might see; and that they which see might be made blind. John 9:39

The promises of God come sounding down along the lines to us, assuring us that we may reach heaven if we will abide in Christ. Look up; it is fatal to look down. Looking down, the earth reels and sways beneath you, and nothing is sure. A divine hand is reached toward you. The hand of the Infinite is stretched over the battlements of heaven to grasp your hand in its embrace. The mighty Helper is nigh to help the most erring, the most sinful and despairing. Look up by faith, and the light of the glory of God will shine upon you. Do not be discouraged because you see that your character is defective. The closer you come to Jesus, the more faulty you will appear in your own eyes; for your vision will be clearer, and your imperfections will be seen in distinct contrast with his perfect character. Be not discouraged; this is an evidence that Satan's delusions are losing their power, that the vivifying influence of the Spirit of God is arousing you, and that your indifference and ignorance are passing away.

Whatever may have been your past experience, however discouraging may be your present circumstances, if you will come to Jesus just as you are, weak, helpless, and despairing, our compassionate Saviour will meet you a great way off, and will throw about you his arms of love and his robe of righteousness.¹⁰

February 9

Beholding Him

And as Moses lifted up the serpent in the wilderness, even so must the Son of man be lifted up: John 3:14

When we become absorbed in worldly things so that we have no thought for Him in whom our hope of eternal life is centered, we separate ourselves from Jesus and from the heavenly angels. ... This is why discouragement so often exists among the professed followers of Christ.

Many attend religious services, and are refreshed and comforted by the word of God; but through neglect of meditation, watchfulness, and prayer, they lose the blessing, and find themselves more destitute than before they received it. ...

It would be well for us to spend a thoughtful hour each day in contemplation of the life of Christ. We should take it point by point, and let the imagination grasp each scene, especially the closing ones. As we thus dwell upon His great sacrifice for us, our confidence in Him will be more constant, our love will be quickened, and we shall be more deeply imbued with His spirit. ...

If we are Christ's, our sweetest thoughts will be of Him. We shall love to talk of Him; and as we speak to one another of His love, our hearts will be softened by divine influences. Beholding the beauty of His character, we shall be "changed into the same image from glory to glory." 2 Cor. 3:18.[11]

February 10

Speechless

And he saith unto him, Friend, how camest thou in hither not having a wedding garment? And he was speechless. Matthew 22:12

When the king came in to view the guests, the real character of all was revealed. For every guest at the feast there had been provided a wedding garment. This garment was a gift from the king. ...

By the king's examination of the guests at the feast is represented a work of judgment. ... But not all who profess to be Christians are true disciples. Before the final reward is given, it must be decided who are fitted to share the inheritance of the righteous. ...

It is while men are still dwelling upon the earth that the work of investigative judgment takes place in the courts of heaven. The lives of all His professed followers pass in review before God. All are examined according to the record of the books of heaven, and according to his deeds the destiny of each is forever fixed.

By the wedding garment in the parable is represented the pure, spotless character which Christ's true followers will possess. To the church it is given "that she should be arrayed in fine linen, clean and white," "not having spot, or wrinkle, or any such thing." Revelation 19:8; Ephesians 5:27. The fine linen, says the Scripture, "is the righteousness of saints." Revelation 19:8. It is the righteousness of Christ, His own unblemished character, that through faith is imparted to all who receive Him as their personal Saviour.[12]

February 11

Garments of Salvation

... But when he was yet a great way off, his father saw him, and had compassion, and ran, and fell on his neck, and kissed him. Luke 15:20

But while he is yet "a great way off" the father discerns his form. ... He "had compassion, and ran, and fell on his neck" in a long, clinging, tender embrace.

The father ... takes from his own shoulders the broad, rich mantle, and wraps it around the son's wasted form, and the youth sobs out his repentance, saying, "Father, I have sinned against heaven, and in thy sight, and am no more worthy to be called thy son." ...

The father said to his servants, "Bring forth the best robe, and put it on him; and put a ring on his hand, and shoes on his feet; and bring hither the fatted calf, and kill it; and let us eat and be merry; for this my son was dead, and is alive again; he was lost, and is found." ...

If you take even one step toward Him in repentance, He will hasten to enfold you in His arms of infinite love. His ear is open to the cry of the contrite soul. The very first reaching out of the heart after God is known to Him. Never a prayer is offered, however faltering, never a tear is shed, however secret, never a sincere desire after God is cherished, however feeble, but the Spirit of God goes forth to meet it. ...

Your heavenly Father will take from you the garments defiled by sin ... [and] will clothe you with "the garments of salvation," and cover you with "the robe of righteousness." Isaiah 61:10. ...[13]

February 12

To Fulfill the Law

Think not that I am come to destroy the law, or the prophets: I am not come to destroy, but to fulfil. Matthew 5:17

The law lays men under obligation to God; it reaches to the thoughts and feelings; and it will produce conviction of sin in every one who is sensible of having transgressed it requirements. If the law extended to the outward conduct only, men would not be guilty in their wrong thoughts, desires, and designs. But the law requires that the soul itself be pure and the mind holy, that the thoughts and feelings may be in accordance with the standard of love and righteousness.

Christ ... came to fulfil all righteousness, and, as the head of humanity, to show man that he can do the same work, meeting every specification of the requirements of God. Through the measure of his grace furnished to the human agent, not one need miss heaven. Perfection of character is attainable by every one who strives for it. This is made the very foundation of the new covenant of the gospel. [14]

There can be and must be a withdrawal from conformity to the world, a shunning of all appearance of evil, so that no occasion shall be given for gainsayers. ...

There is nothing that Satan fears so much as that the people of God shall clear the way by removing every hindrance, so that the Lord can pour out His Spirit upon a languishing church and an impenitent congregation.[15]

February 13

Seeking His Righteousness

If we confess our sins, he is faithful and just to forgive us our sins, and to cleanse us from all unrighteousness. 1 John 1:9

Sin of a private character is to be confessed to Christ, the only mediator between God and man. For "if any man sin, we have an advocate with the Father, Jesus Christ the righteous." 1 John 2:1. ... Wrong done to a fellow being should be made right with the one who has been offended. ...[16]

If we stand in the great day of the Lord, with Christ as our refuge, our high tower, we must put away all envy, all strife for the supremacy. We must utterly destroy the roots of these unholy things; that they may not again spring up into life. We must place ourselves wholly on the side of the Lord. ...

There are many, many, who are unready for the Lord's appearing. If they continue to act like the wicked, to cherish the principles of the wicked, they will be punished with the wicked. If they betray the truth of God, causing the messages given by Him to become an uncertain thing, can He shield them from disasters by sea and by land? No, no!

Awake, my brethren, awake, Seek righteousness, and stand under the broad shield of Omnipotence. This is your only safety. God calls upon you to seek Him with humility of heart. Read Daniel's prayer, and see if your experience will stand the test of fire.[17]

February 14

Treated As We Deserve

For God so loved the world, that he gave his only begotten Son, that whosoever believeth in him should not perish, but have everlasting life. John 3:16

Taking humanity upon Him, Christ came to be one with humanity and at the same time to reveal our heavenly Father to sinful human beings. He was in all things made like unto His brethren. He became flesh, even as we are. He was hungry and thirsty and weary. He was sustained by food and refreshed by sleep. He shared the lot of men, and yet He was the blameless Son of God. ...

Tender, compassionate, sympathetic, ever considerate of others, He represented the character of God, and was constantly engaged in service for God and man. [18]

In stooping to take upon Himself humanity, Christ revealed a character the opposite of the character of Satan. ... As the high priest laid aside his gorgeous pontifical robes, and officiated in the white linen dress of the common priest, so Christ took the form of a servant, and offered sacrifice, Himself the priest, Himself the victim. ...

Christ was treated as we deserve, that we might be treated as He deserves. He was condemned for our sins, in which He had no share, that we might be justified by His righteousness, in which we had no share. He suffered the death which was ours, that we might receive the life which was His. "With His stripes we are healed."[19]

February 15

Will You Give It To Him?

The kingdom of heaven is like unto a merchant man, seeking goodly pearls: Who, when he had found one pearl of great price, went and sold all that he had, and bought it. Matthew 13:45, 46

Christ must be revealed to the sinner as the Saviour dying for the sins of the world; and as we behold the Lamb of God upon the cross of Calvary, the mystery of redemption begins to unfold to our minds and the goodness of God leads us to repentance. In dying for sinners, Christ manifested a love that is incomprehensible; and as the sinner beholds this love, it softens the heart, impresses the mind, and inspires contrition in the soul. [20]

Christ ... saw in lost humanity the pearl of price. In man, defiled and ruined by sin, He saw the possibilities of redemption. Hearts that have been the battleground of the conflict with Satan, and that have been rescued by the power of love, are more precious to the Redeemer than are those who have never fallen. God looked upon humanity, not as vile and worthless; He looked upon it in Christ, saw it as it might become through redeeming love. He collected all the riches of the universe, and laid them down in order to buy the pearl. ... "For they shall be as the stones of a crown, lifted up as an ensign upon His land." Zechariah 9:16. "They shall be Mine, saith the Lord of hosts, in that day when I make up My jewels." Malachi 3:17. [21] Jesus, who has bought you with an infinite price, asks you to give him your heart. Will you give it to him?[22]

February 16

Learn How to Believe

Jesus said unto him, If thou canst believe, all things are possible to him that believeth. Mark 9:23

We want in the name of Jesus to break down the barriers between our souls and God and then the peace of Christ will abide in our hearts by faith. We want to present ourselves in all humility before God, and get rid of everything like pride, selfishness, evil surmising, evil speaking, and all iniquity. Jesus will not take His abode in the heart where sin is enthroned. We want less of self and more of Jesus. We want to learn how to believe — that it is simply taking God at His word — but it is impossible to learn this unless we place ourselves in that position where we will be submissive to God. Our will must be on God's side, not on the side of Satan. The result of proving the forgiving love of God is to be perfectly reconciled to God's will. Then the human will and the divine become united. …

You should have a clear apprehension of the gospel. The religious life is not one of gloom and of sadness, but of peace and joy coupled with Christlike dignity and holy solemnity. We are not encouraged by our Saviour to cherish doubts and fears and distressing forebodings; these bring no relief to the soul and should be rebuked rather than praised. … If we ever needed the Holy Ghost to be with us, if we ever needed to preach in the demonstration of the Spirit, it is at this very time. … We need to dwell more upon present truth and the preparation essential in order that sinners may be saved.[23]

February 17

Willing

For it is God which worketh in you both to will and to do of his good pleasure. Philippians 2:13

Your part is to put your will on the side of Christ. When you yield your will to His, He immediately takes possession of you, and works in you to will and to do of His good pleasure. Your nature is brought under the control of His Spirit. Even your thoughts are subject to Him. If you cannot control your impulses, your emotions, as you may desire, you can control the will, and thus an entire change will be wrought in your life. When you yield up your will to Christ, your life is hid with Christ in God. It is allied to the power which is above all principalities and powers. You have a strength from God that holds you fast to His strength; and a new life, even the life of faith, is possible to you.[24]

Making God's will his will, he will reveal in his life the transforming power of the grace of Christ. In all the circumstances of life, he will take Christ's example as his guide. …

Christ says, "He that loveth his life shall lose it; and he that hateth his life in this world shall keep it unto life eternal" (John 12:25). By earnest, thoughtful efforts to help where help is needed, the true Christian shows his love for God and for his fellow beings. He may lose his life in service. But when Christ comes to gather His jewels to Himself, he will find it again.²⁵

February 18

True Forgiveness

Let the wicked forsake his way, and the unrighteous man his thoughts: and let him return unto the LORD, and he will have mercy upon him; and to our God, for he will abundantly pardon. Isaiah 55:7

[F]orgiveness has a broader meaning than many suppose. When God gives the promise that He "will abundantly pardon," He adds, as if the meaning of that promise exceeded all that we could comprehend: "My thoughts are not your thoughts, neither are your ways My ways, saith the Lord. For as the heavens are higher than the earth, so are My ways higher than your ways, and My thoughts than your thoughts." Isaiah 55:7-9. God's forgiveness is not merely a judicial act by which He sets us free from condemnation. It is not only forgiveness for sin, but reclaiming from sin. It is the outflow of redeeming love that transforms the heart. … "As far as the east is from the west, so far hath He removed our transgressions from us." Psalm 103:12.

God in Christ gave Himself for our sins. He suffered the cruel death of the cross, bore for us the burden of guilt, "the just for the unjust," that He might reveal to us His love and draw us to Himself. … Let Christ, the divine Life, dwell in you and through you reveal the heaven-born love that will inspire hope in the hopeless and bring heaven's peace to the sin-stricken heart. As we come to God, this is the condition which meets us at the threshold, that, receiving mercy from Him, we yield ourselves to reveal His grace to others.²⁶

February 19

Submission to His Will

But as many as received him, to them gave he power to become the sons of God, even to them that believe on his name: John 1:12

A character formed according to the divine likeness is the only treasure that we can take from this world to the next. Those who are under the instruction of Christ in this world will take every divine attainment with them to the heavenly mansions. ... How important, then, is the development of character in this life.

The heavenly intelligences will work with the human agent who seeks with determined faith that perfection of character which will reach out to perfection in action. To everyone engaged in this work Christ says, I am at your right hand to help you.

As the will of man co-operates with the will of God, it becomes omnipotent. Whatever is to be done at His command may be accomplished in His strength. All His biddings are enablings.[27]

The believing soul comes into perfect submission to the will of God. The Majesty of heaven condescends to a holy, familiar intercourse with him who seeks God with the whole heart, and the child of God, through the abundant manifestation of His grace, is softened into a childlike dependence. You must commit your soul and body unto God with perfect trust in His power and willingness to bless you, helpless and unworthy as you are. "As many as received Him, to them gave He power to become the sons of God, even to them that believe on His name."[28]

February 20

Feeling Is Not Faith

If we confess our sins, he is faithful and just to forgive us our sins, and to cleanse us from all unrighteousness. 1 John 1:9

When you confess your sins, it is your privilege to believe this promise, but not because you have a happy flight of feeling. Feeling is not faith. Faith is just as distinct from feeling as the east is from the west. You are to believe that God will accept you when you fulfill his conditions, believing his word because he has spoken it. ...

We should make a complete surrender to God, that he may fashion us according to his will. We should seek him earnestly, and not permit anything to divert the mind, until we know that we are indeed the children of Heaven. Why not make up your mind that you will not retain anything that separates the soul from God? Say, "Here is my heart. I open the door. Come in, Lord Jesus, come in. I am thine, and thou art mine." If you will do this, he has promised that he will put a new song in your mouth, even praise unto your God.

You are to reflect glory to God, and through his grace live day by day a life that will be pleasing before Heaven. The light of Christ is to illuminate your pathway. If you fulfill his conditions, he says, "Thy righteousness shall go before thee; the glory of the Lord shall be thy rearward." ...

Surrender everything to Christ, and let your life be hid with Christ in God. Then you will be a power for good.[29]

February 21

The Only Way

[T]*o him that worketh not, but believeth on him that justifieth the ungodly, his faith is counted for righteousness. Romans 4:5*

Without the grace of Christ, the sinner is in a hopeless condition; nothing can be done for him; but through divine grace, supernatural power is imparted to the man, and works in mind and heart and character. ... It is through grace that we are brought into fellowship with Christ, to be associated with Him in the work of salvation. ... When the sinner believes that Christ is his personal Saviour, then, according to His unfailing promises, God pardons his sin, and justifies him freely. ...

Righteousness is obedience to the law. The law demands righteousness, and this the sinner owes to the law; but he is incapable of rendering it. The only way in which he can attain to righteousness is through faith. By faith he can bring to God the merits of Christ, and the Lord places the obedience of His Son to the sinner's account. Christ's righteousness is accepted in place of man's failure, and God receives, pardons, justifies, the repentant, believing soul, treats him as though he were righteous, and loves him as He loves His Son. This is how faith is accounted righteousness; and the pardoned soul goes on from grace to grace, from light to a greater light. ...

[W]hen we accept Christ, good works will appear as fruitful evidence that we are in the way of life, that Christ is our way, and that we are treading the true path that leads to heaven.[30]

February 22

Implicit Trust

[H]*e is able also to save them to the uttermost that come unto God by him ...*
Hebrews 7:25

We cannot dishonor our Saviour more than by doubting that he will save us. Whatever may have been our life of transgression, however deep may be the stain of our sin, there is One who is able to save to the uttermost all that come unto God by him. Jesus is the remedy for sin. ... Salvation is the gift of God through Christ, and the promise is, "Whosoever believeth on him shall not perish, but have eternal life."

It is not enough to have a nominal faith. We must have faith that will appropriate the life-giving power to our souls. ... We should be able to say, "He is my Saviour; he died for me; I look to him as my complete Saviour and live." We are to look to Christ day by day. We are to regard him as our example in all things. This is faith. The true believer in Christ is represented by a branch connected with a living vine. The sap and nourishment of the vine extends through every vein and fiber of the branch, and thus the branch becomes knit with the life of the vine, and bears precious fruit. Every soul that abides in Christ will do the works of Christ. Those who love God will keep his commandments; for Christ has said, "I have kept my Father's commandments." ...

We honor our Lord and Master when we place implicit confidence in him. ... If we accept the message of love that has come to us in invitations, exhortation, and reproof, it will prove life and healing to our souls.[31]

February 23

Free Indeed

If the Son therefore shall make you free, ye shall be free indeed. John 8:36

In the divine arrangement God does nothing without the cooperation of man. He compels no man's will. That must be given to the Lord completely, else the Lord is not able to accomplish His divine work that He would do through the human agency. ... The Christian life is one of daily surrender, submission, and continual overcoming, gaining fresh victories every day. This is the growing up into Christ, fashioning the life into the divine Model.[32]

Christ came to break the shackles of sin-slavery from the soul. "If the Son therefore shall make you free, ye shall be free indeed." "The law of the Spirit of life in Christ Jesus" sets us "free from the law of sin and death." Romans 8:2.

In the work of redemption there is no compulsion. No external force is employed. ... In the change that takes place when the soul surrenders to Christ, there is the highest sense of freedom. The expulsion of sin is the act of the soul itself. ...

The only condition upon which the freedom of man is possible is that of becoming one with Christ. "The truth shall make you free;" and Christ is the truth. ... The divine law, to which we are brought into subjection, is "the law of liberty." James 2:12.[33]

February 24

The Holy Ghost Upon You

[A]fter that the Holy Ghost is come upon you: and ye shall be witnesses ...unto the uttermost part of the earth. Acts 1:8

We are not to walk with God for a time, and then part from his company, and walk in the sparks of our own kindling. ... No one of us will gain the victory without persevering, untiring effort, proportionate to the value of the object which we seek, even eternal life.

The dispensation in which we are now living is to be, to those that ask, the dispensation of the Holy Spirit. Ask for his blessing. It is time we were more intense in our devotion. To us is committed the arduous, but happy, glorious work of revealing Christ to those who are in darkness. We are called to proclaim the special truths for this time. For all this the outpouring of the Spirit is essential. We should pray for it. The Lord expects us to ask him.[34]

I saw that many were neglecting the preparation so needful and were looking to the time of "refreshing" and the "latter rain" to fit them to stand in the day of the Lord and to live in His sight. Oh, how many I saw in the time of trouble without a shelter! ... I saw that none could share the "refreshing" unless they obtain the victory over every besetment, over pride, selfishness, love of the world, and over every wrong word and action. We should, therefore, be drawing nearer and nearer to the Lord and be earnestly seeking that preparation necessary to enable us to stand in the battle in the day of the Lord.[35]

February 25

Into All Truth

Howbeit when he, the Spirit of truth, is come, he will guide you into all truth.
John 16:13

The Lord Jesus, who is the image of the invisible God, gave his own life to save perishing man, and, oh, what light, what power, he brings with him! In him dwells all the fullness of the Godhead, bodily. What a mystery of mysteries! It is difficult for the reason to grasp the majesty of Christ, the mystery of redemption. The shameful cross has been upraised, the nails have been driven through his hands and feet, the cruel spear has pierced to his heart, and the redemption price has been paid for the human race. The spotless Lamb of God bore our sins in his own body upon the tree; he carried our sorrows. Redemption is an inexhaustible theme, worthy of our closest contemplation. It passes the comprehension of the deepest thought, the stretch of the most vivid imagination. ... Although great and talented authors have made known wonderful truths, and have presented increased light to the people, still in our day we shall find new ideas, and ample fields in which to work, for the theme of salvation is inexhaustible. ...

We shall never reach a period when there is no increased light for us. The sayings of Christ were always far-reaching in their import. ...

The truth is constantly unfolding and presenting new features to different minds. All who dig in the mines of truth, will constantly discover rich and precious gems.[36]

February 26

Let Your Light Shine

Let your light so shine before men, that they may see your good works, and glorify your Father which is in heaven. Matthew 5:16

Christ declared himself to be the light of the world. To his disciples he gave a part in the work of shedding light on a sin-darkened world. "Ye are the light of the world," he declared. "Let your light so shine before men, that they may see your good works, and glorify your Father which is in heaven." ...

By his death [Christ] opened a fountain in which all may wash their robes of character, and make them white. ... In his name they [are] to go forth to carry out his purpose of bringing many souls to a knowledge of the truth. ...

The Lord expects those who believe in Christ to co-operate with divine instrumentalities, and thus reveal a strength that the worldling can not reveal. ...

The work that Christ did on this earth his followers are to do. With the power and efficacy brought by the Holy Spirit they are to carry forward his plan for the restoration of the divine image in humanity. The Lord will do great things for them when they work under the Holy Spirit's guidance. But they must place their entire dependence on God.[37]

February 27

Washed in the Blood

...These are they which came out of great tribulation, and have washed their robes, and made them white in the blood of the Lamb. Revelation 7:14

Here is a work for man to do. He must face the mirror of God's law, discern the defects in his moral character and put away his sins, washing his robes of character in the blood of the Lamb. Envy, pride, malice, deceit, strife, crime will be cleansed from the heart that is recipient of the love of Christ, and cherishes the hope of being made like him when we shall see him as he is. ...

But the influence of a gospel hope will not lead the sinner to look upon the salvation of Christ as a matter of free grace, while he continues to live in transgression of the law of God. When the light of truth dawns upon his mind, and he fully understands the requirements of God, and realizes the extent of his transgressions, he will reform his ways, become loyal to God through the strength obtained from his Saviour, and lead a new and purer life. Those who overcome in the name of Jesus will stand about the great white throne, with crowns of immortal glory, waving the palm branches of victory. … While mercy lingers, I beseech you to make the most of the probationary time left you, in preparing for eternity, that life may not be an utter failure, and that in the time of solemn scrutiny you may be found with those who are accepted of God, and are called the sons of God.[38]

February 28

Glory to Glory

But we all, with open face beholding as in a glass the glory of the Lord, are changed into the same image from glory to glory, even as by the Spirit of the Lord. 2 Corinthians 3:18

We have the companionship of the divine presence, and as we realize this presence, our thoughts are brought into captivity to Jesus Christ. Our spiritual exercises are in accordance with the vividness of our sense of this companionship. Enoch walked with God in this way: and Christ is dwelling in our hearts by faith when we will consider what he is to us, and what a work he has wrought out for us in the plan of redemption. We shall be most happy in cultivating a sense of this great gift of God to our world and to us personally.

These thoughts have a controlling power upon the whole character. I want to impress upon your mind that you may have a divine companion with you, if you will, always. … As the mind dwells upon Christ, the character is molded after the divine similitude. The thoughts are pervaded with a sense of his goodness, his love. We contemplate his character, and thus he is in all our thoughts. His love encloses us. … By beholding, we are conformed to the divine similitude, even the likeness of Christ. To all with whom we associate we reflect the bright and cheerful beams of his righteousness. We have become transformed in character; for heart, soul, and mind, are irradiated by the reflection of him who loved us, and gave himself for us. Here again there is the realization of a personal, living influence dwelling in our hearts by faith.[39]

March 1

Even as Your Father

Be ye therefore perfect, even as your Father which is in heaven is perfect.
Matthew 5:48

God has made provision that we may become like unto Him, and He will accomplish this for all who do not interpose a perverse will and thus frustrate His grace. ...

By the revelation of the attractive loveliness of Christ, by the knowledge of His love expressed to us while we were yet sinners, the stubborn heart is melted and subdued, and the sinner is transformed and becomes a child of heaven. God does not employ compulsory measures; love is the agent which He uses to expel sin from the heart. ...

The Jews had been wearily toiling to reach perfection by their own efforts, and they had failed. Christ had already told them that their righteousness could never enter the kingdom of heaven. ... Be perfect as God is perfect. The law is but a transcript of the character of God. ...

God is love. Like rays of light from the sun, love and light and joy flow out from Him to all His creatures. ...

Jesus said, Be perfect as your Father is perfect. ... In Christ dwells "all the fullness of the Godhead bodily" (Colossians 2:9); and the life of Jesus is made manifest "in our mortal flesh" (2 Corinthians 4:11). That life in you will produce the same character and manifest the same works as it did in Him.[1]

March 2

Sons of God

... if ye through the Spirit do mortify the deeds of the body, ye shall live. For as many as are led by the Spirit of God, they are the sons of God. Romans 8:13, 14

If man will cooperate with God by returning willingly to his loyalty, and obeying the commandments, God will receive him as a son. Through the provision Christ has made by taking the punishment due to man, we may be reinstated in God's favor, being made partakers of the divine nature. If we repent of our transgression, and receive Christ as the Life-giver, our personal Saviour, we become one with him, and our will is brought into harmony with the divine will. We become partakers of the life of Christ, which is eternal. We derive immortality from God by receiving the life of Christ for in Christ dwells all the fulness of the Godhead bodily. This life is the mystical union and cooperation of the divine with the human.

As children of the first Adam, we partake of the dying nature of Adam. But through the imparted life of Christ, man has been given opportunity to win back again the lost gift of life, and to stand in his original position before God, a partaker of the divine nature. "As many as received him," writes John, "to them gave he power to become the sons of God, even to them that believe on his name." "He that hath the Son hath life; and he that hath not the Son of God hath not life." "I am come," said Christ, "that they might have life, and that they might have it more abundantly."²

March 3

Transformation

… be ye transformed by the renewing of your mind, that ye may prove what is that good, and acceptable, and perfect, will of God. Romans 12:2

Earnest men and women, filled with courage and devotion, are needed in the Master's service. The call comes to us, "Be not conformed to this world; but be ye transformed by the renewing of your mind." As we obey this command, the power of the Holy Spirit will come upon mind and body, bringing us into conformity to the will of Christ, and renewing us in His likeness. The hereditary and cultivated tendencies to wrong will die, and Christ will be formed within, the hope of glory. …

We are not to trust in our own wisdom, but in the wisdom of God. This will bring into the character the patience, kindness, and love of Christ. … There is to be constant growth in grace. We are to make constant advancement in preparing for the future, immortal life. ….

Let us strive to help those connected with us. To this work let us devote our tact and ingenuity. Let us reach higher and still higher for purity and devotion, our hearts filled with a desire to know the will of God. Let us consecrate our all to the service of humanity. We shall receive our reward in the future life. Reveal the living charm of the Saviour's love. Represent Christ by revealing faith and hope and love. In short, copy the Pattern.³

March 4

Knowledge Shall be Increased

But thou, O Daniel, shut up the words, and seal the book, even to the time of the end: many shall run to and fro, and knowledge shall be increased. Daniel 12:4

As the message of Christ's first advent announced the kingdom of His grace, so the message of His second advent announces the kingdom of His glory. And the second message, like the first, is based on the prophecies. The words of the angel to Daniel relating to the last days were to be understood in the time of the end. At that time, "many shall run to and fro, and knowledge shall be increased." "The wicked shall do wickedly: and none of the wicked shall understand; but the wise shall understand." Daniel 12:4, 10. ...

We have reached the period foretold in these scriptures. The time of the end is come, the visions of the prophets are unsealed, and their solemn warnings point us to our Lord's coming in glory as near at hand.

The Jews misinterpreted and misapplied the word of God, and they knew not the time of their visitation. ... [T]oday the kingdom of this world absorbs men's thoughts, and they take no note of the rapidly fulfilling prophecies and the tokens of the swift-coming kingdom of God. ...

While we are not to know the hour of our Lord's return, we may know when it is near. "Therefore let us not sleep, as do others; but let us watch and be sober." 1 Thessalonians 5:4-6.[4]

March 5

The Bread

[M]an doth not live by bread only, but by every word that proceedeth out of the mouth of the LORD doth man live. Deuteronomy 8:3

If you would become acquainted with the Saviour, study the Holy Scriptures.

Fill the whole heart with the words of God. They are the living water, quenching your burning thirst. They are the living bread from heaven. ...

The infinite mercy and love of Jesus, the sacrifice made in our behalf, call for the most serious and solemn reflection. We should dwell upon the character of our dear Redeemer and Intercessor. ... As we thus contemplate heavenly themes, our faith and love will grow stronger, and our prayers will be more and more acceptable to God, because they will be more and more mixed with faith and love. They will be intelligent and fervent. There will be more constant confidence in Jesus, and a daily, living experience in His power to save to the uttermost all that come unto God by Him.

As we meditate upon the perfections of the Saviour, we shall desire to be wholly transformed and renewed in the image of His purity. There will be a hungering and thirsting of soul to become like Him whom we adore. The more our thoughts are upon Christ, the more we shall speak of Him to others and represent Him to the world.[5]

March 6

Unto the Perfect Day

But the path of the just is as the shining light, that shineth more and more unto the perfect day. Proverbs 4:18

In a special sense Seventh-day Adventists have been set in this world as watchmen and light bearers. To them has been entrusted the last message of mercy for a perishing world. On them is shining wonderful light from the Word of God. What manner of persons, then, ought they to be?

It is the purpose of God to glorify himself in his people before the world. He longs to make them channels through which he can pour his boundless love and mercy. But are we what God would have us? — No, we are not. The members of our churches in every place need to examine themselves closely, and surrender their lives unreservedly to God. … When God's people bring the righteousness of Christ into the daily life, sinners will be converted, and victories over the enemy will be gained.

God calls for light bearers, who will fill the world with the light and peace and joy that come from Christ. … Such ones will reveal in their lives the virtues of Christ's character.

There needs to be a deeper work of grace in the hearts of God's people. Less of self, and more of Christ, must be seen. … The religion of the Bible must be interwoven with all that we do and say.[6]

March 7

Rising

Arise, shine; for thy light is come, and the glory of the LORD is risen upon thee. Isaiah 60:1

The Lord in compassion is seeking to enlighten the understanding of those who are now groping in the darkness of error. He is delaying His judgments upon an impenitent world, in order that His light bearers may seek and save that which is lost. He is now calling upon His church on the earth to awake from the lethargy that Satan has sought to bring upon them, and fulfill their heaven-appointed work of enlightening the world. His message to His church at this time is, "Arise, shine; for thy light is come, and the glory of the Lord is risen upon thee." To meet the conditions existing at the time when darkness covers the earth, and gross darkness the people, the church of God has been commissioned to cooperate with God in shedding abroad the light of Bible truth. To those who seek to do their part faithfully as bearers of precious light, is given the assurance: "The Lord shall rise upon thee, and His glory shall be seen upon thee. And the Gentiles shall come to thy light, and kings to the brightness of thy rising."

The world today is in crying need of a revelation of Christ Jesus in the person of His saints. … [T]here is a world to be saved by the light of gospel truth; and as the message of truth that is to call men out of darkness into God's marvelous light is given by the church, the lives of its members, sanctified by the Spirit of truth, are to bear witness to the verity of the messages proclaimed.[7]

March 8

Let Your Light Shine

Let your light so shine before men, that they may see your good works, and glorify your Father which is in heaven. Matthew 5:16

Christ declared himself to be the light of the world. To his disciples he gave a part in the work of shedding light on a sin-darkened world. "Ye are the light of the world," he declared. "Let your light so shine before men, that they may see your good works, and glorify your Father which is in heaven." …

By his death [Christ] opened a fountain in which all may wash their robes of character, and make them white. … In his name they [are] to go forth to carry out his purpose of bringing many souls to a knowledge of the truth. …

The Lord expects those who believe in Christ to co-operate with divine instrumentalities, and thus reveal a strength that the worldling can not reveal. …

The work that Christ did on this earth his followers are to do. With the power and efficacy brought by the Holy Spirit they are to carry forward his plan for the restoration of the divine image in humanity. The Lord will do great things for them when they work under the Holy Spirit's guidance. But they must place their entire dependence on God.[8]

March 9

Dawning Light

For God, who commanded the light to shine out of darkness, hath shined in our hearts, to give the light of the knowledge of the glory of God in the face of Jesus Christ. 2 Corinthians 4:6

This glorious Light of the world was to bring salvation to every nation, kindred, tongue, and people. Of the work before Him, the prophet heard the Eternal Father declare: "It is a light thing that thou shouldest be my servant to raise up the tribes of Jacob, and to restore the preserved of Israel: I will also give thee for a light to the Gentiles, that thou mayest be my salvation unto the end of the earth. ...

Looking on still farther through the ages, the prophet beheld the literal fulfillment of these glorious promises. He saw the bearers of the glad tidings of salvation going to the ends of the earth, to every kindred and people. ...

The day of deliverance is at hand. ... Among all nations, kindreds, and tongues, he sees men and women who are praying for light and knowledge. Their souls are unsatisfied: long have they fed on ashes. ... [T]hey are honest in heart, and desire to learn a better way. Although in the depths of heathenism, with no knowledge of the written law of God or of his Son Jesus, they have revealed in manifold ways the working of a divine power on mind and character. ...

Heaven's plan of salvation is broad enough to embrace the whole world. God longs to breathe into prostrate humanity the breath of life.⁹

March 10

Washed in the Blood

... These are they which came out of great tribulation, and have washed their robes, and made them white in the blood of the Lamb. Revelation 7:14

Here is a work for man to do. He must face the mirror of God's law, discern the defects in his moral character and put away his sins, washing his robes of character in the blood of the Lamb. Envy, pride, malice, deceit, strife, crime will be cleansed from the heart that is recipient of the love of Christ, and cherishes the hope of being made like him when we shall see him as he is. ...

But the influence of a gospel hope will not lead the sinner to look upon the salvation of Christ as a matter of free grace, while he continues to live in transgression of the law of God. When the light of truth dawns upon his mind, and he fully understands the requirements of God, and realizes the extent of his transgressions, he will reform his ways, become loyal to God through the strength obtained from his Saviour, and lead a new and purer life. Those who overcome in the name of Jesus will stand about the great white throne, with crowns of immortal glory, waving the palm branches of victory. ... While mercy lingers ... make the most of the probationary time left you, in preparing for eternity, that life may not be an utter failure, and that in the time of solemn scrutiny you may be found with those who are accepted of God, and are called the sons of God.¹⁰

March 11

Revealing His Righteousness

For I am not ashamed of the gospel of Christ: for ... therein is the righteousness of God revealed ... Romans 1:16, 17

Every truly converted soul will be intensely desirous to bring others from the darkness of error into the marvelous light of the righteousness of Jesus Christ. The great outpouring of the Spirit of God, which lightens the whole earth with his glory, will not come until we have an enlightened people, that know by experience what it means to be laborers together with God. When we have entire, whole-hearted consecration to the service of Christ, God will recognize the fact by an outpouring of his Spirit without measure; but this will not be while the largest portion of the church are not laborers together with God.[11]

By a study of the word, we are to see Him as He is, and, charmed with the view of His divine perfection, we are to grow into the same image. ... The likeness of God is revealed in the perfect character of His Son, that we may understand what it means to be made in the likeness of the image of God, and what we may become if by constantly beholding we allow ourselves to be changed from "glory to glory."

It is our privilege, by an earnest study of the word, to learn wherein we are not manifesting the principles of that word in our lives. And as the mirror reveals to us our defects, we are to seek by earnest prayer and faith to put them away. ... Beholding day by day the glory of the Lord, we are molded into conformity to His Spirit and will. [12]

March 12

The Gift of God

...God hath given to us eternal life, and this life is in his Son. 1 John 5:11

When men and women can more fully comprehend the magnitude of the great sacrifice which was made by the Majesty of Heaven in dying in man's stead, then will the plan of salvation be magnified, and reflections of Calvary will awaken sacred and living emotions in the Christian's heart. Praises to God and the Lamb will be in their hearts and upon their lips. Pride and self-worship cannot flourish in the hearts that keep fresh in memory the scenes of Calvary. This world will appear of but little value to those who appreciate the great price of man's redemption.

Christ has shown that his love was stronger than death. Even when suffering the most fearful conflicts with the powers of darkness, his love for perishing sinners increased. He endured the hidings of his Father's countenance, until he was led to exclaim in the bitterness of his soul, "My God, my God, why hast thou forsaken me?"

It is when we most fully comprehend the love of God that we best realize the sinfulness of sin, and the fullness of salvation. When we see the length of the chain that was let down for us, and understand something of the merits of that infinite sacrifice that Christ has made for us, the heart is melted with tenderness and contrition.[13]

March 13

Exceeding Sorrowful

... My soul is exceeding sorrowful, even unto death: tarry ye here, and watch with me. Matthew 26:38

The withdrawal of the divine countenance from the Saviour in this hour of supreme anguish pierced His heart with a sorrow that can never be fully understood by man. So great was this agony that His physical pain was hardly felt. ...

The Saviour could not see through the portals of the tomb. Hope did not present to Him His coming forth from the grave a conqueror, or tell Him of the Father's acceptance of the sacrifice. He feared that sin was so offensive to God that Their separation was to be eternal.[14]

Daily He suffers the agonies of the crucifixion. Daily men and women are piercing Him by dishonoring Him, by refusing to do His will.

The Lord desires us to be men and women in Christ Jesus. Our natural dispositions are to be softened and subdued by His grace. Then we shall not be continually crucifying Him afresh. ... If we now follow Him, doing His will in all things, we shall in the world to come live with Him forever. Let us keep Him constantly in view. It should be our life-purpose to glorify Christ. This is the great purpose that has inspired Christians in every age. It is by cherishing this purpose that we make sure of eternal salvation. Let us learn to know Him whom to know aright is peace and joy and life everlasting.[15]

March 14

Looking Unto Jesus

[L]et us lay aside every weight, and the sin which doth so easily beset us, and let us run with patience the race that is set before us, Looking unto Jesus the author and finisher of our faith ... Hebrews 12:1, 2

Let us fix our eyes upon him; for he is full of grace and truth, and he will let all his goodness pass before us while he hides us in the cleft of the Rock. Then we shall endure as seeing him who is invisible, and by beholding him, we shall be changed into his image. The reason that we carelessly indulge in sin is that we do not see Jesus. We would not lightly regard sin, did we appreciate the fact that sin wounds our Lord. Did we know Jesus by an experimental knowledge, we would not esteem duty as of small importance; but would manifest faithful integrity in the performance of every service. A right estimate of the character of God would enable us rightly to represent him to the world. …

We abide in Christ by faith, by simple childlike trust in his pledged word. Perfect faith, and the surrender of self to God are subjects that should be made very plain to those who are slow to comprehend spiritual things. Faith is not feeling. "Faith is the substance of things hoped for, the evidence of things not seen." The religion that takes the position of secluded enjoyment, that is satisfied to contemplate the religion of Jesus Christ, and that keeps its possessor from an experimental knowledge of its saving power, is a deception.[16]

March 15

Wounded Afresh

Blessed are they that mourn: for they shall be comforted. Matthew 5:4

We often sorrow because our evil deeds bring unpleasant consequences to ourselves; but this is not repentance. Real sorrow for sin is the result of the working of the Holy Spirit. The Spirit reveals the ingratitude of the heart that has slighted and grieved the Saviour, and brings us in contrition to the foot of the cross. By every sin Jesus is wounded afresh; and as we look upon Him whom we have pierced, we mourn for the sins that have brought anguish upon Him. Such mourning will lead to the renunciation of sin. …

[Such sorrow] is the strength which binds the penitent to the Infinite One with links that cannot be broken. … This sorrow heralds a joy which will be a living fountain in the soul. "Only acknowledge thine iniquity, that thou hast transgressed against the Lord thy God;" "and I will not cause Mine anger to fall upon you: for I am merciful, saith the Lord." Jeremiah 3:13, 12. "Unto them that mourn in Zion," He has appointed to give "beauty for ashes, the oil of joy for mourning, the garment of praise for the spirit of heaviness." Isaiah 61:3.[17]

Our natural dispositions are to be softened and subdued by His grace. Then we shall not be continually crucifying Him afresh. … It should be our life-purpose to glorify Christ. … Let us learn to know Him whom to know aright is peace and joy and life everlasting.[18]

March 16

Sufferings of Christ

That I may know him, and the power of his resurrection, and the fellowship of his sufferings, being made conformable unto his death; Phillipians 3:10

Those who think of the result of hastening or hindering the gospel think of it in relation to themselves and to the world. Few think of its relation to God. Few give thought to the suffering that sin has caused our Creator. All heaven suffered in Christ's agony; but that suffering did not begin or end with His manifestation in humanity. The cross is a revelation to our dull senses of the pain that, from its very inception, sin has brought to the heart of God. Every departure from the right, every deed of cruelty, every failure of humanity to reach His ideal, brings grief to Him. When there came upon Israel the calamities that were the sure result of separation from God … it is said that "His soul was grieved for the misery of Israel." "In all their affliction He was afflicted: . . . and He bare them, and carried them all the days of old." Judges 10:16; Isaiah 63:9. …

Our world is a … scene of misery that we dare not allow even our thoughts to dwell upon. Did we realize it as it is, the burden would be too terrible. Yet God feels it all. In order to destroy sin and its results He gave His best Beloved, and He has put it in our power, through co-operation with Him, to bring this scene of misery to an end. "This gospel of the kingdom shall be preached in all the world for a witness unto all nations; and then shall the end come." Matthew 24:14.[19]

March 17

The Robe

I counsel thee to buy of me … white raiment, that thou mayest be clothed, and that the shame of thy nakedness do not appear; … Revelation 3:18

The white robe of innocence was worn by our first parents when they were placed by God in holy Eden. They lived in perfect conformity to the will of God. All the strength of their affections was given to their heavenly Father. A beautiful soft light, the light of God, enshrouded the holy pair. This robe of light was a symbol of their spiritual garments of heavenly innocence. Had they remained true to God it would ever have continued to enshroud them. But when sin entered, they severed their connection with God, and the light that had encircled them departed. Naked and ashamed, they tried to supply the place of the heavenly garments by sewing together fig leaves for a covering.

But this they can never do. Nothing can man devise to supply the place of his lost robe of innocence. No fig-leaf garment, no worldly citizen dress, can be worn by those who sit down with Christ and angels at the marriage supper of the Lamb.

Only the covering which Christ Himself has provided can make us meet to appear in God's presence. This covering, the robe of His own righteousness, Christ will put upon every repenting, believing soul. "I counsel thee," He says, "to buy of Me … white raiment, that thou mayest be clothed, and that the shame of thy nakedness do not appear." Revelation 3:18.[20]

March 18

White Raiment

… Jesus Christ, who … washed us from our sins in his own blood, Revelation 1:5

Many who are without spiritual life have their names on the church records, but they are not written in the Lamb's book of life. … Unless they trust in the righteousness of Christ as their only security; unless they copy his character, labor in his spirit, they are naked, they have not on the robe of his righteousness. The dead are often made to pass for the living; for those who are working out what they term salvation after their own ideas, have not God working in them to will and to do of his good pleasure.[21]

This robe, woven in the loom of heaven, has in it not one thread of human devising. Christ in His humanity wrought out a perfect character, and this character He offers to impart to us. "All our righteousness are as filthy rags." Isaiah 64:6. Everything that we of ourselves can do is defiled by sin. But the Son of God "was manifested to take away our sins; and in Him is no sin." … When we submit ourselves to Christ, the heart is united with His heart, the will is merged in His will, the mind becomes one with His mind, the thoughts are brought into captivity to Him; we live His life. This is what it means to be clothed with the garment of His righteousness. Then as the Lord looks upon us He sees, not the fig-leaf garment, not the nakedness and deformity of sin, but His own robe of righteousness, which is perfect obedience to the law of Jehovah.[22]

March 19

Clean and White

Thou hast a few names even in Sardis which have not defiled their garments; and they shall walk with me in white: for they are worthy. Revelation 3:4

The robe of Christ's righteousness is prepared for all those who will exchange their own sinful, filthy garments for the robe Jesus has prepared for them. This garment was furnished at great cost by the Son of God, and he presents it as a free gift to any one, rich or poor, high or low, wise or ignorant, who will exchange his sin-defiled garments for this robe of matchless purity. …

The clinging to the defiled garments and refusing the pure, spotless robes of Christ's righteousness is the love of sin. Not one can stand before God at his appearing in these garments of sin. … [Y]ou must be earnest in building up a character that will fit you for those mansions. … All must be without spot who enter that haven of bliss.

If you are to sit at Christ's table, and feast on the provisions he has furnished at the marriage supper of the Lamb, you must have a special garment, called the wedding garment, which is the white robe of Christ's righteousness. Every one who has on this robe is entitled to enter the city of God; … Will you lay off your self-righteous garments and accept of Jesus Christ as your Saviour? In doing this, you accept the righteousness of the Lord Jesus, and despising your own garments of sin and uncleanness, put on the garments of Christ's righteousness.[23]

March 20

The Work in the Sanctuary

And there was given me a reed like unto a rod: and the angel stood, saying, Rise, and measure the temple of God, and the altar, and them that worship therein.
Revelation 11:1

A revival of true godliness among us is the greatest and most urgent of all our needs. … There must be earnest effort to obtain the blessing of the Lord, not because God is not willing to bestow his blessing upon us, but because we are unprepared to receive it. Our Heavenly Father is more willing to give his Holy Spirit to them that ask him, than are earthly parents to give good gifts to their children. But it is our work, by confession, humiliation, repentance, and earnest prayer, to fulfill the conditions upon which God has promised to grant us his blessing. … While the people are so destitute of God's Holy Spirit, they cannot appreciate the preaching of the word; but when the Spirit's power touches their hearts, then the discourses given will not be without effect. Guided by the teachings of God's word, with the manifestation of his Spirit, in the exercise of sound discretion, those who attend our meetings will gain a precious experience, and returning home will be prepared to exert a healthful influence. The old standard-bearers knew what it was to wrestle with God in prayer, and to enjoy the out-pouring of his Spirit. … How is it with the rising generation? are they converted to God? Are we awake to the work that is going on in the heavenly Sanctuary, or are we waiting for some compelling power to come upon the church before we shall arouse?[24]

March 21

Cleansing the Soul Temple

These things I have spoken unto you, that in me ye might have peace. In the world ye shall have tribulation: but be of good cheer; I have overcome the world.
John 16:33

As Christ's earthly ministry drew to a close ... He sought to encourage them and to prepare them for the future. ... He knew that they would suffer persecution, that they would be cast out of the synagogues, and would be thrown into prison. He knew that for witnessing to Him as the Messiah, some of them would suffer death. And something of this He told them. ...

As Christ's representatives the apostles were to make a decided impression on the world. ... Humbling themselves, they would declare that He whom the Jews had crucified was the Prince of life, the Son of the living God, and that in His name they did the works that He had done. ...

In His parting conversation with His disciples on the night before the crucifixion the Saviour made no reference to the suffering that He had endured and must yet endure. He did not speak of the humiliation that was before Him, but sought to bring to their minds that which would strengthen their faith, leading them to look forward to the joys that await the overcomer. He rejoiced in the consciousness that He could and would do more for His followers than He had promised; that from Him would flow forth love and compassion, cleansing the soul temple, and making men like Him in character; that His truth, armed with the power of the Spirit, would go forth conquering and to conquer.[25]

March 22

Precious Trials

That the trial of your faith, being much more precious than of gold that perisheth ... 1 Peter 1:7

We must not think that we shall escape trials; for the apostle says, "That the trial of your faith, being much more precious than of gold that perisheth, though it be tried with fire, might be found unto praise and honor and glory at the appearing of Jesus Christ." Gold is tried in the fire, that it may be purified from dross; but faith that is purified by trial, is more precious than refined gold. Then let us look upon trials in a reasonable way. Let us not come through them with murmuring and discontent. Let us not make mistakes in getting out of them. In times of trial we must cling to God and his promises. ...

Christ is cleansing the temple in heaven from the sins of the people, and we must work in harmony with him upon the earth, cleansing the soul temple from its moral defilement. If we will work thus, we shall find that the sweet influence of God's Spirit will be wrought into our life. Grace and peace and strength will take the place of strife and weakness, and instead of talking of discouragement and gloom, we shall speak of God's light and love and joy. We shall be looking at the things that are not seen, which are not temporal, but eternal. When we engage in this work, the angels of God will draw near to communicate divine power, and combine heavenly strength with human weakness. Then we shall grow into the image of our Lord.[26]

March 23

A Great High Priest

Seeing then that we have a great high priest, that is passed into the heavens, Jesus the Son of God, let us hold fast our profession. Hebrews 4:14

Satan invents unnumbered schemes to occupy our minds, that they may not dwell upon the very work with which we ought to be best acquainted. The archdeceiver hates the great truths that bring to view an atoning sacrifice and an all-powerful mediator. He knows that with him everything depends on his diverting minds from Jesus and His truth.

Those who would share the benefits of the Saviour's mediation should permit nothing to interfere with their duty to perfect holiness in the fear of God. The precious hours, instead of being given to pleasure, to display, or to gain seeking, should be devoted to an earnest, prayerful study of the word of truth. The subject of the sanctuary and the investigative judgment should be clearly understood by the people of God. All need a knowledge for themselves of the position and work of their great High Priest. Otherwise it will be impossible for them to exercise the faith which is essential at this time or to occupy the position which God designs them to fill. Every individual has a soul to save or to lose. Each has a case pending at the bar of God. Each must meet the great Judge face to face. How important, then, that every mind contemplate often the solemn scene when the judgment shall sit and the books shall be opened, when, with Daniel, every individual must stand in his lot, at the end of the days.[27]

March 24

Enter by Faith

[W]e ... have a strong consolation ... both sure and stedfast ... which entereth ... within the veil; ... even Jesus ... an high priest ... Hebrews 6:18 - 20

The sanctuary in heaven is the very center of Christ's work in behalf of men. ...

The intercession of Christ in man's behalf in the sanctuary above is as essential to the plan of salvation as was His death upon the cross. ... We must by faith enter within the veil, "whither the forerunner is for us entered." Hebrews 6:20. There the light from the cross of Calvary is reflected. There we may gain a clearer insight into the mysteries of redemption. ...

"He that covereth his sins shall not prosper: but whoso confesseth and forsaketh them shall have mercy." Proverbs 28:13. If those who hide and excuse their faults could see how Satan exults over them, how he taunts Christ and holy angels with their course, they would make haste to confess their sins and to put them away. Through defects in the character, Satan works to gain control of the whole mind, and he knows that if these defects are cherished, he will succeed. Therefore he is constantly seeking to deceive the followers of Christ with his fatal sophistry that it is impossible for them to overcome. But Jesus pleads in their behalf His wounded hands, His bruised body; and He declares to all who would follow Him: "My grace is sufficient for thee." 2 Corinthians 12:9. ... Let none, then, regard their defects as incurable. God will give faith and grace to overcome them.[28]

March 25

A Pure Heart

Who shall ascend into the hill of the LORD? or who shall stand in his holy place?
He that hath clean hands, and a pure heart; Psalm 7:3, 4

We are now living in the great day of atonement. In the typical service, while the high priest was making the atonement for Israel, all were required to afflict their souls by repentance of sin and humiliation before the Lord, lest they be cut off from among the people. In like manner, all who would have their names retained in the book of life should now, in the few remaining days of their probation, afflict their souls before God by sorrow for sin and true repentance. There must be deep, faithful searching of heart. The light, frivolous spirit indulged by so many professed Christians must be put away. ... Everyone must be tested and found without spot or wrinkle or any such thing. ...

The judgment is now passing in the sanctuary above. ... Soon — none know how soon — it will pass to the cases of the living. In the awful presence of God our lives are to come up in review. ...

Silently, unnoticed as the midnight thief, will come the decisive hour which marks the fixing of every man's destiny, the final withdrawal of mercy's offer to guilty men.

Perilous is the condition of those who, growing weary of their watch, turn to the attractions of the world.[29]

March 26

Freedom

[in the fiftieth year] in the day of atonement ... ye shall ... proclaim liberty throughout all the land unto all the inhabitants thereof: ... and ye shall return every man unto his possession, and ye shall return every man unto his family.
Leviticus 25:8-10

In ancient times criminals were sometimes sold into slavery by the judges; in some cases, debtors were sold by their creditors; and poverty even led persons to sell themselves or their children.[30]

"On the tenth day of the seventh month, in the Day of Atonement," the trumpet of the jubilee was sounded. Throughout the land ...the sound was heard, calling upon all the children of Jacob to welcome the year of release. ...

[A]ll landed property [was returned] to the family of the original possessor ... or his heirs in the year of jubilee.[31]

Adam fell under the dominion of Satan. He brought sin into the world, and death by sin. God gave his only begotten Son to save man. This he did that he might be just, and yet the justifier of all who accept Christ. Man sold himself to Satan, but Jesus bought back the race.[32]

March 27

Pray One for Another

And another angel came and stood at the altar, having a golden censer; and there was given unto him much incense, that he should offer it with the prayers of all saints upon the golden altar which was before the throne. Revelation 8:3

Men of courage are wanted now; men who will venture something for the truth's sake; men who will be sober, but not gloomy and desponding; men who will watch unto prayer, and whose prayers will be mingled with living, active faith. ... But no lightness, no trifling, should be indulged in; no low witticism should escape our lips, for these things give Satan great advantage. And we are living in the solemn hour of the Judgment, when we should afflict our souls, confess our errors, repent of our sins, and pray one for another that we may be healed.[33]

We are in the great day of atonement, and the sacred work of Christ for the people of God that is going on at the present time in the heavenly sanctuary should be our constant study. We should teach our children what the typical Day of Atonement signified and that it was a special season of great humiliation and confession of sins before God. The antitypical day of atonement is to be of the same character. ... The great work is before us of leading the people away from worldly customs and practices, up higher and higher, to spirituality, piety, and earnest work for God. It is your work to proclaim the message of the third angel, to sound the last note of warning to the world. May the Lord bless you with spiritual eyesight.[34]

March 28

Nearer to Eternity

...The LORD shall endure for ever: he hath prepared his throne for judgment. And he shall judge the world in righteousness, he shall minister judgment to the people in uprightness. Psalm 9:7, 8

Every day that passes brings us nearer the last great important day. We are one year nearer the judgment, nearer eternity ... Are we also drawing nearer to God? Are we watching unto prayer? ... Every day we have been associating with men and women who are judgment bound. Each day may have been the dividing line to some soul; someone may have made the decision which shall determine his future destiny. What has been our influence over these fellow travelers? What efforts have we put forth to bring them to Christ?

It is a solemn thing to die, but a far more solemn thing to live. Every thought and word and deed of our lives will meet us again. What we make of ourselves in probationary time, that we must remain to all eternity. Death brings dissolution to the body, but makes no change in the character. The coming of Christ does not change our characters; it only fixes them forever beyond all change. ...

My brethren and sisters, awake, I beseech you, from the sleep of death. It is too late to devote the strength of brain, bone, and muscle to self-serving. Let not the last day find you destitute of heavenly treasure. Seek to push the triumphs of the cross, seek to enlighten souls, labor for the salvation of your fellow beings, and your work will abide the trying test of fire.[35]

March 29

The Acceptable Year

*The Spirit of the Lord GOD is upon me; because the LORD hath anointed me ...
Isaiah 61:1*

The mission of the people of God in this age is outlined in the words of inspiration that describe the work of the Messiah: "The spirit of the Lord God is upon me, because the Lord hath anointed me to preach good tidings unto the meek; he hath sent me to heal the brokenhearted, to proclaim liberty to the captives, and the opening of the prison to them that are bound; to proclaim the acceptable year of the Lord, and the day of vengeance of our God; to comfort all that mourn, to appoint unto them that mourn in Zion, to give unto them beauty for ashes, the oil of joy for mourning, the garment of praise for the spirit of heaviness; …"

There is an extensive work to be done in imparting a knowledge of the gospel message in all our cities of America … and not only in America, but in all parts of the world. …

The word of God is represented as a light. His servants are declared to be light-bearers. …

But before the precious light can shine to all that are in the house, there is needed a spirit of re-conversion in many of our people. …

"Arise, shine; for thy light is come, and the glory of the Lord is risen upon thee. …"[36]

March 30

A Glorious Church

Christ also loved the church, and gave himself for it; That he might sanctify and cleanse it with the washing of water by the word, That he might present it to himself a glorious church … Ephesians 5:25-27

All who have truly repented of sin, and by faith claimed the blood of Christ as their atoning sacrifice, have had pardon entered against their names in the books of heaven; as they have become partakers of the righteousness of Christ, and their characters are found to be in harmony with the law of God, their sins will be blotted out, and they themselves will be accounted worthy of eternal life. The Lord declares, by the prophet Isaiah: "I, even I, am He that blotteth out thy transgressions for Mine own sake, and will not remember thy sins." Isaiah 43:25. Said Jesus: "He that overcometh, the same shall be clothed in white raiment; and I will not blot out his name out of the book of life, but I will confess his name before My Father, and before His angels." … Revelation 3:5 …

Christ will clothe His faithful ones with His own righteousness, that He may present them to His Father "a glorious church, not having spot, or wrinkle, or any such thing." Ephesians 5:27. …

The work of the investigative judgment and the blotting out of sins is to be accomplished before the second advent of the Lord. … [T]he apostle Peter distinctly states that the sins of believers will be blotted out "when the times of refreshing shall come from the presence of the Lord; and He shall send Jesus Christ." Acts 3:19, 20.[37]

March 31

Confess Your Faults

He that covereth his sins shall not prosper: but whoso confesseth and forsaketh them shall have mercy. Proverbs 28:13

Christ was manifested as the Saviour of men. The people were not to trust in their own works, in their own righteousness, or in themselves in any way, but in the Lamb of God which taketh away the sins of the world. In Him the Advocate with the Father was revealed. Through Him the invitation was given, "Come now, and let us reason together, saith the Lord: though your sins be as scarlet, they shall be as white as snow; though they be red like crimson, they shall be as wool." This invitation comes sounding down along the lines to us today. Let not pride, or self-esteem, or self-righteousness keep any one from confessing his sins, that he may claim the promise: "He that covereth his sins shall not prosper: but whoso confesseth and forsaketh them shall have mercy." Keep nothing back from God, and neglect not the confession of your faults to the brethren when they have a connection with them. "Confess your faults one to another, and pray one for another, that ye may be healed." Many a sin is left unconfessed, to be confronted in the day of final accounts; better far to see your sins now, to confess them, and put them away, while the atoning Sacrifice pleads in your behalf. Do not dislike to learn the will of God on this subject. The health of your soul, the unity of your brethren, may depend upon the course you pursue in these things. Humble yourselves, therefore, under the mighty hand of God, that He may exalt you in due time, "casting all your care upon Him; for He careth for you."[38]

April 1

While He May be Found

Seek ye the LORD while he may be found, call ye upon him while he is near: Let the wicked forsake his way, and the unrighteous man his thoughts: Isaiah 55:6, 7

Those who exercise but little faith now, are in the greatest danger of falling under the power of satanic delusions and the decree to compel the conscience. And even if they endure the test they will be plunged into deeper distress and anguish in the time of trouble, because they have never made it a habit to trust in God. The lessons of faith which they have neglected they will be forced to learn under a terrible pressure of discouragement.

We should now acquaint ourselves with God by proving His promises. Angels record every prayer that is earnest and sincere. We should rather dispense with selfish gratifications than neglect communion with God.[1]

God will not impart to men divine light while they are content to remain in darkness. In order to receive God's help, man must realize his weakness and deficiency; he must apply his own mind to the great change to be wrought in himself; he must be aroused to earnest and persevering prayer and effort. Wrong habits and customs must be shaken off; and it is only by determined endeavor to correct these errors and to conform to right principles that the victory can be gained. ... All who are fitted for usefulness must be trained by the severest mental and moral discipline, and God will assist them by uniting divine power with human effort.[2]

April 2

Ye Shall Afflict Your Souls

For on that day shall the priest make an atonement for you, to cleanse you, that ye may be clean from all your sins before the LORD. It shall be a Sabbath of rest unto you, and ye shall afflict your souls... Leviticus 16:30, 31

The system of Jewish economy was the gospel in figure, a presentation of Christianity which was to be developed as fast as the minds of the people could comprehend spiritual light. ... To this day there are still aspects of truth which are dimly seen, connections that are not understood, and far-reaching depths in the law of God that are uncomprehended. There is immeasurable breadth, dignity, and glory in the law of God; and yet the religious world has set aside this law, as did the Jews, to exalt the traditions and commandments of men. ...

A man may have a knowledge of the Scriptures which will not make him wise unto salvation, although he may be able to master his opponents in public controversy. If he does not have a yearning of soul after God; if he does not search his own heart as with a lighted candle, fearing that any wrong should lurk there; if he is not possessed with a desire to answer the prayer of Christ, that His disciples may be one as He is one with the Father, that the world may believe that Jesus is the Christ, — he flatters himself in vain that he is a Christian. ... Nothing but divine power can regenerate the human heart and character, and imbue the soul with the love of Christ ...[3]

April 3

Ye Shall Be Clean

Then will I sprinkle clean water upon you, and ye shall be clean: from all your filthiness, and from all your idols, will I cleanse you. A new heart also will I give you, and a new spirit will I put within you: and I will take away the stony heart out of your flesh, and I will give you an heart of flesh. Ezekiel 36:25, 26

It is only through a living connection with the Source of all wisdom and light, that men may become wise unto salvation, and this living connection must be continually maintained ...

Though the light of God is shining in more distinct rays than ever before, and will shine more and more clearly as we near the close of earth's history, those who will be able to discern truth from error, will be men who are often upon their knees, seeking wisdom from God. ...

The promise of the Lord is, "Then will I sprinkle clean water upon you, and ye shall be clean: ...

The end of earth's history is right upon us, and O that all might fully come into the light! O that all might be moved by the Spirit from above! ... Only a remnant of probationary time is left us, and at this late day, shall our love for God and his truth grow cold? Shall our light flicker and die out in darkness, because we have not the oil of grace in our vessels with our lamps?[4]

April 4

He Will Subdue Our Iniquities

Who is a God like unto thee ... he will have compassion upon us; he will subdue our iniquities; and thou wilt cast all their sins into the depths of the sea.
Micah 7:18, 19

he courts of the temple at Jerusalem, filled with the tumult of unholy traffic, represented all too truly the temple of the heart, defiled by the presence of sensual passion and unholy thoughts. In cleansing the temple from the world's buyers and sellers, Jesus announced His mission to cleanse the heart from the defilement of sin, — from the earthly desires, the selfish lusts, the evil habits, that corrupt the soul. ... He is like a refiner's fire, and like fullers' soap: and He shall sit as a refiner and purifier of silver: and He shall purify the sons of Levi, and purge them as gold and silver." Malachi 3:1-3.

"Know ye not that ye are the temple of God, and that the Spirit of God dwelleth in you? If any man defile the temple of God, him shall God destroy; for the temple of God is holy, which temple ye are." 1 Corinthians 3:16, 17. ... Only Christ can cleanse the soul temple. ... "Behold, I stand at the door, and knock: if any man hear My voice, and open the door, I will come in to him." Revelation 3:20. ... "I will dwell in them, and walk in them; . . . and they shall be My people." "He will subdue our iniquities; and Thou wilt cast all their sins into the depths of the sea." 2 Corinthians 6:16; Micah 7:19. His presence will cleanse and sanctify the soul, so that it may be a holy temple unto the Lord, and "an habitation of God through the Spirit." Ephesians 2:21, 22.⁵

April 5

We Shall Be Like Him

[W]hen he shall appear, we shall be like him; for we shall see him as he is. And every man that hath this hope in him purifieth himself, even as he is pure.
1 John 3:3, 4

What is it to serve God? — It is to resemble Him in character, to imitate Him. ... Those who serve God strive earnestly to obey His will. ...

The church is Christ's instrumentality in this world. By it He seeks to represent the divine character. ... The faith that works by love and purifies the soul is the only true faith. The faith that does not produce fruit, that does not reveal the Christlikeness, is a false faith.

God is love, and all who truly serve Him will reveal His purity of character. They will be transformed into His image. ... The children of God are patient. They are merciful, even as Christ is merciful. They are kind, pitiful, tender-hearted, and firm as a rock to principle. ...

But until men see their defects in the mirror of God's law, until they realize that they must meet that law in character, they can not truly serve God. ... They will not feel it essential to be free from sin. ... The Son of God came to our world in human form to show man that divinity and humanity combined can obtain the victory over sin. Through Him we may be partakers of the divine nature, having escaped the corruption that is in the world through lust.[6]

April 6

Counted Worthy

[We] pray always for you, that our God would count you worthy of this calling, and fulfil all the good pleasure of his goodness, and the work of faith with power: 2 Thessalonians 1:11

Moral perfection is required of all. Never should we lower the standard of righteousness in order to accommodate inherited or cultivated tendencies to wrong-doing. We need to understand that imperfection of character is sin. All righteous attributes of character dwell in God as a perfect, harmonious whole, and every one who receives Christ as a personal Saviour is privileged to possess these attributes. ...

But Christ has given us no assurance that to attain perfection of character is an easy matter. ... A noble character is earned by individual effort through the merits and grace of Christ. God gives the talents, the powers of the mind; we form the character. It is formed by hard, stern battles with self. Conflict after conflict must be waged against hereditary tendencies. We shall have to criticize ourselves closely, and allow not one unfavorable trait to remain uncorrected.

Let no one say, I cannot remedy my defects of character. If you come to this decision, you will certainly fail of obtaining everlasting life. The impossibility lies in your own will. If you will not, then you can not overcome. ...

A character formed according to the divine likeness is the only treasure that we can take from this world to the next.[7]

April 7

The Cleansing

I tell you ... except ye repent, ye shall all likewise perish. Luke 13:3

All who endeavor to excuse or conceal their sins, and permit them to remain upon the books of heaven, unconfessed and unforgiven, will be overcome by Satan. ...

Those who are unwilling to forsake every sin and to seek earnestly for God's blessing, will not obtain it. But all who will lay hold of God's promises ..., and be as earnest and persevering ..., will succeed ...[8]

God requires His people to cleanse themselves from all filthiness of the flesh and spirit, perfecting holiness in the fear of the Lord. All those who are indifferent and excuse themselves from this work, waiting for the Lord to do for them that which He requires them to do for themselves, will be found wanting when the meek of the earth, who have wrought His judgments, are hid in the day of the Lord's anger.

I was shown that if God's people make no efforts on their part, but wait for the refreshing to come upon them and remove their wrongs and correct their errors; if they depend upon that to cleanse them from filthiness of the flesh and spirit, and fit them to engage in the loud cry of the third angel, they will be found wanting. The refreshing or power of God comes only on those who have prepared themselves for it by doing the work which God bids them, namely, cleansing themselves from all filthiness of the flesh and spirit, perfecting holiness in the fear of God.⁹

April 8

Grace

For sin shall not have dominion over you: for ye are not under the law, but under grace. Romans 6:14

God's law reaches the feelings and motives, as well as the outward acts. It reveals the secrets of the heart, flashing light upon things before buried in darkness. God knows every thought, every purpose, every plan, every motive. The books of heaven record the sins that would have been committed had there been opportunity. God will bring every work into judgment, with every secret thing. By His law He measures the character of every man. …

There are those who … talk of the grace of Christ, but they know not the meaning of grace; for God does not use His grace to make void the law. Satan has confused their minds, leading them to look upon the law as a yoke of bondage, a hindrance to spirituality. …

In his own strength the sinner can not meet the demands of God. He must go for help to the One who paid the ransom for him. It is impossible for him of himself to keep the law. But Christ can give him strength to do this. …

Christ is our hope. Those who trust in Him are cleansed. … Christ did not die to encourage man in rebellion against God, but to provide a way whereby he might keep the whole law. His garment of spotless righteousness clothes the repenting, believing sinner.¹⁰

April 9

Heart Searching

And I saw the dead, small and great, stand before God; and the books were opened: ... and the dead were judged out of those things which were written in the books, according to their works. Revelation 20:12

Then men will have a clear, sharp remembrance of all their transactions in this life. Not a word or a deed will escape their memory. Those will be trying times. And while we are not to mourn over the time of trouble to come, let us, as Christ's followers, search our hearts as with a lighted candle to see what manner of spirit we are of. For our present and eternal good, let us criticize our actions, to see how they stand in the light of the law of God. For this law is our standard. Let every soul search his own heart.[11]

The eye is the sensitive conscience, the inner light, of the mind. Upon its correct view of things the spiritual healthfulness of the whole soul and being depends. The "eye-salve," the Word of God, makes the conscience smart under its application; for it convicts of sin. But the smarting is necessary that the healing may follow, and the eye be single to the glory of God. The sinner, beholding himself in God's great moral looking-glass, sees himself as God views him, and exercises repentance toward God and faith toward our Lord Jesus Christ.

This is the work of the Holy Spirit. Said Christ: "... And when he is come, he will reprove the world of sin, and of righteousness, and of judgment: ..."[12]

April 10

The Grand Work of Instruction

[Y]e were not redeemed with corruptible things ... But with the precious blood of Christ, as of a lamb without blemish and without spot: 1 Peter 1:18, 19

From the Holy of Holies, there goes on the grand work of instruction. The angels of God are communicating to men. Christ officiates in the sanctuary. We do not follow Him into the sanctuary as we should. ... There must be a purifying of the soul here upon the earth, in harmony with Christ's cleansing of the sanctuary in heaven. There we shall see more clearly as we are seen. We shall know as we are known.

That which our people must have interwoven with their life and character is the unfolding of the plan of redemption, and more elevated conceptions of God and His holiness brought into the life. The washing of the robes of character in the blood of the Lamb is a work that we must attend to earnestly while every defect of character is to be put away. Thus are we working out our own salvation with fear and trembling. The Lord is working in us to will and to do of His good pleasure. We need Jesus abiding in the heart, a constant, living well-spring; then the streams flowing from the living fountain will be pure, sweet, and heavenly. Then the foretaste of heaven will be given to the humble in heart. ...[13]

[D]eep movings of the Spirit of God [are] needed to operate upon the heart to mold character, to open the communication between God and the soul...[14]

April 11

The Science of Prayer

And you, being dead in your sins and the uncircumcision of your flesh, hath he quickened together with him, having forgiven you all trespasses; Colossians 2:13

As fast as his people can bear it, the Lord reveals to them their errors in doctrine and their defects of character.[15] Night after night, scenes have been presented to me of little companies pleading with God. He would show them some idol they had been cherishing. Some would give this up, and some would not. But the light of heaven shone from the faces of those who would put away their idols. Then other idols would be shown to them, and again some would put these away. But the light of heaven shown upon all who would give up all for Christ.[16]

Through faith in Christ, every deficiency of character may be supplied, every defilement cleansed, every fault corrected, every excellence developed.

Prayer and faith are closely allied, and they need to be studied together. In the prayer of faith there is a divine science; it is a science that everyone who would make his lifework a success must understand. ...

For the pardon of sin, for the Holy Spirit, for a Christlike temper, for wisdom and strength to do His work, for any gift He has promised, we may ask; then we are to believe that we receive, and return thanks to God that we have received.[17]

April 12

Motives

[W]e shall all stand before the judgment seat of Christ. Romans 14:10

When the light shines, making manifest and reproving the errors that were undiscovered, there must be a corresponding change in the life and character. The mistakes that are the natural result of blindness of mind are, when pointed out, no longer sins of ignorance or errors of judgment; but unless there are decided reforms in accordance with the light given, they then become presumptuous sins. ... When the light is received and acted upon, you will be crucified to sin, being dead indeed unto the world, but alive to God. Your idols will be abandoned, and your example will be on the side of self-denial rather than that of self-indulgence.[18]

By a close scrutiny of [our] daily life under all circumstances [we] would know [our] own motives, the principles which actuate them. This daily review of our acts, to see whether conscience approves or condemns, is necessary for all who wish to arrive at the perfection of Christian character. Many acts which pass for good works, even deeds of benevolence, will, when closely investigated, be found to be prompted by wrong motives. ... The Searcher of hearts inspects motives, and often the deeds which are highly applauded by men are recorded by Him as springing from selfish motives and base hypocrisy. Every act of our lives, whether excellent and praiseworthy or deserving of censure, is judged by the Searcher of hearts according to the motives which prompted it.[19]

April 13

To Give Repentance

Him hath God exalted ... to give repentance ... and forgiveness of sins. Acts 5:31

When our earthly labors are ended, and Christ shall come for His faithful children, we shall then shine forth as the sun in the kingdom of our Father. But before that time shall come, everything that is imperfect in us will have been seen and put away. All envy and jealousy and evil surmising and every selfish plan will have been banished from the life.[20]

It is the virtue that goes forth from Christ, that leads to genuine repentance. Peter made the matter clear in his statement to the Israelites when he said, "Him hath God exalted with His right hand to be a Prince and a Saviour, for to give repentance to Israel, and forgiveness of sins." Acts 5:31. We can no more repent without the Spirit of Christ to awaken the conscience than we can be pardoned without Christ. ...

He is the only one that can implant in the heart enmity against sin. Every desire for truth and purity, every conviction of our own sinfulness, is an evidence that His Spirit is moving upon our hearts.

[A]s we behold the Lamb of God upon the cross of Calvary, the mystery of redemption begins to unfold to our minds and the goodness of God leads us to repentance. In dying for sinners, Christ manifested a love that is incomprehensible; and as the sinner beholds this love, it softens the heart, impresses the mind, and inspires contrition in the soul.[21]

April 14

Law and Grace

Do we then make void the law through faith? God forbid: yea, we establish the law. Romans 3:31

It is the sophistry of Satan that the death of Christ brought in grace to take the place of the law. The death of Jesus did not change, or annul, or lessen in the slightest degree, the law of ten commandments. That precious grace offered to men through a Saviour's blood, establishes the law of God. ...

Jesus, our substitute, consented to bear for man the penalty of the law transgressed. He clothed his divinity with humanity, and thus became the Son of man, a Saviour and Redeemer. The very fact of the death of God's dear Son to redeem man, shows the immutability of the divine law. ... The doctrine which teaches freedom, through grace, to break the law, is a fatal delusion. Every transgressor of God's law is a sinner, and none can be sanctified while living in known sin.

The condescension and agony of God's dear Son were not endured to purchase for man liberty to transgress the Father's law and yet sit down with Christ in his throne. It was that through his merits, and the exercise of repentance and faith, the most guilty sinner might receive pardon, and obtain strength to live a life of obedience. The sinner is not saved in his sins, but from his sins.[22]

April 15

Cast Out

Thou hast made us as the offscouring and refuse in the midst of the people. All our enemies have opened their mouths against us. Lamentations 3:45,46

Satan well knows that all whom he can lead to neglect prayer and the searching of the Scriptures, will be overcome by his attacks. Therefore he invents every possible device to engross the mind. There has ever been a class professing godliness, who, instead of following on to know the truth, make it their religion to seek some fault of character or error of faith in those with whom they do not agree. Such are Satan's right-hand helpers. Accusers of the brethren are not few, and they are always active when God is at work and His servants are rendering Him true homage. They will put a false coloring upon the words and acts of those who love and obey the truth. They will represent the most earnest, zealous, self-denying servants of Christ as deceived or deceivers. It is their work to misrepresent the motives of every true and noble deed, to circulate insinuations, and arouse suspicion in the minds of the inexperienced. In every conceivable manner they will seek to cause that which is pure and righteous to be regarded as foul and deceptive. [23]

The enemies of Christ are many, who, while they claim to be righteous, have not the righteousness of Christ. They disguise themselves as angels of light, but they are ministers of sin.[24]

April 16

Understanding the Plan

But if we walk in the light, as he is in the light, we have fellowship one with another, and the blood of Jesus Christ his Son cleanseth us from all sin. 1 John 1:7

We need to be enlightened in regard to the plan of salvation. There is not one in one hundred who understands for himself the Bible truth on this subject that is so necessary to our present and eternal welfare. When light begins to shine forth to make clear the plan of redemption to the people, the enemy works with all diligence that the light may be shut away from the hearts of men. If we come to the word of God with a teachable, humble spirit, the rubbish of error will be swept away, and gems of truth, long hidden from our eyes, will be discovered. ...

The enemy of man and God is not willing that this truth should be clearly presented; for he knows that if the people receive it fully, his power will be broken. ... God's people must have that faith which will lay hold of divine power; "for by grace are ye saved through faith; and that not of yourselves: it is the gift of God." Not all will receive the light, forsake their sins, and believe the words of eternal life, and without drawing back, go on from one truth to another, until guided into all truth. Those who believe that God for Christ's sake has forgiven their sins, should not, through temptation, fail to press on to fight the good fight of faith. Their faith should grow stronger until their Christian life, as well as their words, shall declare, "The blood of Jesus Christ cleanseth me from all sin."[25]

April 17

Do You Believe?

Jesus ... said unto him, Dost thou believe on the Son of God? John 9:35

Today let the question come home to the heart of every one who professes the name of Christ, "Dost thou believe in the Son of God?" Not, "Do you admit that Jesus is the Redeemer of the world?" Not to soothe your conscience and the consciences of others by saying, "I believe," and think that is all there is to be done. ... Do you bring him into your life, and weave him into your character, until you are one with Christ? Many accept Jesus as an article of belief, but they have no saving faith in him as their sacrifice and Saviour.

You may say that you believe in Jesus, when you have an appreciation of the cost of salvation. You may make this claim, when you feel that Jesus died for you on the cruel cross of Calvary; when you have an intelligent, understanding faith that his death makes it possible for you to cease from sin, and to perfect a righteous character through the grace of God, bestowed upon you as the purchase of Christ's blood. The eyes of fallen men may be anointed with the eye-salve of spiritual comprehension, and they may see themselves as they really are, — poor, and miserable, and blind, and naked. ...

The plan of salvation is not appreciated as it should be. ... It is made altogether a cheap affair; whereas to unite the human with the divine, required an exertion of Omnipotence.[26]

April 18

Jacob's Ladder

And he saith unto him, Verily, verily, I say unto you, Hereafter ye shall see heaven open, and the angels of God ascending and descending upon the Son of man.
John 1:51

Christ is the ladder which Jacob saw whose base rested on the earth and whose topmost round reached the highest heavens. This shows the appointed method of salvation. We are to climb round after round of this ladder. If any one of us (shall finally be) saved, it will be by clinging to Jesus as to the rounds of a ladder. Christ is made unto the believer wisdom and righteousness, sanctification and redemption....

We must as faithful messengers of God, plead with Him constantly to be kept by His power. If we swerve a single inch from duty we are in danger of following on in a course of sin that ends in perdition. There is hope for every one of us, but only in one way by fastening ourselves to Christ, and exerting every energy to attain to the perfection of His character. This goody goody religion that makes light of sin and that is forever dwelling upon the love of God to the sinner, encourages the sinner to believe that God will save him while he continues in sin and he knows it to be sin. This is the way that many are doing who profess to believe present truth. The truth is kept apart from their life, and that is the reason it has no more power to convict and convert the soul. There must be a straining of every nerve and spirit and muscle to leave the world, its customs, its practices, and its fashions....[27]

April 19

Half-Hearted

And then will I profess unto them, I never knew you: depart from me, ye that work iniquity. Matthew 7:23

There are a large number of professed Christians who would feel surprised and deeply injured if they were shown the light in which God regards them. They are spiritually dead, while professing to live. They are false lights — signs that point in the wrong direction. To these I would lift my voice in warning. Study your Bibles, analyze your motives and principles, before it is too late. When you repent and become converted, you will see and appreciate the true Light, which lighteth every man that cometh into the world. The half-hearted, pleasure-loving professor of religion is the very best agent Satan has to allure souls away from the straight gate and from the narrow path. Such have proved the ruin of souls they might have saved had they walked in the footprints of the Light of life.

And yet these persons think that because they have a form of godliness, they are accepted of God. But God does not receive such as his sons and daughters. [28]

Half-hearted Christians are worse than infidels; for their deceptive words and non-committal position may lead many astray. The infidel shows his colors. The luke-warm Christian deceives both parties. He is neither a good worldling nor a good Christian. Satan uses him to do a work that no one else can do. [29]

April 20

The Law of Liberty

But whoso looketh into the perfect law of liberty, and continueth therein, he being not a forgetful hearer, but a doer of the work, this man shall be blessed in his deed. James 2:25

The state of the character must be compared with the great moral standard of righteousness. There must be a searching out of the peculiar sins which have been offensive to God, which have dishonored his name, and quenched the light of his Spirit, and killed the first love from the soul. …

There are many who profess to be Christians, while they are living a sinful, immoral life; but their profession will not cover them in the day of God. There is a large class who trample upon God's law, who break its precepts, and teach others to do the same, terming it a "yoke of bondage;" while with words they exalt Jesus, and talk of being saved by grace. These are the ones who are turning the grace of Christ into lasciviousness. All such teaching has a tendency to enfeeble the moral tone of the religious world, and accounts for the miserable, heartless, outward form that is taking the place of the genuine piety that God desires in his people. How many come under the condemnation of the words of Christ! "I would that thou wert cold or hot. So then because thou art lukewarm, and neither cold nor hot, I will spew thee out of my mouth. Because thou sayest, I am rich, and increased with goods, and have need of nothing; and knowest not that thou art wretched, and miserable, and poor, and blind, and naked." [30]

April 21

Influenced by the Unrighteous

The great day of the LORD is near, it is near, and hasteth greatly, even the voice of the day of the LORD: the mighty man shall cry there bitterly. Zephaniah 1:14

The prophet, looking down the ages, had this time presented before his vision. The nations of this age have been the recipients of unprecedented mercies. The choicest of heaven's blessings have been given them, but increased pride, covetousness, idolatry, contempt of God, and base ingratitude are written against them. They are fast closing up their account with God.

But that which causes me to tremble is the fact that those who have had the greatest light and privileges have become contaminated by the prevailing iniquity. Influenced by the unrighteous around them, many, even of those who profess the truth, have grown cold and are borne down by the strong current of evil. The universal scorn thrown upon true piety and holiness leads those who do not connect closely with God to lose their reverence for His law. … As the disrespect for God's law becomes more manifest, the line of demarcation between its observers and the world becomes more distinct. Love for the divine precepts increases with one class according as contempt for them increases with another class.

The crisis is fast approaching. … Although loath to punish, nevertheless He will punish, and that speedily. Those who walk in the light will see signs of the approaching peril; but they are …to labor diligently to save others, looking with strong faith to God for help. [31]

April 22

Impending Wrath

And the dragon was wroth with the woman, and went to make war with the remnant of her seed, which keep the commandments of God, and have the testimony of Jesus Christ. Revelation 12:17

Today the signs of the times declare that we are standing on the threshold of great and solemn events. Everything in our world is in agitation. …

Rulers and statesmen, men who occupy positions of trust and authority, thinking men and women of all classes, have their attention fixed upon the events taking place about us. … They observe the intensity that is taking possession of every earthly element, and they realize that something great and decisive is about to take place — that the world is on the verge of a stupendous crisis.

Angels are now restraining the winds of strife, until the world shall be warned of its coming doom; but a storm is gathering, ready to burst upon the earth, and when God shall bid his angels loose the winds, there will be such a scene of strife as no pen can picture. [32]

The agencies of evil are combining their forces and consolidating. They are strengthening for the last great crisis. Great changes are soon to take place in our world, and the final movements will be rapid ones.[33]

April 23

And He Spake as a Dragon

And he causeth all, both small and great, rich and poor, free and bond, to receive a mark in their right hand, or in their foreheads: Revelation 13:16

This vision that Christ presented to John, presenting the commandments of God and the faith of Jesus, is to be definitely proclaimed to all nations, peoples, and tongues. The churches, represented by Babylon, are represented as having fallen from their spiritual state to become a persecuting power against those who keep the commandments of God and have the testimony of Jesus Christ. To John this persecuting power is represented as having horns like a lamb, but as speaking like a dragon. …

As we near the close of time, there will be greater and still greater external parade of heathen power; heathen deities will manifest their signal power, and will exhibit themselves before the cities of the world, and this delineation has already begun to be fulfilled. …

One of the marked characteristics of these false religious powers in that while they profess to have the character and features of a lamb, while they profess to be allied to heaven, they reveal by their actions that they have the heart of a dragon, that they are instigated by and united with satanic power, the same power that created war in heaven ...[34]

April 24

A Kingdom Rising

The beast ... shall ascend out of the bottomless pit ... and they that dwell on the earth shall wonder ... Revelation 17:8

As the condition of the church and the world was opened before me, and I beheld the fearful scenes that lie just before us, I was alarmed at the outlook.... I was shown the heresies which are to arise, the delusions that will prevail, the miracle-working power of Satan — the false Christs that will appear — that will deceive the greater part even of the religious world, and that would, if it were possible, draw away even the elect.[35]

[T]he church must and will fight against seen and unseen foes. Satan's agencies in human form are on the ground. Men have confederated to oppose the Lord of hosts. These confederacies will continue until Christ shall leave his place of intercession before the mercy-seat, and shall put on the garments of vengeance. Satanic agencies are in every city, busily organizing into parties those opposed to the law of God. Professed saints and avowed unbelievers take their stand with these parties. This is not time for the people of God to be weaklings. We can not afford to be off our guard for one moment.[36]

Satan will use every opportunity to seduce men from their allegiance to God. He and the angels who fell with him will appear on the earth as men, seeking to deceive. ... We, too, have a part to act. We shall surely be overcome unless we fight manfully the battles of the Lord.[37]

April 25

Supernatural Experiences

And Jesus answering them began to say, Take heed lest any man deceive you:
Mark 13:5

Satan will have power to bring the appearance of a form before us purporting to be our relatives and friends that now sleep in Jesus. It will be made to appear as though they were present, the words they uttered while here, which we were familiar with, will be spoken, and the same tone of voice, which they had while living, will fall upon the ear. All this is to deceive the saints, and ensnare them into the belief of this delusion.

I saw that the saints ... must understand the state of the dead; for the spirits of devils will yet appear to them, professing to be beloved friends and relatives, who will declare to them that the Sabbath has been changed, and, also, other unscriptural doctrines. They will do all in their power to excite sympathy, and work miracles before them, to confirm what they declare. The people of God must be prepared to withstand these spirits with the Bible truth, that the dead know not any thing, and that they are the spirits of devils. ... We must seek wisdom from on high that we may stand in this day of error and delusion.

I saw that we must examine well the foundation of our hope, for we shall have to give a reason for it from the scriptures; for we shall see this delusion spreading, and we shall have to contend with it face to face. And unless we are prepared for it, we shall be ensnared and overcome.[38]

April 26

More Frequent and Disastrous

For they have sown the wind, and they shall reap the whirlwind: it hath no stalk: the bud shall yield no meal: if so be it yield, the strangers shall swallow it up.
Hosea 8:7

Satan works through the elements also to garner his harvest of unprepared souls. He has studied the secrets of the laboratories of nature, and he uses all his power to control the elements as far as God allows. When he was suffered to afflict Job, how quickly flocks and herds, servants, houses, children, were swept away, one trouble succeeding another as in a moment. ... Satan has control of all whom God does not especially guard. He will favor and prosper some in order to further his own designs, and he will bring trouble upon others and lead men to believe that it is God who is afflicting them.

While appearing to the children of men as a great physician who can heal all their maladies, he will bring disease and disaster, until populous cities are reduced to ruin and desolation. Even now he is at work. In accidents and calamities by sea and by land, in great conflagrations, in fierce tornadoes and terrific hailstorms, in tempests, floods, cyclones, tidal waves, and earthquakes, in every place and in a thousand forms, Satan is exercising his power. He sweeps away the ripening harvest, and famine and distress follow. He imparts to the air a deadly taint, and thousands perish by the pestilence. These visitations are to become more and more frequent and disastrous.[39]

April 27

Iniquity Shall Abound

And because iniquity shall abound, the love of many shall wax cold.
Matthew 24:12

[T]he doctrine that men are released from obedience to God's requirements has weakened the force of moral obligation and opened the floodgates of iniquity upon the world. Lawlessness, dissipation, and corruption are sweeping in upon us like an overwhelming tide. ... [Satan's] banner waves, even in professedly Christian households. There is envy, evil surmising, hypocrisy, estrangement, emulation, strife, betrayal of sacred trusts, indulgence of lust. The whole system of religious principles and doctrines, which should form the foundation and framework of social life, seems to be a tottering mass, ready to fall to ruin. The vilest of criminals, when thrown into prison for their offenses, are often made the recipients of gifts and attentions as if they had attained an enviable distinction. Great publicity is given to their character and crimes. The press publishes the revolting details of vice, thus initiating others into the practice of fraud, robbery, and murder; and Satan exults in the success of his hellish schemes. The infatuation of vice, the wanton taking of life, the terrible increase of intemperance and iniquity of every order and degree, should arouse all who fear God, to inquire what can be done to stay the tide of evil. ...

By introducing the belief that God's law is not binding, [Satan] as effectually leads men to transgress as if they were wholly ignorant of its precepts. [40]

April 28

Economic Crisis

Your gold and silver is cankered; ... Ye have heaped treasure together for the last days. James 5:3

The centralizing of wealth and power; the vast combinations for the enriching of the few at the expense of the many; the combinations of the poorer classes for the defense of their interests and claims; the spirit of unrest, of riot and bloodshed; the world-wide dissemination of the same teachings that led to the French Revolution — all are tending to involve the whole world in a struggle similar to that which convulsed France.[41]

The agencies of evil are combining their forces and consolidating. They are strengthening for the last great crisis. Great changes are soon to take place in our world, and the final movements will be rapid ones.

There are not many, even among educators and statesmen, who comprehend the causes that underlie the present state of society. Those who hold the reins of government are not able to solve the problem of moral corruption, poverty, pauperism, and increasing crime. They are struggling in vain to place business operations on a more secure basis. If men would give more heed to the teaching of God's word, they would find a solution of the problems that perplex them.

The Scriptures describe the condition of the world just before Christ's second coming. Of the men who by robbery and extortion are amassing great riches …[42]

April 29

Poverty

For nation shall rise against nation, and kingdom against kingdom: and there shall be earthquakes in divers places, and there shall be famines and troubles: these are the beginnings of sorrows. Mark 13:8

Poverty is coming upon this world, and there will be a time of trouble such as never was since there was a nation. There will be wars and rumours of wars, and the faces of men will gather paleness. You may have to suffer; but God will not forsake you in your need. He will test your faith. We are not to live to please ourselves. We are here to manifest Christ to the world, to represent Him and His power to mankind.[43]

The Lord has shown me that some of his children would fear when they see the price of food rising, and they would buy food and lay it by for the time of trouble. Then in a time of need, I saw them go to their food and look at it, and it had bred worms, and was full of living creatures, and not fit for use. About one week since, the Lord showed me in vision, that houses and lands would be of no use in the time of trouble, and in that time they could not be disposed of. I saw it was the will of God that the saints should cut loose from every encumbrance — dispose of their houses and lands before the time of trouble comes, and make a covenant with God by sacrifice. I saw they would sell if they laid their property on the altar and earnestly inquired for duty. Then God will teach them when to dispose of these things. Then they will be free in the time of trouble, and have no clogs to weigh them down.[44]

April 30

Blasphemies

And there was given unto him a mouth speaking great things and blasphemies...
Revelation 13:5

And as the claims of the fourth commandment are urged upon the people, it is found that the observance of the seventh-day Sabbath is enjoined; and as the only way to free themselves from a duty which they are unwilling to perform, many popular teachers declare that the law of God is no longer binding. Thus they cast away the law and the Sabbath together. As the work of Sabbath reform extends, this rejection of the divine law to avoid the claims of the fourth commandment will become well-nigh universal. The teachings of religious leaders have opened the door to infidelity, to spiritualism, and to contempt for God's holy law; and upon these leaders rests a fearful responsibility for the iniquity that exists in the Christian world.

Yet this very class put forth the claim that the fast-spreading corruption is largely attributable to the desecration of the so-called "Christian sabbath," and that the enforcement of Sunday observance would greatly improve the morals of society. This claim is especially urged in America, where the doctrine of the true Sabbath has been most widely preached. ... The leaders of the Sunday movement ... advocate reforms which the people need, principles which are in harmony with the Bible ... [but nothing] can justify them in setting aside the commandments of God for the precepts of men. 45

May 1

The Sabbath Question

And it was given unto him to make war with the saints, and to overcome them: ...
Revelation 13:7

Says the great deceiver: "We must watch those who are calling the attention of the people to the Sabbath of Jehovah; they will lead many to see the claims of the law of God; and the same light which reveals the true Sabbath, reveals also the ministration of Christ in the heavenly sanctuary, and shows that the last work for man's salvation is now going forward. Hold the minds of the people in darkness till that work is ended, and we shall secure the world and the church also.

"The Sabbath is the great question which is to decide the destiny of souls. We must exalt the Sabbath of our creating. We have caused it to be accepted by both worldlings and church-members; now the church must be led to unite with the world in its support. We must work by signs and wonders to blind their eyes to the truth, and lead them to lay aside reason and the fear of God, and follow custom and tradition. ...

"But our principal concern is to silence this sect of Sabbath-keepers. ... We will enlist great men and worldly-wise men upon our side, and induce those in authority to carry out our purposes. Then the Sabbath which I have set up shall be enforced by laws the most severe and exacting. Those who disregard them shall be driven out from the cities and villages, and made to suffer hunger and privation. When once we have the power, we will show that we can do with those who will not swerve from their allegiance to God. ..."[1]

May 2

For the One

And if so be that he find it, verily I say unto you, he rejoiceth more of that sheep, than of the ninety and nine which went not astray. Matthew 18:13

There is a great work to be done, and every effort possible must be made to reveal Christ as the sin-pardoning Saviour, Christ as the Sin Bearer, Christ as the bright and morning Star; and the Lord will give us favor before the world until our work is done.

While the angels hold the four winds, we are to work with all our capabilities. We must bear our message without any delay. We must give evidence to the heavenly universe, and to men in this degenerate age, that our religion is a faith and a power of which Christ is the Author and His word the divine oracle. Human souls are hanging in the balance. They will either be subjects for the kingdom of God or slaves to the despotism of Satan. All are to have the privilege of laying hold of the hope set before them in the gospel, and how can they hear without a preacher? The human family is in need of a moral renovation, a preparation of character, that they may stand in God's presence. There are souls ready to perish because of the theoretical errors which are prevailing, and which are calculated to counterwork the gospel message. Who will now fully consecrate themselves to become laborers together with God? …

One soul is of more value to heaven than a whole world of property, houses, lands, money. For the conversion of one soul we should tax our resources to the utmost.[2]

May 3

The Fear

Men's hearts failing them for fear, and for looking after those things which are coming on the earth: for the powers of heaven shall be shaken. Luke 21:26

Christ upon the Mount of Olives rehearsed the fearful judgments that were to precede his second coming … While these prophecies received a partial fulfillment at the destruction of Jerusalem, they have a more direct application in the last days.

John also was a witness of the terrible scenes that will take place as signs of Christ's coming. He saw armies mustering for battle, and men's hearts failing them for fear. He saw the earth moved out of its place, the mountains carried into the midst of the sea, the waves thereof roaring and troubled, and the mountains shaking with the swelling thereof. He saw the vials of God's wrath opened, and pestilence, famine, and death come upon the inhabitants of the earth. …

Hurricanes, storms, tempests, fire and flood, disasters by sea and land, follow each other in quick succession. …

We are standing on the threshold of great and solemn events. … The scenes to be enacted in our world are not even dreamed of. Satan is at work through human agencies. Those who are making so great efforts to change the Constitution and secure a law enforcing the first day of the week little realize what will be the result. A crisis is just upon us.[3]

May 4

The Test

… [Y]e may be blameless and harmless, the sons of God, without rebuke, in the midst of a crooked and perverse nation, among whom ye shine as lights in the world; Philippians 2:15

The time is not far distant when the test will come to every soul. The observance of the false sabbath will be urged upon us. The contest will be between the commandments of God and the commandments of men. Those who step by step have yielded to worldly demands and conformed to worldly customs will then yield to the powers that be, rather than subject themselves to derision, insult, threatened imprisonment and death. At this time the gold will be separated from the dross. True godliness will be clearly distinguished from the appearance and tinsel of it. ... Those who have assumed the ornaments of the sanctuary, but are not clothed with Christ's righteousness, will then appear in the shame of their own nakedness.

Among earth's inhabitants, scattered in every land, there are those who have not bowed the knee to Baal. ... Even now they are appearing in every nation, among every tongue and people, and in the hour of deepest apostasy, when Satan's supreme effort is made to "cause all, both small and great, rich and poor, free and bond," to receive under penalty of death the sign of allegiance to a false rest day, these faithful ones, "blameless and harmless, the sons of God, without rebuke," will "shine as lights in the world." The darker the night the more brilliantly will they shine.[4]

May 5

The Day of Trouble

An end is come, the end is come ... behold, it is come. ... the time is come, the day of trouble is near ... Ezekiel 7:6, 7

Soon grievous troubles will arise among the nations.—trouble that will not cease until Jesus comes. As never before, we need to press together, serving him who has prepared his throne in the heavens, and whose kingdom ruleth over all. ...

The judgments of God are in the land. The wars and rumors of wars, the destruction by fire and flood, say clearly that the time of trouble, which is to increase until the end, is very near at hand.[5]

Just as fast as God's Spirit is taken away, Satan's cruel work will be done upon land and sea. Judgments by fire and flood will increase in fearfulness; for Satan claims his harvest of souls in the destruction.[6]

[E]arthquakes, tempests, tidal waves, pestilence, and famine have multiplied. The most awful destructions, by fire and flood, are following one another in quick succession. The terrible disasters that are taking place from week to week speak to us in earnest tones of warning, declaring that the end is near, that something great and decisive will soon of necessity take place.

Probationary time will not continue much longer. Now God is withdrawing his restraining hand from the earth.[7]

May 6

Calamities Will Come

And Lot went out ... and said, Up, get you out of this place; for the LORD will destroy this city. But he seemed as one that mocked ... Genesis 19:14

I am bidden to declare the message that cities full of transgression, and sinful in the extreme, will be destroyed by earthquakes, by fire, by flood. All the world will be warned that there is a God who will display His authority as God. His unseen agencies will cause destruction, devastation, and death. All the accumulated riches will be as nothingness.

Notwithstanding the scientific care with which men safeguard buildings from destruction, one touch of the great and rightful Ruler will bring to nothingness the idolatrous possessions that have been laid up in a sightly and magnificent display. The devices of men will come to naught.

The injustice in our world, the masterly power man has taken unto himself, the oppressive, man-made unions that bring confusion and violence and strife, and the manipulation of a power to rule men and to acquire means through underhand deceptions — these conditions God cannot pass by with silence. ... He keeps a strict account of every lie framed, and when He takes matters in His hand, He will deal in accordance with every man's secret and hidden devising.

Bible history is to be repeated. Calamities will come—calamities most awful, most unexpected; and these destructions will follow one after another.[8]

May 7

The Synagogue of Satan

If the world hate you, ye know that it hated me before it hated you. John 15:18

The world will be enraged at them in the same way that they were enraged at Christ ... Those who love and keep the commandments of God are most obnoxious to the synagogue of Satan, and the powers of evil will manifest their hatred toward them to the fullest extent possible. ... The forces of darkness will unite with human agents who have given themselves into the control of Satan, and the same scenes that were exhibited at the trial, rejection, and crucifixion of Christ will be revived. Through yielding to satanic influences, men will be transformed into fiends; ... [they] will become the habitation of dragons, and Satan will see in an apostate race his masterpiece of evil, — men who reflect his own image.[9]

Satan puts his interpretation upon events, and they think, as he would have them, that the calamities which fill the land are a result of Sunday-breaking. Thinking to appease the wrath of God, these influential men make laws enforcing Sunday observance. They think that by exalting this false rest day higher and still higher, compelling obedience to the Sunday law, the spurious sabbath, they are doing God service. ...

The chosen people of God will be proved and tried before they are pronounced good and faithful servants, worthy to inherit eternal life with its endowment of heavenly riches.[10]

May 8

Against the Covenant

... and they shall place the abomination that maketh desolate. Daniel 11:31

Troublous times are before us. ... Soon the scenes of trouble spoken of in the prophecies will take place. The prophecy in the eleventh of Daniel has nearly reached its complete fulfillment. Much of the history that has taken place in fulfillment of this prophecy will be repeated. In the thirtieth verse a power is spoken of that "shall be grieved, and return, and have indignation against the holy covenant: so shall he do; he shall even return, and have intelligence with them that forsake the holy covenant." ...

[T]hey shall place the abomination that maketh desolate. And such as do wickedly against the covenant shall he corrupt by flatteries: but the people that do know their God shall be strong, and do exploits. And they that understand among the people shall instruct many: yet they shall fall by the sword, and by flame, by captivity, and by spoil, many days. ... And the king ... and he shall exalt himself, and magnify himself above every god, and shall speak marvellous things against the God of gods, and shall prosper till the indignation be accomplished... [Dan. 11:31-36]

Scenes similar to those described in these words will take place. ... Let all read and understand the prophecies of this book, for we are now entering upon the time of trouble spoken of...[11]

May 9

Sunday Worship

[H]e shall speak great words against the most High ... and think to change times and laws: Daniel 7:25

Satan says, "I will work at cross purposes with God. I will empower my followers to set aside God's memorial, the seventh-day Sabbath. Thus I will show the world that the day sanctified and blessed by God has been changed. … I will obliterate the memory of it. I will place in its stead a day that does not bear the credentials of God, a day that cannot be a sign between God and His people. I will lead those who accept this day to place upon it the sanctity that God placed upon the seventh day.

"Through my vicegerent, I will exalt myself. The first day will be extolled, and the Protestant world will receive this spurious sabbath as genuine. Through the nonobservance of the Sabbath that God instituted, I will bring His law into contempt. The words, 'A sign between Me and you throughout your generations,' I will make to serve on the side of my sabbath.

"Thus the world will become mine. I will be the ruler of the earth, the prince of the world. I will so control the minds under my power that God's Sabbath shall be a special object of contempt. A sign? I will make the observance of the seventh day a sign of disloyalty to the authorities of earth. Human laws will be made so stringent that men and women will not dare to observe the seventh-day Sabbath. For fear of wanting food and clothing, they will join with the world in transgressing God's law. The earth will be wholly under my dominion."[12]

May 10

Growing Into Power

And I beheld another beast coming up out of the earth; and he had two horns like a lamb, and he spake as a dragon. Revelation 13:11

Protestants little know what they are doing when they propose to accept the aid of Rome in the work of Sunday exaltation. While they are bent upon the accomplishment of their purpose, Rome is aiming to re-establish her power, to recover her lost supremacy. Let the principle once be established in the United States that the church may employ or control the power of the state; that religious observances may be enforced by secular laws; in short, that the authority of church and state is to dominate the conscience, and the triumph of Rome in this country is assured.

God's word has given warning of the impending danger; let this be unheeded, and the Protestant world will learn what the purposes of Rome really are, only when it is too late to escape the snare. She is silently growing into power. Her doctrines are exerting their influence in legislative halls, in the churches, and in the hearts of men. She is piling up her lofty and massive structures in the secret recesses of which her former persecutions will be repeated. Stealthily and unsuspectedly she is strengthening her forces to further her own ends when the time shall come for her to strike. All that she desires is vantage ground, and this is already being given her. We shall soon see and shall feel what the purpose of the Roman element is. Whoever shall believe and obey the word of God will thereby incur reproach and persecution.[13]

May 11

Babylon's Wrath

And they worshipped the dragon which gave power unto the beast: and they worshipped the beast, saying, Who is like unto the beast? who is able to make war with him? Revelation 13:4

The great deceiver will persuade men that those who serve God are causing these evils. ... It will be declared that men are offending God by the violation of the Sunday sabbath; that this sin has brought calamities which will not cease until Sunday observance shall be strictly enforced; and that those who present the claims of the fourth commandment, thus destroying reverence for Sunday, are troublers of the people, preventing their restoration to divine favor and temporal prosperity. ... As the wrath of the people shall be excited by false charges, they will pursue a course toward God's ambassadors very similar to that which apostate Israel pursued toward Elijah.

The miracle-working power manifested through spiritualism will exert its influence against those who choose to obey God rather than men. Communications from the spirits will declare that God has sent them to convince the rejecters of Sunday of their error, affirming that the laws of the land should be obeyed as the law of God. They will lament the great wickedness in the world and second the testimony of religious teachers that the degraded state of morals is caused by the desecration of Sunday. Great will be the indignation excited against all who refuse to accept their testimony.[14]

May 12

As In the Days of Noah

And as it was in the days of Noe, so shall it be also in the days of the Son of man. Luke 17:26

The law of God is made void. We see and hear of confusion and perplexity, want and famine, earthquakes and floods; terrible outrages will be committed by men; passion, not reason, bears sway. ... Already fire and flood are destroying thousands of lives and the property that has been selfishly accumulated by the oppression of the poor. The Lord is soon to cut short His work and put an end to sin. Oh, that the scenes which have come before me of the iniquities practiced in these last days, might make a deep impression on the minds of God's professing people. As it was in the days of Noah, so shall it be when the Son of man shall be revealed. The Lord is removing His restrictions from the earth, and soon there will be death and destruction, increasing crime, and cruel, evil working against the rich who have exalted themselves against the poor. Those who are without God's protection will find no safety in any place or position. Human agents are being trained and are using their inventive power to put in operation the most powerful machinery to wound and to kill. [15]

The earth's crust will be rent by the outbursts of the elements concealed in the bowels of the earth. These elements, once broken loose, will sweep away the treasures of those who for years have been adding to their wealth by securing large possessions at starvation prices from those in their employ.[16]

May 13

Forming the Image

... The servant is not greater than his lord. If they have persecuted me, they will also persecute you; ... John 15:20

In a Sunday law there is possibility for great suffering to those who observe the seventh day. The working out of Satan's plans will bring persecution to the people of God.[17] The Lord has shown me clearly that the image of the beast will be formed before probation closes; for it is to be the great test for the people of God, by which their eternal destiny will be decided.[18]

God has revealed what is to take place in the last days, that his people may be prepared to stand against the tempest of opposition and wrath. ... The Sunday movement is now making its way in darkness. The leaders are concealing the true issue, and many who unite in the movement do not themselves see whither the under-current is tending. Its professions are mild, and apparently Christian; but when it shall speak, it will reveal the spirit of the dragon. ...

Through fraud and falsehood Satan is now using those who claim to be Christians to divorce the world from God's mercy. They are working in blindness. They do not see that if [the] government ... brings into the Constitution, principles that will propagate papal falsehood and papal delusion, they are plunging into the Roman horrors of the Dark Ages.[19]

May 14

The Image

Now the brother shall betray the brother to death, and the father the son; and children shall rise up against their parents, and shall cause them to be put to death. Mark 13:12

In order for the United States to form an image of the beast, the religious power must so control the civil government that the authority of the state will also be employed by the church to accomplish her own ends.[20]

By the decree enforcing the institution of the papacy in violation of the law of God, our nation will disconnect herself fully from righteousness. When Protestantism shall stretch her hand across the gulf to grasp the hand of the Roman power, when she shall reach over the abyss to clasp hands with spiritualism, when, under the influence of this threefold union, our country shall repudiate every principle of its Constitution as a Protestant and republican government, and shall make provision for the propagation of papal falsehoods and delusions, then we may know that the time has come for the marvelous working of Satan and that the end is near. ...

[T]his apostasy be a sign to us that the limit of God's forbearance is reached, that the measure of our nation's iniquity is full, and that the angel of mercy is about to take her flight, never to return. The people of God will then be plunged into those scenes of affliction and distress which prophets have described as the time of Jacob's trouble. [21]

May 15

National Apostasy

And he ... causeth the earth and them which dwell therein to worship the first beast, whose deadly wound was healed. Revelation 13:12

Very soon our nation will attempt to enforce upon all the observance of the first day of the week as a sacred day. In doing this they will not scruple to compel men against the voice of their own conscience to observe the day the nation declares to be the Sabbath.[22]

The dignitaries of church and state will unite to bribe, persuade, or compel all classes to honor the Sunday. The lack of divine authority will be supplied by oppressive enactments. Political corruption is destroying love of justice and regard for truth; and even in free America, rulers and legislators, in order to secure public favor, will yield to the popular demand for a law enforcing Sunday observance. Liberty of conscience, which has cost so great a sacrifice, will no longer be respected.[23]

The Roman Catholic principles will be taken under the care and protection of the State. This national apostasy will speedily be followed by national ruin. The protest of Bible truth will be no longer tolerated by those who have made not the law of God their rule of life. Then will the voice be heard from the graves of martyrs, represented by the souls which John saw slain for the word of God and the testimony of Jesus Christ which they held; then the prayer will ascend from every true child of God, "It is time, Lord, for thee to work: for they have made void thy law."[24]

May 16

The Loud Cry

And I heard a loud voice saying in heaven, Now is come salvation, and strength, and the kingdom of our God, and the power of his Christ ... Revelation 12:10

As men depart further and further from God, Satan is permitted to have power over the children of disobedience. He hurls destruction among men. There is calamity by land and sea. Property and life are destroyed by fire and flood. Satan resolves to charge this upon those who refuse to bow to the idol which he has set up. His agents point to Seventh-day Adventists as the cause of the trouble. "These people stand out in defiance of law," they say. "They desecrate Sunday. Were they compelled to obey the law for Sunday observance, there would be a cessation of these terrible judgments."

The civil power is called to the aid of the Church in persecuting those who keep holy the seventh day. ... The decree goes forth that no man shall be allowed to buy or sell save he that has the mark or the number of the Beast.

As God's people approach the final crisis, they must with increasing power proclaim the message He has given them. ... God's requirements must be laid before those who are transgressing His law. They must be made to understand that this is a life and death question. God's remnant people are to fill the earth with the cry of the third angel.[25]

May 17

The Sunday Movement

Rivers of waters run down mine eyes, because they keep not thy law.
Psalm 119:136

As the claims of the fourth commandment are urged upon the people, it is found that the observance of the seventh-day Sabbath is enjoined; and as the only way to free themselves from a duty which they are unwilling to perform, many popular teachers declare that the law of God is no longer binding. Thus they cast away the law and the Sabbath together. As the work of Sabbath reform extends, this rejection of the divine law to avoid the claims of the fourth commandment will become well-nigh universal. The teachings of religious leaders have opened the door to infidelity, to spiritualism, and to contempt for God's holy law; and upon these leaders rests a fearful responsibility for the iniquity that exists in the Christian world.

Yet this very class put forth the claim that the fast-spreading corruption is largely attributable to the desecration of the so-called "Christian sabbath," and that the enforcement of Sunday observance would greatly improve the morals of society. This claim is especially urged in America, where the doctrine of the true Sabbath has been most widely preached. ... The leaders of the Sunday movement may advocate reforms which the people need, principles which are in harmony with the Bible; yet while there is with these a requirement which is contrary to God's law ... Nothing can justify them in setting aside the commandments of God for the precepts of men. [26]

May 18

War With the Remnant

And the dragon was wroth with the woman, and went to make war with the remnant of her seed, which keep the commandments of God, and have the testimony of Jesus Christ. Revelation 12:17

Those who honor the Bible Sabbath will be denounced as enemies of law and order, as breaking down the moral restraints of society, causing anarchy and corruption, and calling down the judgments of God upon the earth. Their conscientious scruples will be pronounced obstinacy, stubbornness, and contempt of authority. ... Ministers who deny the obligation of the divine law will present from the pulpit the duty of yielding obedience to the civil authorities as ordained of God. In legislative halls and courts of justice, commandment keepers will be misrepresented and condemned. A false coloring will be given to their words; the worst construction will be put upon their motives.

As the Protestant churches reject the clear, Scriptural arguments in defense of God's law, they will long to silence those whose faith they cannot overthrow by the Bible. Though they blind their own eyes to the fact, they are now adopting a course which will lead to the persecution of those who conscientiously refuse to do what the rest of the Christian world are doing, and acknowledge the claims of the papal sabbath. ...

The lack of divine authority will be supplied by oppressive enactments. ... [R]ulers and legislators, in order to secure public favor, will yield to the popular demand for a law enforcing Sunday observance.[27]

May 19

The Cities

And the angel took the censer, and filled it with fire of the altar, and cast it into the earth: and there were voices, and thunderings, and lightnings, and an earthquake. Revelation 8:5

In the visions of the night a very impressive scene passed before me. I saw an immense ball of fire fall among some beautiful mansions, causing their instant destruction. I heard someone say: "We knew that the judgments of God were coming upon the earth, but we did not know that they would come so soon." Others, with agonized voices, said: "You knew! Why then did you not tell us? We did not know." On every side I heard similar words of reproach spoken. [28]

O that God's people had a sense of the impending destruction of thousands of cities, now almost given to idolatry! …

Transgression has almost reached its limit. Confusion fills the world, and a great terror is soon to come upon human beings. The end is very near. We who know the truth should be preparing for what is soon to break upon the world as an overwhelming surprise.[29]

The inhabitants of the ungodly cities so soon to be visited by calamities have been cruelly neglected. The time is near when large cities will be swept away, and all should be warned of these coming judgments. But who is giving to the accomplishment of this work the wholehearted service that God requires? [30]

May 20

Fire

Likewise also as it was in the days of Lot; they did eat, they drank, they bought, they sold, they planted, they builded; But the same day that Lot went out of Sodom it rained fire and brimstone from heaven, and destroyed them all. Even thus shall it be in the day when the Son of man is revealed. Luke 17:28-30

Let all who would understand the meaning of these things read the eleventh chapter of Revelation. Read every verse, and learn the things that are yet to take place in the cities. Read also the scenes portrayed in the eighteenth chapter of the same book.[31]

The time is near when the large cities will be visited by the judgments of God. In a little while these cities will be terribly shaken. No matter how large or how strong their buildings, no matter how many safeguards against fire may have been provided, let God touch these buildings, and in a few minutes or a few hours they are in ruins.

The ungodly cities of our world are to be swept away by the besom of destruction. In the calamities that are now befalling immense buildings and large portions of cities God is showing us what will come upon the whole earth. He has told us: "Now learn a parable of the fig tree; When his branch is yet tender, and putteth forth leaves, ye know that summer is nigh: so likewise ye, when ye shall see all these things, know that it [the coming of the Son of man] is near, even at the doors." Matthew 24:32, 33. [32]

May 21

Vengeance

For these be the days of vengeance, that all things which are written may be fulfilled. Luke 21:22

On one occasion, when in New York City, I was in the night season called upon to behold buildings rising story after story toward heaven. These buildings were warranted to be fireproof, and they were erected to glorify the owners and builders. Higher and still higher these buildings rose, and in them the most costly material was used. ...

As these lofty buildings went up, the owners rejoiced with ambitious pride that they had money to use in gratifying self and provoking the envy of their neighbors. Much of the money that they thus invested had been obtained through exaction, through grinding down the poor. ... The time is coming when in their fraud and insolence men will reach a point that the Lord will not permit them to pass, and they will learn that there is a limit to the forbearance of Jehovah.

The scene that next passed before me was an alarm of fire. Men looked at the lofty and supposedly fire-proof buildings and said: "They are perfectly safe." But these buildings were consumed as if made of pitch. ...

No material can be used in the erection of buildings that will preserve them from destruction when God's appointed time comes to send retribution on men for their disregard of His law and for their selfish ambition.[33]

May 22

Judgments in Quick Succession

A fire devoureth before them; and behind them a flame burneth ... yea, and nothing shall escape them. Joel 2:3

In tender compassion God himself is speaking to an impenitent world through judgments; and he will continue to speak in this manner. For many years we have known that the great cities would be visited with divine judgments because of long-continued disobedience. …

The time of God's destructive judgments is the time of mercy for those who have no opportunity to learn what is truth. Tenderly will the Lord look upon them. His heart of mercy is touched; his hand is still stretched out to save, while the door is closed to those who would not enter. Large numbers will be admitted who in these last days hear the truth for the first time. …

In quick succession the judgments of God will follow one another, — fire and flood and earthquakes, with war and bloodshed. Something great and decisive will soon of necessity take place."

[God] is holding back his judgments, waiting for the message of warning to be sounded to all. There are many who have not yet heard the testing truths for this time. The last call of mercy is to be given more fully to our world. The truths of the eighteenth and nineteenth chapters of Revelation should be read and understood by all."[34]

May 23

War, Famine and Pestilence

For thus saith the Lord GOD; How much more when I send my four sore judgments upon Jerusalem, the sword, and the famine, and the noisome beast, and the pestilence, to cut off from it man and beast? Ezekiel 14:21

I saw the sword, famine, pestilence, and great confusion in the land. The wicked thought that we had brought the judgments down on them. They rose up and took counsel to rid the earth of us, thinking that then the evil would be stayed.[35]

Strife, war, and bloodshed, with famine and pestilence, raged everywhere. … War caused famine. Want and bloodshed caused pestilence. And then men's hearts failed them for fear, "and for looking after those things which are coming on the earth."[36]

In the last great conflict of the controversy with Satan those who are loyal to God will see every earthly support cut off. Because they refuse to break His law in obedience to earthly powers, they will be forbidden to buy or sell. It will finally be decreed that they shall be put to death. … But to the obedient is given the promise, "He shall dwell on high: his place of defense shall be the munitions of rocks: bread shall be given him; his waters shall be sure." Isa. 33:16. By this promise the children of God will live. When the earth shall be wasted with famine, they shall be fed. "They shall not be ashamed in the evil time: and in the days of famine they shall be satisfied." Ps. 37:19.[37]

May 24

One Day

Therefore shall her plagues come in one day ... for strong is the Lord God who judgeth her. Revelation 18:8

Probationary time will not continue much longer. Now God is withdrawing his restraining hand from the earth. Long has he been speaking to men and women through the agency of his Holy Spirit; but they have not heeded the call. Now he is speaking to his people, and to the world, by his judgments. The time of these judgments is a time of mercy for those who have not yet had opportunity to learn what is truth. Tenderly will the Lord look upon them. His heart of mercy is touched; his hand is still stretched out to save. Large numbers will be admitted to the fold of safety who in these last days will hear the truth for the first time.

The Lord calls upon those who believe in him to be workers together with him. ... Shall we allow the signs of the end to be fulfilled without telling people of what is coming upon the earth? ... Unless we ourselves do our duty to those around us, the day of God will come upon us as a thief. Confusion fills the world, and a great terror is soon to come upon human beings. The end is very near. We who know the truth should be preparing for what is soon to break upon the world as an overwhelming surprise. ...

The message that means so much to the dwellers upon earth will be heard and understood. Men will know what is truth. Onward, and still onward, the work will advance, until the whole earth shall have been warned. And then shall the end come.[38]

May 25

What Is the Seal?

... Hurt not the earth, neither the sea, nor the trees, till we have sealed the servants of our God in their foreheads. Revelation 7:3

In the issue of the great contest two parties are developed, those who "worship the beast and his image," and receive his mark, and those who receive "the seal of the living God," who have the Father's name written in their foreheads. This is not a visible mark. The time has come when all who have an interest in their soul's salvation should earnestly and solemnly inquire, What is the seal of God?[39] The living righteous will receive the seal of God prior to the close of probation. [40]

We are standing on the threshold of great and solemn events. ... — events which it was declared should shortly precede the great day of God. ... The great day of God is hasting greatly.

But although the nations are mustering their forces for war and bloodshed, the command to the angels is still in force, that they hold the four winds until the servants of God are sealed in their foreheads.

We should study more earnestly the character of our Saviour. ... We should desire to reflect his image in kindness, in courtesy, in gentleness, and love, then "when he shall appear, we shall be like him; for we shall see him as he is. And every man that hath this hope in him purifieth himself, even as he is pure." In a little while every one who is a child of God will have his seal placed upon him. [41]

May 26

The Mystery

[T]he mystery which hath been hid from ages and from generations ... now is made manifest to his saints: ... which is Christ in you, the hope of glory:
Colossians 1:26, 27

Those who imagine that because Christ has done all that is necessary in the way of merit, there remains nothing for them to do in the way of complying with the conditions, are deceiving their own souls. Said Christ, "I sanctify myself, that they also might be sanctified through the truth."

The servants of Christ have a sacred work. They must copy his character and his ways and plans of reaching men. God does not want them to labor with their own finite power, but in his strength; he wants them to represent to the world, in their own characters, the Saviour's purity, benevolence, and love. ... "Without me," says Christ, "ye can do nothing." In him we can do all things. ...

The divine must be blended with all our work in the cause of our Master. ... We may reach higher; we may conform to the divine Model; we may be channels to communicate the living water to thirsting souls; we may so build that neither storm nor tempest can move us from the foundation, for we are united to the Eternal Rock. [42]

May 27

The Best Robe

But the father said to his servants, Bring forth the best robe, and put it on him ...
Luke 15:22

Have you wandered far from God? Have you sought to feast upon the fruits of transgression, only to find them turn to ashes upon your lips? ... Return to your Father's house. He invites you, saying, "Return unto Me; for I have redeemed thee." Isa. 44:22.

Do not listen to the enemy's suggestion to stay away from Christ until you have made yourself better; until you are good enough to come to God. ... When Satan points to your filthy garments, repeat the promise of Jesus, "Him that cometh to Me I will in no wise cast out." John 6:37. Tell the enemy that the blood of Jesus Christ cleanses from all sin. ...

Your heavenly Father will take from you the garments defiled by sin. ... And the word is spoken by the Lord, "Take away the filthy garments from him. And unto him He said, Behold, I have caused thine iniquity to pass from thee, and I will clothe thee with change of raiment. ..." Zech. 3:4, 5. Even so God will clothe you with "the garments of salvation," and cover you with "the robe of righteousness." Isa. 61:10. ...

"As the bridegroom rejoiceth over the bride, so shall thy God rejoice over thee." Isa. 62:5. ... And heaven and earth shall unite in the Father's song of rejoicing: "For this My son was dead, and is alive again; he was lost, and is found." [43]

May 28

The Wedding Garment

I counsel thee to buy of me ... white raiment, that thou mayest be clothed ...
that the shame of thy nakedness do not appear... Revelation 3:18

By the wedding garment in the parable is represented the pure, spotless character which Christ's true followers will possess. To the church it is given "that she should be arrayed in fine linen, clean and white," "not having spot, or wrinkle, or any such thing." Rev. 19:8; Eph. 5:27. The fine linen, says the Scripture, "is the righteousness of saints." Rev. 19:8. It is the righteousness of Christ, His own unblemished character, that through faith is imparted to all who receive Him as their personal Saviour. ...

Only the covering which Christ Himself has provided can make us meet to appear in God's presence. This covering, the robe of His own righteousness, Christ will put upon every repenting, believing soul. "I counsel thee," He says, "to buy of Me ... white raiment, that thou mayest be clothed, and that the shame of thy nakedness do not appear." Rev. 3:18.

This robe, woven in the loom of heaven, has in it not one thread of human devising. Christ in His humanity wrought out a perfect character, and this character He offers to impart to us. "All our righteousness are as filthy rags." Isa. 64:6. Everything that we of ourselves can do is defiled by sin. But the Son of God "was manifested to take away our sins; and in Him is no sin."[44]

May 29

In My Name

And whatsoever ye shall ask in my name, that will I do, that the Father may be glorified in the Son. John 14:13

In Christ's name His followers are to stand before God. ... Because of the imputed righteousness of Christ they are accounted precious. ...

The Lord ... desires His chosen heritage to value themselves according to the price He has placed upon them. ... He is well pleased when they make the very highest demands upon Him, that they may glorify His name. ...

But to pray in Christ's name means much. It means that we are to accept His character, manifest His spirit, and work His works. The Saviour's promise is given on condition. "If ye love Me," He says, "keep My commandments." ...

All true obedience comes from the heart. It was heart work with Christ. And if we consent, He will so identify Himself with our thoughts and aims, so blend our hearts and minds into conformity to His will, that when obeying Him we shall be but carrying out our own impulses. The will, refined and sanctified, will find its highest delight in doing His service. When we know God as it is our privilege to know Him, our life will be a life of continual obedience. Through an appreciation of the character of Christ, through communion with God, sin will become hateful to us.[45]

May 30

All Thy Heart

Jesus said unto him, Thou shalt love the Lord thy God with all thy heart, and with all thy soul, and with all thy mind. Matthew 22:37

No one can be truly righteous unless his soul reflects the image of God, and manifests love for all nations, kindreds, tongues, and people; for "God so loved the world, that he gave his only begotten Son, that whosoever believeth in him, should not perish, but have everlasting life." ... He who has the love of God shed abroad in his heart, will reflect the purity and love which exist in Jehovah, and which Christ represented in our world. He who has the love of God in his heart has no enmity against the law of God, but renders willing obedience to all his commandments, and this constitutes Christianity. He who has supreme love to God will reveal love to his fellow-men, who belong to God both by creation and by redemption.

Love is the fulfilling of the law; and it is the duty of every child of God to render obedience to his commandments. ...

Those who love God, have the seal of God in their foreheads, and work the works of God. Would that all who profess Christianity knew what it means to love God practically. ... They would have a powerful influence upon the life and character of those around them, which would work as leaven amid the mass of humanity, transforming others through the power of Jesus Christ.⁴⁶

May 31

His Father's Name

And I looked, and, lo, a Lamb stood on the mount Sion, and with him an hundred forty and four thousand, having his Father's name written in their foreheads. Revelation 14:1

"And I looked, and lo, a Lamb stood on the mount Sion, and with Him an hundred and forty and four thousand, having His Father's name written in their foreheads. ... These were redeemed from among men, being the firstfruits unto God and to the Lamb. And in their mouth was found no guile: for they are without fault before the throne of God" [Rev. 14:1-5].

This Scripture represents the character of the people of God for these last days. The everlasting gospel is to be preached, and it is to be practiced in true missionary work carried forward not after the wisdom that men may devise, but after the wisdom of God. All who walk in safe paths are to understand that the third angel's message is of consequence to the whole world, and must be carried to the world in clear, straight lines, and in its distinctive features, as Christ revealed it to John.

[Rev. 14:6-12, quoted.] This is the message we have to bear; this is the work we have to do. This is the message God has kept before the Seventh-day Adventist people. The truth of this message will not decrease, but will increase in force and importance as we are brought down to the close of the work of God on earth.⁴⁷

June 1

From Every Nation

... I saw four angels standing on the four corners of the earth, holding the four winds of the earth ... Revelation 7:1

Already the restraining Spirit of God is being withdrawn from the earth. Hurricanes, storms, tempests, fire and flood, disasters by sea and land, follow each other in quick succession. ... Men cannot discern the sentinel angels restraining the four winds that they may not blow until the servants of God are sealed; but when God shall bid his angels loose the winds, there will be such a scene of his avenging wrath as no pen can picture.

We are standing on the threshold of great and solemn events. ... There is soon to open before us a period of overwhelming interest to all living. The controversies of the past are to be revived. New controversies will arise. The scenes to be enacted in our world are not even dreamed of. Satan is at work through human agencies. Those who are making so great efforts to change the Constitution and secure a law enforcing the first day of the week little realize what will be the result. A crisis is just upon us.[1]

The message of the renewing power of God's grace will belt the world. Those that will be sealed will be from every nation and kindred and tongue and people. From every country will be gathered men and women who will stand before the throne of God and before the Lamb ... But before this work can be accomplished, we must experience right here in our own country the work of the Holy Spirit upon our hearts.[2]

June 2

As Wax

... I will put my laws into their mind, and write them in their hearts: and I will be to them a God, and they shall be to me a people: Hebrews 8:10

The pure and holy garments are not prepared to be put on by any one after he has entered the gate of the city. All who enter will have on the robe of Christ's righteousness and the name of God will be seen in their foreheads. This name is the symbol which the apostle saw in vision, and signifies the yielding of the mind to intelligent and loyal obedience to all of God's commandments.[3]

We are to work out our "own salvation with fear and trembling, for it is God that worketh in you to will and to do of His good pleasure." ... To the extent of our ability, we are to make manifest the truth and love and excellence of the divine character. As wax takes the impression of the seal, so the soul is to take the impression of the Spirit of God and retain the image of Christ.

We are to grow daily in spiritual loveliness. We shall fail often in our efforts to copy the divine Pattern. We shall often have to bow down to weep at the feet of Jesus, because of our shortcomings and mistakes; but we are not to be discouraged; we are to pray more fervently, believe more fully, and try again with more steadfastness to grow into the likeness of our Lord. As we distrust our own power, we shall trust the power of our Redeemer ...⁴

June 3

Not Having Spot or Wrinkle

... they shall walk with me in white: for they are worthy. Revelation 3:4

The divine Intercessor presents the plea that all who have overcome through faith in His blood be forgiven their transgressions, that they be restored to their Eden home, and crowned as joint heirs with Himself to "the first dominion." Micah 4:8. ... He asks for His people not only pardon and justification, full and complete, but a share in His glory and a seat upon His throne.

While Jesus is pleading for the subjects of His grace, Satan accuses them before God as transgressors. ... Now he points to the record of their lives, to the defects of character, the unlikeness to Christ, which has dishonored their Redeemer, to all the sins that he has tempted them to commit, and because of these he claims them as his subjects.

Jesus ... lifts His wounded hands before the Father and the holy angels, saying: I know them by name. I have graven them on the palms of My hands. ... And to the accuser of His people He declares: "The Lord rebuke thee, O Satan; even the Lord that hath chosen Jerusalem rebuke thee: is not this a brand plucked out of the fire?" Zechariah 3:2. Christ will clothe His faithful ones with His own righteousness, that He may present them to His Father "a glorious church, not having spot, or wrinkle, or any such thing." Ephesians 5:27. Their names stand enrolled in the book of life, and concerning them it is written: "They shall walk with Me in white: for they are worthy." Revelation 3:4. ⁵

June 4

Fitted For Translation

And he shall sit as a refiner and purifier of silver: and he shall purify the sons of Levi, and purge them as gold and silver, that they may offer unto the LORD an offering in righteousness. Malachi 3:3

God leads His people on, step by step. He brings them up to different points calculated to manifest what is in the heart. Some endure at one point, but fall off at the next. At every advanced point the heart is tested and tried a little closer. If the professed people of God find their hearts opposed to this straight work, it should convince them that they have a work to do to overcome, if they would not be spewed out of the mouth of the Lord. Said the angel: "God will bring His work closer and closer to test and prove every one of His people." Some are willing to receive one point; but when God brings them to another testing point, they shrink from it and stand back, because they find that it strikes directly at some cherished idol. Here they have opportunity to see what is in their hearts that shuts out Jesus. They prize something higher than the truth, and their hearts are not prepared to receive Jesus. Individuals are tested and proved a length of time to see if they will sacrifice their idols and heed the counsel of the True Witness. If any will not be purified through obeying the truth, and overcome their selfishness, their pride, and evil passions, the angels of God have the charge: "They are joined to their idols, let them alone," … Those who come up to every point, and stand every test, and overcome, be the price what it may, have heeded the counsel of the True Witness, and they will receive the latter rain, and thus be fitted for translation.[6]

June 5

Settling Into the Truth

… These were redeemed from among men, being the firstfruits unto God and to the Lamb. Revelation 14:4

Satan is working to the utmost to make himself as God, and to destroy all who oppose his power. And today the world is bowing before him. His power is received as the power of God. The prophecy of the Revelation is being fulfilled, that "all the world wondered after the beast."

But the cloud of judicial wrath hangs over it, containing the elements that destroyed Sodom. John saw this multitude. This demon-worship was revealed to him, and it seemed as if the whole world were standing on the brink of perdition. But as he looked with intense interest, he beheld the company of God's commandment keeping people. They had upon their foreheads the seal of the living God, and he exclaimed, "Here is the patience of the saints: here are they that keep the commandments of God, and have the faith of Jesus."[7]

There is a spirit of desperation, of war and bloodshed, and that spirit will increase until the very close of time. Just as soon as the people of God are sealed in their foreheads, — it is not any seal or mark that can be seen, but a settling into the truth, both intellectually and spiritually, so they cannot be moved, — just as soon as God's people are sealed and prepared for the shaking, it will come. Indeed, it has begun already; the judgments of God are now upon the land, to give us warning, that we may know what is coming.[8]

June 6

Not Even a Thought

Casting down imaginations, and every high thing that exalteth itself against the knowledge of God, and bringing into captivity every thought to the obedience of Christ; 2 Corinthians 10:5

The "time of trouble, such as never was," is soon to open upon us; and we shall need an experience which we do not now possess and which many are too indolent to obtain. It is often the case that trouble is greater in anticipation than in reality; but this is not true of the crisis before us. The most vivid presentation cannot reach the magnitude of the ordeal. In that time of trial, every soul must stand for himself before God. ...

Now, while our great High Priest is making the atonement for us, we should seek to become perfect in Christ. Not even by a thought could our Saviour be brought to yield to the power of temptation. ... Satan could find nothing in the Son of God that would enable him to gain the victory. He had kept His Father's commandments, and there was no sin in Him that Satan could use to his advantage. This is the condition in which those must be found who shall stand in the time of trouble.

It is in this life that we are to separate sin from us, through faith in the atoning blood of Christ. Our precious Saviour invites us to join ourselves to Him, to unite our weakness to His strength, our ignorance to His wisdom, our unworthiness to His merits. ... It rests with us to co-operate with the agencies which Heaven employs in the work of conforming our characters to the divine model.[9]

June 7

Great Shaking

For in my jealousy and in the fire of my wrath have I spoken, Surely in that day there shall be a great shaking ... Isaiah 38:19

I saw some, with strong faith and agonizing cries, pleading with God. Their countenances were pale, and marked with deep anxiety, expressive of their internal struggle. ...

Evil angels crowded around, pressing darkness upon them to shut out Jesus from their view, that their eyes might be drawn to the darkness that surrounded them, and thus they be led to distrust God ...

As the praying ones continued their earnest cries, at times a ray of light from Jesus came to them, to encourage their hearts, and light up their countenances. Some, I saw, did not participate in this work of agonizing and pleading. ... They were not resisting the darkness around them, and it shut them in like a thick cloud. The angels of God left these, and went to the aid of the earnest, praying ones. ...

I asked the meaning of the shaking I had seen, and was shown that it would be caused by the straight testimony called forth by the counsel of the True Witness to the Laodiceans. This will have its effect upon the heart of the receiver, and will lead him to exalt the standard and pour forth the straight truth. ... They will rise up against it, and this is what will cause a shaking among God's people.

This testimony must work deep repentance; all who truly receive it will obey it, and be purified.[10]

June 8

Give Glory to God

And they shall see his face; and his name shall be in their foreheads.
Revelation 22:4

Before the world, God is developing us as living witnesses to what men and women may become through the grace of Christ. ... The divine Teacher says, "Be ye therefore perfect, even as your Father which is in heaven is perfect." Would Christ tantalize us by requiring of us an impossibility? — Never, never! ... He can enable us to do this, for He declares, "All power is given unto Me in heaven and in earth." ...

The glory of God is His character. While Moses was in the mount, earnestly interceding with God, He prayed, "I beseech Thee, show me Thy glory." In answer God declared "I will make all My goodness pass before thee, and I will proclaim the name of the Lord before thee;

...." The glory of God — His character — was then revealed ... Christ desires His followers to reveal in their lives this same character. ...

Today it is still His purpose to sanctify and cleanse His church "with the washing of water by the Word, that He might present it to Himself a glorious church, not having spot, or wrinkle, or any such thing; but that it should be holy and without blemish." No greater gift than the character that He revealed, can Christ ask His Father to bestow upon those who believe on Him.[11]

June 9

The Seal and The Mark

... I gave them my sabbaths, to be a sign between me and them, that they might know that I am the LORD that sanctify them. Ezekiel 20:12

The seal of God, the token or sign of His authority, is found in the fourth commandment. This is the only precept of the Decalogue that points to God as the Creator of the heavens and the earth, and clearly distinguishes the true God from all false gods. Throughout the Scriptures the fact of God's creative power is cited as proof that He is above all heathen deities.

The Sabbath enjoined by the fourth commandment was instituted to commemorate the work of creation ... The Sabbath of the fourth commandment is the seal of the living God. It points to God as the Creator, and is the sign of His rightful authority over the beings He has made.

What, then, is the mark of the beast, if it is not the spurious sabbath which the world has accepted in the place of the true?

The prophetic declaration that the Papacy was to exalt itself above all that is called God, or that is worshiped, has been strikingly fulfilled in the changing of the Sabbath from the seventh to the first day of the week. ...

Roman Catholics acknowledge that the change in the Sabbath was made by their church, and they cite this very change as evidence of the supreme authority of this church. [12]

June 10

To Him That Keepeth My Works

And he that overcometh, and keepeth my works unto the end, to him will I give power over the nations: Revelation 2:26

The seal of the living God will be placed upon those only who bear a likeness to Christ in character.[13]

Not all who profess to keep the Sabbath will be sealed. There are many even among those who teach the truth to others who will not receive the seal of God in their foreheads. They had the light of truth, they knew their Master's will, they understood every point of our faith, but they had not corresponding works. These who were so familiar with prophecy and the treasures of divine wisdom should have acted their faith. ...

Jesus is the only true pattern. Everyone must now search the Bible for himself upon his knees before God, with the humble, teachable heart of a child, if he would know what the Lord requires of him. ...

Not one of us will ever receive the seal of God while our characters have one spot or stain upon them. ...[14]

Those that overcome the world, the flesh, and the devil, will be the favored ones who shall receive the seal of the living God. ... Only those who, in their attitude before God, are filling the position of those who are repenting and confessing their sins in the great anti-typical day of atonement, will be recognized and marked as worthy of God's protection. [15]

June 11

Holiness Inwrought

...The LORD said unto him, Go ... and set a mark upon the foreheads of the men that sigh and that cry for all the abominations that be done ... Ezekiel 9:4

This sealing of the servants of God is the same that was shown to Ezekiel in vision. John also had been a witness of this most startling revelation. He saw the sea and the waves roaring, and men's hearts failing them for fear. ... He was shown plagues, pestilence, famine, and death performing their terrible mission.

The same angel who visited Sodom is sounding the note of warning, "Escape for thy life." The bottles of God's wrath cannot be poured out to destroy the wicked and their works until all the people of God have been judged, and the cases of the living as well as the dead are decided. And even after the saints are sealed with the seal of the living God, His elect will have trials individually. Personal afflictions will come; but the furnace is closely watched by an eye that will not suffer the gold to be consumed. The indelible mark of God is upon them. God can plead that His own name is written there. The Lord has shut them in. Their destination is inscribed — "God, New Jerusalem." They are God's property, His possession.

Will this seal be put upon the impure in mind, the fornicator, the adulterer, the man who covets his neighbor's wife? Let your souls answer the question, Does my character correspond to the qualifications essential that I may receive a passport to the mansions Christ has prepared for those who are fitted for them? Holiness must be inwrought in our character. [16]

June 12

The Seal and the Mark

... my Sabbaths ... shall be a sign between me and you, that ye may know that I am the LORD your God. Ezekiel 20:20

Satan is making desperate efforts to make himself god, to speak and act like God, to appear as one who has a right to control the consciences of men. He strives with all his power to place a human institution in the position of God's holy rest-day. Under the jurisdiction of the man of sin, men have exalted a false standard in complete opposition to God's enactment. Each Sabbath institution bears the name of its author, an ineffaceable mark showing the authority of each. ...

Thus the distinction is drawn between the loyal and the disloyal. Those who desire to have the seal of God in their foreheads must keep the Sabbath of the Fourth Commandment. Thus they are distinguished from the disloyal, who have accepted a man-made institution in place of the true Sabbath. The observance of God's rest-day is a mark of distinction between him that serveth God and him that serveth Him not. ...

The substitution of the false for the true is the last act in the drama. When this substitution becomes universal, God will reveal himself. When ... the powers of this earth try to force men to keep the first day of the week, know that the time has come for God to work. He will arise in His majesty, and will shake terribly the earth. He will come out of His place to punish the inhabitants of the world for their iniquity.[17]

June 13

Stewards of the Mysteries

Let a man so account of us, as of the ministers of Christ, and stewards of the mysteries of God. 1 Corinthians 4:1

We should understand better the mysteries of redemption. Mysteries into which angels desire to look, which prophets and kings and righteous men desired to understand, the church will carry in messages from God to the world. The prophets prophesied of these things, and they longed to understand that which they foretold, but to them this privilege was not given. They longed to see what we see, and hear what we hear, but they could not.

Souls that have borne the likeness of Satan, have been transformed into the image of God. The change is itself the miracle of miracles. A change wrought by the Word, it is one of the deepest mysteries of the Word. We can not understand it; we can only believe, that, as declared by the Scriptures, it is "Christ in you, the hope of glory."

A knowledge of this mystery furnishes a key to every other. It opens to the soul the treasures of the universe, the possibilities of infinite development.

And this development is gained through the constant unfolding to us of the character of God — the glory and mystery of the written Word.[18]

Gospel religion is Christ in the life — a living, active principle. It is the grace of Christ revealed in character and wrought out in good works.[19]

June 14

Mystery of Love

[W]e speak the wisdom of God in a mystery ... which God ordained before the world unto our glory 1 Corinthians 2:7

When we seek for appropriate language in which to describe the love of God, we find words too tame, to weak, too far beneath the theme.... In attempting any description of this love, we feel that we are as an infant lisping its first words. ... This love is ... the mystery of God in the flesh, God in Christ, and divinity in humanity. Christ bowed down in unparalleled humility, that in his exaltation to the throne of God, he might also exalt those who believe in him, to a seat with him upon his throne. All who look upon Jesus in faith ... shall be made whole.

The themes of redemption are momentous themes, and only those who are spiritually minded can discern their depth and significance. ... Faith and prayer are necessary in order that we may behold the deep things of God. ... [W]e catch but limited views of the experience it is our privilege to have. How little do we comprehend what is meant by the prayer of the apostle, when he says, "That he would grant you, according to the riches of his glory, to be strengthened with might by his spirit in the inner man; that Christ may dwell in your hearts by faith; that ye, being rooted and grounded in love, may be able to comprehend with all saints what is the breadth, and length, and depth, and height; and to know the love of Christ, which passeth knowledge, that ye might be filled with all the fullness of God. ..."[20]

June 15

Bearing the Dying

*I will dwell in them, and walk in them; and I will be their God, and they shall be
my people. 2 Corinthians 6:16*

We bear about in our body the dying of the Lord Jesus, which is life and salvation and righteousness to us. Wherever we go, we bear the abiding presence of … Christ by a living faith. … [A]s we realize his presence, our thoughts are brought into captivity to him. Our experience in divine things will be in proportion to the vividness of our sense of his companionship. … Christ dwells in our hearts by faith when we appreciate what he is to us, and what a work he has wrought out for us in the plan of redemption. Then we shall be most happy in cultivating a sense of this great Gift of God to our world, and to us personally.

Thoughts of this order have a controlling power on our character. … The thoughts are pervaded with a sense of his goodness, his love. … By beholding, we are conformed to the divine similitude, even to the likeness of Christ. …

Jesus is to us an abiding presence, controlling our thoughts and actions. We are imbued with the instruction of the greatest Teacher the world ever knew. … The words of Christ are spirit and life. We can not then center our thoughts upon self; it is no more we that live, but Christ that liveth in us, and he is the hope of glory. Self is dead, but Christ is a living Saviour. Continuing to look unto Jesus, we reflect his image to all around us.[21]

June 16

The Revelation

*[K]now the love of Christ, which passeth knowledge, that ye might be filled with
all the fulness of God. Ephesians 3:19*

The last rays of merciful light, the last message of mercy to be given to the world, is a revelation of His character of love. …

The religion of Christ means more than the forgiveness of sin; it means taking away our sins, and filling the vacuum with the graces of the Holy Spirit. It means divine illumination, rejoicing in God. It means a heart emptied of self, and blessed with the abiding presence of Christ. When Christ reigns in the soul, there is purity, freedom from sin. The glory, the fullness, the completeness of the gospel plan is fulfilled in the life. The acceptance of the Saviour brings a glow of perfect peace, perfect love, perfect assurance. The beauty and fragrance of the character of Christ revealed in the life testifies that God has indeed sent His Son into the world to be its Saviour. ...

The revelation of His own glory in the form of humanity will bring heaven so near to men that the beauty adorning the inner temple will be seen in every soul in whom the Saviour dwells. Men will be captivated by the glory of an abiding Christ. And in currents of praise and thanksgiving from the many souls thus won to God, glory will flow back to the great Giver.[22]

June 17

The Great Harvest

And I looked, and behold a white cloud, and upon the cloud one sat like unto the Son of man, having on his head a golden crown, and in his hand a sharp sickle. Revelation 14:14

As the plant receives the sunshine, the dew, and the rain, we are to open our hearts to the Holy Spirit. ... If we keep our minds stayed upon Christ, He will come unto us "as the rain, as the latter and former rain unto the earth." Hosea 6:3. ... By constantly relying upon Christ as our personal Saviour, we shall grow up into Him in all things who is our head. ...

Christ is seeking to reproduce Himself in the hearts of men; and He does this through those who believe in Him. The object of the Christian life is fruit bearing — the reproduction of Christ's character in the believer, that it may be reproduced in others. ...

"The fruit of the Spirit is love, joy, peace, longsuffering, gentleness, goodness, faith, meekness, temperance." Gal. 5:22, 23. This fruit can never perish, but will produce after its kind a harvest unto eternal life.

"When the fruit is brought forth, immediately he putteth in the sickle, because the harvest is come." Christ is waiting with longing desire for the manifestation of Himself in His church. When the character of Christ shall be perfectly reproduced in His people, then He will come to claim them as His own. [23]

June 18

They Shall Be Filled

Blessed are they which do hunger and thirst after righteousness: for they shall be filled. Matthew 5:6

The work that God has begun in the human heart in giving his light and knowledge, must be continually going forward. Every individual must realize his own necessity. The heart must be emptied of every defilement, and cleansed for the indwelling of the Spirit. It was by the confession and forsaking of sin, by earnest prayer and consecration of themselves to God, that the early disciples prepared for the outpouring of the Holy Spirit on the day of Pentecost. The same work, only in greater degree, must be done now. ... It is God who began the work, and he will finish his work, making man complete in Jesus Christ.[24]

When the laborers have an abiding Christ in their own souls, when all selfishness is dead, when there is no rivalry, no strife for the supremacy, when oneness exists, when they sanctify themselves, so that love for one another is seen and felt, then the showers of the grace of the Holy Spirit will just as surely come upon them as that God's promise will never fail in one jot or tittle.[25]

As they reform, and His love revives in their hearts, His loving answers will come to their requests. ... His rich blessing will rest upon them, and in bright rays they will reflect the light of heaven. Then a multitude not of their faith, seeing that God is with His people, will unite with them in serving the Redeemer.[26]

June 19

Deep Heart Searching

These all continued with one accord in prayer and supplication ... Acts 1:14

As the disciples waited for the fulfillment of the promise, they humbled their hearts in true repentance and confessed their unbelief. ... They reproached themselves for their misapprehension of the Saviour. ... As they meditated upon His pure, holy life they felt that no toil would be too hard, no sacrifice too great, if only they could bear witness in their lives to the loveliness of Christ's character. ... But they were comforted by the thought that they were forgiven. And they determined that, so far as possible, they would atone for their unbelief by bravely confessing Him before the world.

The disciples prayed with intense earnestness for a fitness to meet men and in their daily intercourse to speak words that would lead sinners to Christ. Putting away all differences, all desire for the supremacy, they came close together in Christian fellowship. They drew nearer and nearer to God, and as they did this they realized what a privilege had been theirs in being permitted to associate so closely with Christ. ...

These days of preparation were days of deep heart searching. The disciples felt their spiritual need and cried to the Lord for the holy unction that was to fit them for the work of soul saving. They did not ask for a blessing for themselves merely. They were weighted with the burden of the salvation of souls. They realized that the gospel was to be carried to the world, and they claimed the power that Christ had promised.[27]

June 20

The Glad Tidings

... And the Lord added to the church daily such as should be saved. Acts 2:47

What was the result of the outpouring of the Spirit upon the day of Pentecost? – The glad tidings of a risen Saviour were carried to the utmost bounds of the inhabited world. The hearts of the disciples were surcharged with the benevolence so full, so deep, so far-reaching, that it impelled them to go to the ends of the earth … As they proclaimed the truth as it is in Jesus, hearts yielded to the power of the message. The church beheld converts flocking to her from all directions. Backsliders were reconverted. Sinners united with Christians in seeking the pearl of great price. Those who had been the bitterest opponents of the gospel became its champions. The prophecy was fulfilled, that the weak shall be "as David," and the house of David "as the angel of the Lord." Every Christian saw in his brother the divine similitude of love and benevolence. One interest prevailed. One subject of emulation swallowed up all others. The only ambition of the believers was to reveal the likeness of Christ's character and to labor for the enlargement of his kingdom.

Notice that it was after the disciples had come into perfect unity, when they were no longer striving for the highest place, that the Spirit was poured out. They were of one accord. All differences had been put away. And the testimony borne of them after the Spirit had been given was the same.[28]

June 21

Pray For the Holy Spirit

... I will pray the Father, and he shall give you another Comforter, that he may abide with you for ever; John 14:16

We should pray as earnestly for the descent of the Holy Spirit as the disciples prayed on the day of Pentecost. If they needed it at that time, we need it more today. All manner of false doctrines, heresies, and deceptions are misleading the minds of men; and without the Spirit's aid, our efforts to present divine truth will be in vain.

We are living in the time of the Holy Spirit's power. It is seeking to diffuse itself through the agency of humanity, thus increasing its influence in the world. For if any man drinks of the water of life, it will be in him "a well of water springing up into everlasting life;" and the blessing will not be confined to himself, but will be shared by others. …

Let the routine of study or work be secondary, and let every one co-operate with the divine agency, with hearty thanksgiving that God has visited his people. ...

All our sins must be put away. ... Are we willing to renounce our own wisdom, and to receive the kingdom of heaven as a little child? Are we willing to part with our self-righteousness? ... Are we willing to welcome the Holy Spirit's aid, and co-operate with it, putting forth efforts and making sacrifices proportionate to the value of the object to be obtained? [29]

June 22

Abundant Rain

[T]his is that which was spoken by the prophet Joel; ... in the last days, saith God, I will pour out of my Spirit upon all flesh: ... Acts 2:16, 17

The outpouring of the Spirit in the days of the apostles was "the former rain," and glorious was the result. But the latter rain will be more abundant. What is the promise to those living in these last days? "Turn you to the stronghold, ye prisoners of hope: even today do I declare that I will render double unto thee." "Ask ye of the Lord rain in the time of the latter rain; so the Lord shall make bright clouds, and give them showers of rain, to every one grass in the field." Zechariah 9:12; 10:1.[30]

"He will cause to come down for you the rain, the former rain, and the latter rain." In the East the former rain falls at the sowing-time. It is necessary in order that the seed may germinate. Under the influence of the fertilizing showers, the tender shoot springs up. The latter rain, falling near the close of the season, ripens the grain, and prepares it for the sickle. The Lord employs these operations of nature to represent the work of the Holy Spirit. As the dew and the rain are given first to cause the seed to germinate, and then to ripen the harvest, so the Holy Spirit is given to carry forward, from one stage to another, the process of spiritual growth. The ripening of the grain represents the completion of the work of God's grace in the soul. By the power of the Holy Spirit the moral image of God is to be perfected in the character. We are to be wholly transformed into the likeness of Christ.[31]

June 23

Vessels Unto Honor

Thou blind Pharisee, cleanse first that which is within the cup and platter, that the outside of them may be clean also. Matthew 23:26

We have now the invitations of mercy to become vessels unto honor, and then we need not worry about the latter rain; all we have to do is to keep the vessel clean and right side up and prepared for the reception of the heavenly rain, and keep praying, "Let the latter rain come into my vessel. Let the light of the glorious angel which unites with the third angel shine upon me; give me a part in the work; let me sound the proclamation; let me be a co-laborer with Jesus Christ."

Thus seeking God, let me tell you, He is fitting you up all the time, giving you His grace. You need not be worried. You need not be thinking that there is a special time coming when you are to be crucified; the time to be crucified is just now. Every day, every hour, self is to die; self is to be crucified; and then, when the time comes that the test shall come to God's people in earnest, the everlasting arms are around you. ... It is now that self is to be crucified — when there is work to do; when there is some use to be made of every entrusted capability. It is now that we are to empty and thoroughly cleanse the vessel of its impurity. It is now that we are to be made holy unto God. This is our work, this very moment. You are not to wait for any special period for a wonderful work to be done; it is today. I give myself to God today.[32]

June 24

Fitted For the Baptism

[B]ehold, now is the accepted time; behold, now is the day of salvation.
2 Corinthians 6:2

The third angel's message is swelling into a loud cry, and you must not feel at liberty to neglect the present duty, and still entertain the idea that at some future time you will be the recipients of great blessing, when without any effort on your part a wonderful revival will take place. Today you are to give yourselves to God, that he may make of you vessels unto honor, and meet for his service. Today you are to give yourself to God, that you may be emptied of self, emptied of envy, jealousy, evil-surmising, strife, everything that shall be dishonoring to God. Today you are to have your vessel purified that it may be ready for the heavenly dew, ready for the showers of the latter rain; for the latter rain will come, and the blessing of God will fill every soul that is purified from every defilement. It is our work today to yield our souls to Christ, that we may be fitted for the time of refreshing from the presence of the Lord — fitted for the baptism of the Holy Spirit.[33]

It is our part of the work to put ourselves in connection with the divine channel. God is responsible for his part of the work. He is faithful who hath promised. The great and important matter with us is to be of one heart and mind, putting aside all envy and malice, and, as humble supplicants, to watch and wait. Jesus, our Representative and Head, is ready to do for us what he did for the praying, watching ones on the day of Pentecost.[34]

June 25

By My Spirit

*… This is the word of the LORD … Not by might, nor by power, but by my spirit,
saith the LORD of hosts. Ezekiel 4:6*

There is nothing that Satan fears so much as that the people of God shall clear the way by removing every hindrance, so that the Lord can pour out his Spirit upon a languishing church and an impenitent congregation. If Satan had his way, there would never be another awakening, great or small, to the end of time. But we are not ignorant of his devices. It is possible to resist his power. When the way is prepared for the Spirit of God, the blessing will come. Satan can no more hinder a shower of blessing from descending upon God's people than he can close the windows of heaven that rain cannot come upon the earth. Wicked men and devils cannot hinder the work of God, or shut out his presence from the assemblies of his people, if they will, with subdued, contrite hearts, confess and put away their sins, and in faith claim his promises. Every temptation, every opposing influence, whether open or secret, may be successfully resisted, "not by might, nor by power, but by my Spirit, saith the Lord of hosts."[35]

Before the final visitation of God's judgments upon the earth there will be among the people of the Lord such a revival of primitive godliness as has not been witnessed since apostolic times. The Spirit and power of God will be poured out upon His children. … Many, both of ministers and people, will gladly accept those great truths which God has caused to be proclaimed at this time to prepare a people for the Lord's second coming.[36]

June 26

Cleansing, Sealing, Latter Rain

*How much more shall the blood of Christ, who through the eternal Spirit
offered himself without spot to God, purge your conscience from dead works to
serve the living God? Hebrews 9:14*

Not one of us will ever receive the seal of God while our characters have one spot or stain upon them. It is left with us to remedy the defects in our characters, to cleanse the soul temple of every defilement. Then the latter rain will fall upon us as the early rain fell upon the disciples on the Day of Pentecost. …

In this life we must meet fiery trials and make costly sacrifices, but the peace of Christ is the reward. There has been so little self-denial, so little suffering for Christ's sake, that the cross is almost entirely forgotten. We must be partakers with Christ of His sufferings if we would sit down in triumph with Him on His throne. So long as we choose the easy path of self-indulgence and are frightened at self-denial, our faith will never become firm, and we cannot know the peace of Jesus nor the joy that comes through conscious victory. The most exalted of the redeemed host that stand before the throne of God and the Lamb, clad in white, know the conflict of overcoming, for they have come up through great tribulation. Those who have yielded to circumstances rather than engage in this conflict will not know how to stand in that day when anguish will be upon every soul, when, though Noah, Job, and Daniel were in the land, they could save neither son nor daughter, for everyone must deliver his soul by his own righteousness.[37]

June 27

First Fruits

... These were redeemed ... being the firstfruits unto God ... Revelation 14:4

As the people of God afflict their souls before Him, pleading for purity of heart, the command is given, "Take away the filthy garments" from them, and the encouraging words are spoken, "Behold, I have caused thine iniquity to pass from thee, and I will clothe thee with change of raiment." The spotless robe of Christ's righteousness is placed upon the tried, tempted, yet faithful children of God. The despised remnant are clothed in glorious apparel, nevermore to be defiled by the corruptions of the world. Their names are retained in the Lamb's book of life, enrolled among the faithful of all ages. They have resisted the wiles of the deceiver; they have not been turned from their loyalty by the dragon's roar. Now they are eternally secure from the tempter's devices. Their sins are transferred to the originator of sin. And the remnant are not only pardoned and accepted, but honored. "A fair miter" is set upon their heads. They are to be as kings and priests unto God. While Satan was urging his accusations and seeking to destroy this company, holy angels, unseen, were passing to and fro, placing upon them the seal of the living God. These are they that stand upon Mount Zion with the Lamb, having the Father's name written in their foreheads. They sing the new song before the throne, that song which no man can learn save the hundred and forty and four thousand.... "These are they which follow the Lamb whithersoever He goeth. These were redeemed from among men, being the first fruits unto God and to the Lamb." [38]

June 28

Truth With Great Power

... he shall come unto us as the rain, as the latter and former rain unto the earth.
Hosea 6:3

While the work of salvation is closing, trouble will be coming on the earth, and the nations will be angry, yet held in check so as not to prevent the work of the third angel. At that time the "latter rain," or refreshing from the presence of the Lord, will come, to give power to the loud voice of the third angel, and prepare the saints to stand in the period when the seven last plagues shall be poured out.[39]

I was shown those whom I had before seen weeping and praying in agony of spirit. The company of guardian angels around them had been doubled, and they were clothed with an armor from their head to their feet. ... Their countenances expressed the severe conflict which they had endured, the agonizing struggle they had passed through. Yet their features, marked with severe internal anguish, now shone with the light and glory of heaven. They had obtained the victory, and it called forth from them the deepest gratitude and holy, sacred joy. ...

Evil angels still pressed around them, but could have no power over them.

I heard those clothed with the armor speak forth the truth with great power. It had effect. ... I asked what had made this great change. An angel answered, "It is the latter rain, the refreshing from the presence of the Lord, the loud cry of the third angel."[40]

June 29

Pentecost Repeated

Be patient therefore, brethren, unto the coming of the Lord. Behold, the husbandman waiteth for the precious fruit of the earth, and hath long patience for it, until he receive the early and latter rain. James 5:7

It is with an earnest longing that I look forward to the time when the events of the day of Pentecost shall be repeated with even greater power than on that occasion. John says, "I saw another angel come down from heaven, having great power; and the earth was lightened with his glory." Then, as at the Pentecostal season, the people will hear the truth spoken to them, every man in his own tongue. ... Thousands of voices will be imbued with the power to speak forth the wonderful truths of God's word. ... May the Lord help his people to cleanse the soul temple from every defilement, and to maintain such a close connection with him that they may be partakers of the latter rain when it shall be poured out.

As the members of the body of Christ approach the period of their last conflict, "the time of Jacob's trouble," they will grow up into Christ, and will partake largely of his Spirit. As the third message swells to a loud cry, and as great power and glory attends the closing work, the faithful people of God will partake of that glory. It is the latter rain which revives and strengthens them to pass through the time of trouble. Their faces will shine with the glory of that light which attends the third angel.[41]

June 30

Gentiles Shall Come

Then ... thine heart shall fear, and be enlarged; because the abundance of the sea shall be converted unto thee, the forces of the Gentiles shall come unto thee.
Isaiah 60:5

When God's people so fully separate themselves from evil that he can let the light of heaven rest upon them in rich measure, and shine forth from them to the world, then there will be fulfilled, more fully than it has ever been fulfilled in the past, the prophecy of Isaiah, in which the servant of God declared of the remnant church in the last days: "The Gentiles shall come to thy light, and kings to the brightness of thy rising. Lift up thine eyes round about, and see: all they gather themselves together, they come to thee: thy sons shall come from far, and thy daughters shall be nursed at thy side. Then thou shalt see, and flow together, and thine heart shall fear, and be enlarged; because the abundance of the sea shall be converted unto thee, the forces of the Gentiles shall come unto thee." ...

God's faithful messengers are to ... place themselves in close connection with the Great Teacher, that they may be daily taught of God. They are to wrestle with God in earnest prayer for a baptism of the Holy Spirit, that they may meet the needs of a world perishing in sin. ... As the servants of God bear to the world a living message fresh from the throne of glory, the light of truth will shine forth as a lamp that burneth, reaching to all parts of the world.[42]

July 1

The Victory

... they shall walk with me in white: for they are worthy. Revelation 3:4

My attention was then turned to the company I had seen, who were mightily shaken. I was shown those whom I had before seen weeping and praying in agony of spirit. The company of guardian angels around them had been doubled, and they were clothed with an armor from their head to their feet. ... Yet their features, marked with severe internal anguish, now shone with the light and glory of heaven. They had obtained the victory, and it called forth from them the deepest gratitude, and holy, sacred joy. ...

The numbers of this company had lessened. Some had been shaken out and left by the way. The careless and indifferent, who did not join with those who prized victory and salvation enough to perseveringly plead and agonize for it, did not obtain it, and they were left behind in darkness, and their places were immediately filled by others taking hold of the truth and coming into the ranks. Evil angels still pressed around them, but could have no power over them.

I heard those clothed with the armor speak forth the truth with great power. It had effect. ... They had been hungering and thirsting for truth; it was dearer and more precious than life. ...

Great power was with these chosen ones. ... The zeal and power with the people of God had aroused and enraged [the wicked.] ... I saw measures taken against the company who had the light and power of God.[1]

July 2

The Wise Shall Shine

And they that be wise shall shine as the brightness of the firmament; and they that turn many to righteousness as the stars for ever and ever. Daniel 12:3

To be sanctified is to become a partaker of the divine nature, catching the spirit and mind of Jesus, ever learning in the school of Christ. ... It is impossible for any of us by our own power or our own efforts to work this change in ourselves. It is the Holy Spirit, the Comforter, which Jesus said he would send into the world, that changes our character into the image of Christ ...

The converting power of God must be upon our hearts. We must study the life of Christ, and imitate the divine Pattern. We must dwell upon the perfection of his character, and be changed into his image. No one will enter the kingdom of God unless his will is brought into captivity to the will of Christ. ...

In character and life we are to make manifest the requirement of God in humanity; and in order to do this, we must gather up the rays of divine light from the Bible, and let them shine forth to those who are in darkness. ... "And they that be wise shall shine as the brightness of the firmament; and they that turn many to righteousness as the stars forever and ever."[2]

July 3

Thy Kingdom Come

And as they heard these things, he ... spake a parable ... because they thought that the kingdom of God should immediately appear. He said therefore, A certain nobleman went into a far country to receive for himself a kingdom, and to return. Luke 19:11, 12

At his creation Adam was placed in dominion over the earth. But by yielding to temptation, he was brought under the power of Satan. "Of whom a man is overcome, of the same is he brought in bondage." 2 Peter 2:19. When man became Satan's captive, the dominion which he held, passed to his conqueror. Thus Satan became "the god of this world." 2 Corinthians 4:4. He had usurped that dominion over the earth which had been originally given to Adam. But Christ, by His sacrifice paying the penalty of sin, would not only redeem man, but recover the dominion which he had forfeited. ... Says the prophet, "O tower of the flock, the stronghold of the daughter of Zion, unto thee shall it come, even the first dominion." Micah 4:8. ...[3]

Christ sent forth His disciples with the message, "The kingdom of God is at hand." The proclamation of this message is our work. Jesus said, "This Gospel of the kingdom shall be preached in all the world for a witness unto all nations." His kingdom will not come until the good tidings of His grace have been carried to all the earth. Let us proclaim the message, "Behold the Lamb of God, which taketh away the sin of the world." Thus we may hasten the coming of the Saviour. ... The kingdoms of this world will become the kingdoms of our Lord and of His Christ.[4]

July 4

Then Shall the End Come

And this gospel of the kingdom shall be preached in all the world for a witness unto all nations; and then shall the end come. Matthew 24:14

The same devotion, the same self-sacrifice, the same subjection to the claims of the Word of God, that were manifest in the life of Christ, must be seen in the lives of his servants. …

The Lord calls upon his people to arouse out of sleep. The end of all things is at hand. When those who know the truth will be laborers together with God, the fruits of righteousness will appear. …

God desires to refresh his people by the gift of the Holy Spirit, baptizing them anew in his love. …

The message of salvation is not to be proclaimed in a few places only, but throughout the world. …

The kingdoms of this world are soon to become the kingdoms of our Lord and of his Christ. "The seventh angel sounded, and there were great voices in heaven, saying, The kingdoms of this world are become the kingdoms of our Lord, and of his Christ; and he shall reign forever and ever." There is to be a rapid and triumphant spread of the gospel.⁵

July 5

A Great Work

Knowing the time, that now it is high time to awake out of sleep: for now is our salvation nearer than when we believed. The night is far spent, the day is at hand: let us therefore cast off the works of darkness, and let us put on the armour of light. Romans 13:11, 12

The signs of the times are fulfilling; the closing work must be done. A great work will be done in a short time. A message will soon be given by God's appointment that will swell into a loud cry. Then Daniel will stand in his lot, to give his testimony.

The attention of our churches must be aroused. We are standing upon the borders of the greatest event in the world's history, and Satan must not have power over the people of God, causing them to sleep on. The Papacy will appear in its power. All must now arouse and search the Scriptures, for God will make known to His faithful ones what shall be in the last time. The word of the Lord is to come to His people in power.

The signs of the end are fast fulfilling. The time of trouble is very near us now. We are to be brought into strait places in a way in which we have not been brought heretofore. The time of trouble is near, and we are to awake to a realization of this. We are to be sure that our feet are in the narrow path. We need an experience that we have not yet had, that we may have the assurance that the God of all grace is a very present help in time of need. ⁶

July 6

Through Our Schools

*And they shall build the old wastes, they shall raise up the former desolations,
and they shall repair the waste cities, the desolations of many generations.*
Isaiah 61:4

"And thou shalt be called, The repairer of the breach, The restorer of paths to dwell in." ... 58:12. These words of Inspiration present before believers in present truth the work that should now be done in the education of our children and youth. ...

Our work is reformatory; and it is the purpose of God that through the excellence of the work done in our educational institutions the attention of the people shall be called to the last great effort to save the perishing. ...

They should be impressed with the thought that they are formed in the image of their Creator and that Christ is the pattern after which they are to be fashioned. Most earnest attention must be given to the education which will impart a knowledge of salvation, and will conform the life and character to the divine similitude. It is the love of God, the purity of soul woven into the life like threads of gold, that is of true worth. ....

The third angel's message, the great testing truth for this time, is to be taught in all our institutions. God designs that through them this special warning shall be given, and bright beams of light shall shine to the world. Time is short. ... [W]e should watch and pray, and study and heed the lessons that are given us in the books of Daniel and the Revelation.[7]

July 7

As the Waters Cover the Sea

*... the earth shall be full of the knowledge of the LORD, as the waters
cover the sea.* Isaiah 11:9

We are living in the very last days of this earth's history. All the signs that our Saviour predicted would herald his second advent are being fulfilled. ... As we see and sense the perils of the last days, and as the powers of darkness press more heavily than ever upon us, should not we, as Bible believers, do our very best work?

We see before us a special work to be done in the time when the whole earth shall be filled with the light and the glory of the Lord, as the waters cover the sea. The prophecies in the eighteenth of Revelation will soon be fulfilled. During the proclamation of the third angel's message, "another angel" is to "come down from heaven, having great power;" and the earth is to be "lightened with the glory." The Spirit of the Lord will so graciously and universally bless consecrated human instrumentalities, that men, women, and children will open their lips in praise and testimony, filling the earth with the knowledge of God, and with his unsurpassed glory, as the waters cover the sea. ...

God and Christ and the heavenly angels are working with intense activity to hold in check the fierceness of Satan's wrath, that God's plans may not be thwarted. ... Let there be perfect unity in their ranks. Let them press the battle to the gates. As a mighty Conqueror, the Lord will work for them.[8]

July 8

They Shall Come to Thy Light

And the Gentiles shall come to thy light, and kings to the brightness of thy rising.
Isaiah 60:3

God desires that his people shall stand before the world a holy people. Why? – Because there is a world to be saved by the light of gospel truth; and as the message of truth that is to call men out of darkness into God's marvelous light, is given by the church, the lives of its members, sanctified by the Spirit of truth, are to bear witness to the verity of the messages proclaimed. ...

In order to stand as lights in the world, they need to have the clear light of the Sun of Righteousness constantly shining upon them. ...

When God's people so fully separate themselves from evil that he can let the light of heaven rest upon them in rich measure, and shine forth from them to the world, then there will be fulfilled, more fully than it has ever been fulfilled in the past, the prophecy of Isaiah, in which the servant of God declared of the remnant church in the last days: "The Gentiles shall come to thy light, and kings to the brightness of thy rising. Lift up thine eyes round about, and see: all they gather themselves together, they come to thee: thy sons shall come from far, and thy daughters shall be nursed at thy side. Then thou shalt see, and flow together, and thine heart shall fear, and be enlarged; because the abundance of the sea shall be converted unto thee, the forces of the Gentiles shall come unto thee."[9]

July 9

Inherit the Gentiles

Enlarge the place of thy tent ... and thy seed shall inherit the Gentiles ...
Isaiah 54:2, 3

The words of the Lord in the fifty-fourth chapter of Isaiah are for us: "Enlarge the place of thy tent, and let them stretch forth the curtains of thine habitations: spare not, lengthen thy cords, and strengthen thy stakes; for thou shalt break forth on the right hand and on the left; and thy seed shall inherit the Gentiles, and make the desolate cities to be inhabited. … The God of the whole earth shall He be called." Isaiah 54:2-5. …

God's people have a mighty work before them, a work that must continually rise to greater prominence. Our efforts in missionary lines must become far more extensive. … God's people are not to cease their labors until they shall encircle the world.

The vineyard includes the whole world, and every part of it is to be worked. … At this time there should be representatives of present truth in every city and in the remote parts of the earth. The whole earth is to be illuminated with the glory of God's truth. The light is to shine to all lands and all peoples. And it is from those who have received the light that it is to shine forth. The daystar has risen upon us, and we are to flash its light upon the pathway of those in darkness.

A crisis is right upon us. We must now by the Holy Spirit's power proclaim the great truths for these last days. It will not be long before everyone will have heard the warning and made his decision. Then shall the end come.[10]

July 10

Sunrise, Sunset

For from the rising of the sun even unto the going down of the same my name shall be great among the Gentiles; and in every place incense shall be offered unto my name, and a pure offering: for my name shall be great among the heathen, saith the LORD of hosts. Malachi 1:11

The gospel invitation is to be given to all the world, — "to every nation, and kindred, and tongue, and people." The last message of warning and mercy is to lighten the whole earth with its glory. It is to reach all classes of men, rich and poor, high and low. As surely as this message shall be proclaimed in all the earth, so surely shall be fulfilled the prophecy given through Malachi: "From the rising of the sun, even unto the going down of the same, my name shall be great among the Gentiles …"[11]

We have no time to lose. The end is near. The passage from place to place to spread the truth will soon be hedged with dangers on the right hand and on the left. … We must look our work fairly in the face and advance as fast as possible in aggressive warfare. From the light given me of God I know that the powers of darkness are working with intense energy from beneath, and with stealthy tread Satan is advancing to take those who are now asleep, as a wolf taking his prey. We have warnings now which we may give, a work now which we may do; but soon it will be more difficult than we can imagine. God help us to keep in the channel of light, to work with our eyes fastened on Jesus our Leader, and patiently, perseveringly press on to gain the victory.[12]

July 11

Whosoever Will

And whosoever will, let him take the water of life freely. Revelation 22:17

The gospel never employs force in bringing men to Christ. … The power of God's love and grace constrains us to come.[13]

Tell the poor desponding ones who have gone astray that they need not despair. Though they have erred, and have not been building a right character, God has joy to restore them, even the joy of His salvation. … Tell them there is healing, cleansing for every soul. …

Christ will impart to His messengers the same yearning love that He Himself has in seeking for the lost. … There are those who hear the call, but their ears are too dull to take in its meaning. … Many … say, I am not fit to be helped; leave me alone. But the workers must not desist. In tender, pitying love, lay hold of the discouraged and helpless ones. Give them your courage, your hope, your strength. By kindness compel them to come. …

If the servants of God will walk with Him in faith, He will give power to their message. They will be enabled so to present His love and the danger of rejecting the grace of God that men will be constrained to accept the gospel. Christ will perform wonderful miracles if men will but do their God-given part.

We are living in a time when the last message of mercy, the last invitation, is sounding to the children of men. … To every soul Christ's invitation will be given.[14]

July 12

Highways and Hedges

... Go out into the highways and hedges, and compel them to come in ...
Luke 14:23

In Noah's day the warning of the flood was sent to startle men in their wickedness and call them to repentance. So the message of Christ's soon coming is designed to arouse men from their absorption in worldly things. It is intended to awaken them to a sense of eternal realities, that they may give heed to the invitation to the Lord's table.

The gospel invitation is to be given to all the world—"to every nation, and kindred, and tongue, and people." Revelation 14:6. The last message of warning and mercy is to lighten the whole earth with its glory. It is to reach all classes of men, rich and poor, high and low. ...

The world is perishing for want of the gospel. There is a famine for the word of God. There are few who preach the word unmixed with human tradition. ... The Lord calls upon His servants to carry His message to the people. The word of everlasting life must be given to those who are perishing in their sins.

To a great degree this must be accomplished by personal labor. This was Christ's method. His work was largely made up of personal interviews. ...

We are not to wait for souls to come to us; we must seek them out where they are. ... There are multitudes who will never be reached by the gospel unless it is carried to them.[15]

July 13

Teachers and Leaders

... let him that heareth say, Come. And let him that is athirst come. ...
Revelation 22:17

The message is first to be given "in the highways" — to men who have an active part in the world's work, to the teachers and leaders of the people.

Let the Lord's messengers bear this in mind. To the shepherds of the flock, the teachers divinely appointed, it should come as a word to be heeded. Those who belong to the higher ranks of society are to be sought out with tender affection and brotherly regard. Men in business life, in high positions of trust, men with large inventive faculties and scientific insight, men of genius, teachers of the gospel whose minds have not been called to the special truths for this time — these should be the first to hear the call. To them the invitation must be given.

There is a work to be done for the wealthy. They need to be awakened to their responsibility as those entrusted with the gifts of heaven. ... The wealthy man needs your labor in the love and fear of God. Too often he trusts in his riches, and feels not his danger. The eyes of his mind need to be attracted to things of enduring value. ...

None should be neglected because of their apparent devotion to worldly things. Many in high social positions are heartsore, and sick of vanity. ... Many would receive help if the Lord's workers would approach them personally, with a kind manner, a heart made tender by the love of Christ.[16]

July 14

Poor and Lowly

In these lay a great multitude of impotent folk, of blind, halt, withered, waiting for the moving of the water. John 5:3

Christ instructs His messengers to go also to those in the byways and hedges, to the poor and lowly of the earth. In the courts and lanes of the great cities, in the lonely byways of the country, are families and individuals — perhaps strangers in a strange land — who are without church relations, and who, in their loneliness, come to feel that God has forgotten them. They do not understand what they must do to be saved. Many are sunken in sin. Many are in distress. They are pressed with suffering, want, unbelief, despondency. Disease of every type afflicts them, both in body and in soul. They long to find a solace for their troubles, and Satan tempts them to seek it in lusts and pleasures that lead to ruin and death. He is offering them the apples of Sodom, that will turn to ashes upon their lips. They are spending their money for that which is not bread and their labor for that which satisfieth not. ...

Many who appear wholly indifferent to religious things are in heart longing for rest and peace. Although they may have sunken to the very depths of sin, there is a possibility of saving them.

Christ's servants are to follow His example. As He went from place to place, He comforted the suffering and healed the sick. Then He placed before them the great truths in regard to His kingdom. This is the work of His followers. As you relieve the sufferings of the body, you will find ways for ministering to the wants of the soul.[17]

July 15

Greater Than Pentecost

And they went forth, and preached every where, the Lord working with them, and confirming the word with signs following. Amen. Mark 16:20

The great work of the gospel is not to close with less manifestation of the power of God than marked its opening. The prophecies which were fulfilled in the outpouring of the former rain at the opening of the gospel are again to be fulfilled in the latter rain at its close. …

Servants of God, with their faces lighted up and shining with holy consecration, will hasten from place to place to proclaim the message from heaven. By thousands of voices, all over the earth, the warning will be given. Miracles will be wrought, the sick will be healed, and signs and wonders will follow the believers. Satan also works, with lying wonders, even bringing down fire from heaven in the sight of men. Revelation 13:13. Thus the inhabitants of the earth will be brought to take their stand.

The message will be carried not so much by argument as by the deep conviction of the Spirit of God. … [T]he rays of light penetrate everywhere, the truth is seen in its clearness, and the honest children of God sever the bands which have held them. … Notwithstanding the agencies combined against the truth, a large number take their stand upon the Lord's side.[18]

July 16

He Hungered for Sympathy

… repentance and remission of sins should be preached in his name among all nations … Luke 28:47

The solemn, sacred message of warning must be proclaimed in the most difficult fields and in the most sinful cities, in every place where the light of the great threefold gospel message has not yet dawned. … From town to town, from city to city, from country to country, the message of present truth is to be proclaimed, not with outward display, but in the power of the Spirit. … Our time for work is short, and we are to labor with unflagging zeal. …

Christ longs to extend His sway over every human mind. He longs to stamp His image and character upon every soul. When He was on this earth, He hungered for sympathy and co-operation, that His kingdom might extend and embrace the whole world. This earth is His purchased possession, and He would have men free and pure and holy. … And there are triumphs yet to be accomplished through the blood shed for the world, that will bring everlasting glory to God and to the Lamb. The heathen will be given for His inheritance, and the uttermost parts of the earth for His possession. Christ will see of the travail of His soul, and be satisfied. ...

The Lord calls for pastors, teachers, and evangelists. From door to door His servants are to proclaim the message of salvation. ... The world needs to see in Christians an evidence of the power of Christianity. Not merely in a few places, but throughout the world, messages of mercy are needed.[19]

July 17

Thy Light Shall Break Forth

Then shall thy light break forth as the morning ... and ... the glory of the LORD shall be thy rereward. Isaiah 58:8

At this time a message from God is to be proclaimed, a message illuminating in its influence and saving in its power. His character is to be made known. ...

Christ, the outshining of the Father's glory, came to the world as its light. He came to represent God to men, and of Him it is written that He was anointed "with the Holy Ghost and with power," and "went about doing good." ...

This is the work which the prophet Isaiah describes when he says, "Is it not to deal thy bread to the hungry, and that thou bring the poor that are cast out to thy house? when thou seest the naked, that thou cover him; and that thou hide not thyself from thine own flesh? Then shall thy light break forth as the morning, and thine health shall spring forth speedily; and thy righteousness shall go before thee; the glory of the Lord shall be thy rereward." Isaiah 58:7, 8.

Thus in the night of spiritual darkness God's glory is to shine forth through His church in lifting up the bowed down and comforting those that mourn. ...

Practical work will have far more effect than mere sermonizing. We are to give food to the hungry, clothing to the naked, and shelter to the homeless. And we are called to do more than this. The wants of the soul, only the love of Christ can satisfy. If Christ is abiding in us, our hearts will be full of divine sympathy.[20]

July 18

With His Own Blood

Who shall lay any thing to the charge of God's elect? It is God that justifieth. Romans 8:33

Jesus knows the circumstances of every soul. The greater the sinner's guilt, the more he needs the Saviour. His heart of divine love and sympathy is drawn out most of all for the one who is the most hopelessly entangled in the snares of the enemy. With His own blood He has signed the emancipation papers of the race.

Jesus does not desire those who have been purchased at such a cost to become the sport of the enemy's temptations. He does not desire us to be overcome and perish. He who curbed the lions in their den, and walked with His faithful witnesses amid the fiery flames, is just as ready to work in our behalf to subdue every evil in our nature. Today He is standing at the altar of mercy, presenting before God the prayers of those who desire His help. He turns no weeping, contrite one away. Freely will He pardon all who come to Him for forgiveness and restoration. He does not tell to any all that He might reveal, but He bids every trembling soul take courage. Whosoever will, may take hold of God's strength, and make peace with Him, and He will make peace.

The souls that turn to Him for refuge, Jesus lifts above the accusing and the strife of tongues. No man or evil angel can impeach these souls. Christ unites them to His own divine-human nature. They stand beside the great Sin Bearer in the light proceeding from the throne of God.[21]

July 19

The Great Price

... when he had found one pearl of great price, went and sold all that he had, and bought it. Matthew 13:46

When sin struggles for the mastery in the human heart, when guilt oppresses the soul and burdens the conscience, when unbelief clouds the mind, remember that Christ's grace is sufficient to subdue sin and expel the darkness. Jesus, the sin-pardoning Saviour, is our Advocate in the courts of heaven, and he calls upon us to "arise and shine," because his glory has risen upon us. ...

Christ paid an infinite price for us, and he desires his chosen heritage to value themselves according to the price he placed upon them. Do not disappoint Jesus by placing a low estimate upon yourselves. ... All heaven rejoices over the weak, faulty human soul that gives itself to Jesus, and in his strength lives a life of purity.

Our path to the Paradise of God will be often intercepted by the tempter, who is intent on weakening our faith by hiding the rays of the Sun of Righteousness. Our Saviour has warned us that through much tribulation we must enter into the kingdom of God. ...

In the name of Jesus Christ of Nazareth, be strong in the Lord and in the power of his might. Know that he loves you, and will be your constant efficiency. "Arise and shine; for thy light is come."[22]

July 20

Seeking the Lost

What man of you, having an hundred sheep, if he lose one of them, doth not leave the ninety and nine in the wilderness, and go after that which is lost, until he find it? Luke 15:4

Every one that will submit to be ransomed, Christ will rescue from the pit of corruption and from the briers of sin.

Desponding soul, take courage, even though you have done wickedly. Do not think that perhaps God will pardon your transgressions and permit you to come into His presence. God has made the first advance. While you were in rebellion against Him, He went forth to seek you. With the tender heart of the shepherd He left the ninety and nine and went out into the wilderness to find that which was lost. The soul, bruised and wounded and ready to perish, He encircles in His arms of love and joyfully bears it to the fold of safety. …

If the lost sheep is not brought back to the fold, it wanders until it perishes. And many souls go down to ruin for want of a hand stretched out to save. These erring ones may appear hard and reckless; but if they had received the same advantages that others have had, they might have revealed far more nobility of soul, and greater talent for usefulness. Angels pity these wandering ones. Angels weep, while human eyes are dry and hearts are closed to pity.

O the lack of deep, soul-touching sympathy for the tempted and the erring! O for more of Christ's spirit, and for less, far less, of self![23]

July 21

The Sign

… Verily my sabbaths ye shall keep: for it is a sign between me and you … that ye may know that I am the LORD that doth sanctify you. Exodus 31:13

"Wherefore the rather, brethren, give diligence to make your calling and election sure: for if ye do these things ye shall never fall: …" 2 Peter 1:10.

Here is the life-insurance policy for every soul that shall strive in the right way and upon the right principles. They shall never fall, but shall have their eternal life insurance papers in the sign given in Exodus 31:12-18, in the observance of the Lord's Sabbath. This means obedience to all His commandments, for the keeping of the Sabbath which God has sanctified and blessed at Creation, "is a sign between Me and you throughout your generations" "for ever," "that I am the Lord that doth sanctify you." (verses 13, 17.)

Here is our test which God has made, and He will fulfill His word, if human agents will show their love to God in keeping all His commandments. …

"And these words which I command thee this day, shall be in thine heart: … And thou shalt bind them for a sign upon thine hand …"

We must either observe the Sabbath of the fourth commandment, or repudiate the word, and accept a day that He has not sanctified and set apart for our observance.²⁴

July 22

The Hour

… Fear God, and give glory to him; for the hour of his judgment is come: and worship him that made heaven, and earth, and the sea, and the fountains of waters. Revelation 14:7

John in the Revelation foretells the proclamation of the gospel message just before Christ's second coming. He beholds an angel flying "in the midst of heaven, having the everlasting gospel to preach unto them that dwell on the earth, and to every nation, and kindred, and tongue, and people, saying with a loud voice, Fear God, and give glory to Him; for the hour of His judgment is come." Revelation 14:6, 7.²⁵

The announcement, "The hour of His judgment is come," points to the closing work of Christ's ministration for the salvation of men. It heralds a truth which must be proclaimed until the Saviour's intercession shall cease and He shall return to the earth to take His people to Himself. The work of judgment which began in 1844 must continue until the cases of all are decided, both of the living and the dead; hence it will extend to the close of human probation. That men may be prepared to stand in the judgment, the message commands them to "fear God, and give glory to Him," "and worship Him that made heaven, and earth, and the sea, and the fountains of waters." The result of an acceptance of these messages is given in the word: "Here are they that keep the commandments of God, and the faith of Jesus." In order to be prepared for the judgment, it is necessary that men should keep the law of God.²⁶

July 23

Power of Elias

And he shall go before him in the spirit and power of Elias … to make ready a people prepared for the Lord. Luke 1:17

Today, in the spirit and power of Elias and of John the Baptist, messengers of God's appointment are calling the attention of a judgment-bound world to the solemn events soon to take place in connection with the closing hours of probation and the appearance of Christ Jesus as King of kings and Lord of lords. Soon every man is to be judged for the deeds done in the body. The hour of God's judgment has come, and upon the members of His church on earth rests the solemn responsibility of giving warning to those who are standing as it were on the very brink of eternal ruin. To every human being in the wide world who will give heed must be made plain the principles at stake in the great controversy being waged, principles upon which hang the destinies of all mankind.

In these final hours of probation for the sons of men, when the fate of every soul is so soon to be decided forever, the Lord of heaven and earth expects His church to arouse to action as never before. Those who have been made free in Christ through a knowledge of precious truth, are regarded by the Lord Jesus as His chosen ones, favored above all other people on the face of the earth; and He is counting on them to show forth the praises of Him who hath called them out of darkness into marvelous light. The blessings which are so liberally bestowed are to be communicated to others. The good news of salvation is to go to every nation, kindred, tongue, and people.[27]

July 24

Prophesy Again

...Thou must prophesy again before many peoples, and nations, and tongues, and kings. Revelation 10:11

It was the Lion of the tribe of Judah who unsealed the book and gave to John the revelation of what should be in these last days. Daniel stood in his lot to bear his testimony, which was sealed until the time of the end ... [W]hile "many shall be purified, and made white, and tried," "the wicked shall do wickedly: and none of the wicked shall understand." ...

[T]hose in the denominational churches who will not accept the light in regard to the law of God will not understand the proclamation of the first, second, and third angel's messages. ...[28]

This message ... will call the attention of every nation and kindred and tongue and people to a close examination of the Word, and to the true light in regard to the power that has changed the seventh-day Sabbath to a spurious sabbath. ... [God's] law has been discarded ... The Sabbath memorial, declaring who ... the Creator of the heavens and the earth, has been torn down, and a spurious sabbath has been given to the world in its place. ...

Christ came to our world to represent the character of God as it is represented in His holy law; for His law is a transcript of His character. ... The angel that proclaims the everlasting gospel proclaims the law of God; for the gospel of salvation brings men to obedience of the law ...[29]

July 25

Magnify the Law

The LORD is well pleased for his righteousness' sake; he will magnify the law, and make it honourable. Isaiah 42:21

The three angels of Revelation 14 are represented as flying in the midst of heaven, symbolizing the work of those who proclaim the first, second, and third angels' messages. All are linked together. …

The influence of these messages has been deepening and widening, setting in motion the springs of action in thousands of hearts, bringing into existence institutions of learning, publishing houses, and health institutions. …

As America, the land of religious liberty, shall unite with the papacy in forcing the conscience and compelling men to honor the false sabbath, the people of every country on the globe will be led to follow her example. …

The Lord God of heaven will not send upon the world His judgments for disobedience and transgression until He has sent His watchmen to give the warning. He will not close up the period of probation until the message shall be more distinctly proclaimed. The law of God is to be magnified; its claims must be presented in their true, sacred character, that the people may be brought to decide for or against the truth. Yet the work will be cut short in righteousness. The message of Christ's righteousness is to sound from one end of the earth to the other to prepare the way of the Lord. This is the glory of God, which closes the work of the third angel.[30]

July 26

Worship the Image

… To you it is commanded, O people, nations, and languages, That … ye fall down and worship the golden image that Nebuchadnezzar the king hath set up: Daniel 3:4, 5

In this time of well-nigh universal apostasy, God calls upon his messengers to proclaim his law in the spirit and power of Elias. As John the Baptist, in preparing a people for Christ's first advent, called their attention to the ten commandments, so we are to give, with no uncertain sound, the message: "Fear God, and give glory to him; for the hour of his judgment is come." With the earnestness that characterized Elijah the prophet and John the Baptist, we are to strive to prepare the way for Christ's second advent. …[31]

In the warfare to be waged in the last days … the Sabbath of the fourth commandment will be the great point at issue; for in the Sabbath commandment the great Law-giver identifies Himself as the Creator of the heavens and the earth.

By many, the Sabbath of the fourth commandment is made void, being treated as a thing of naught; while the spurious sabbath, the child of the papacy, is exalted. In the place of God's laws, are elevated the laws of the man of sin — laws that are to be received and regarded as the wonderful golden image of Nebuchadnezzar was by the Babylonians. Forming this great image, Nebuchadnezzar commanded that it should receive universal homage from all, both great and small, high and low, rich and poor.[32]

July 27

Keep it Holy

Remember the Sabbath day, to keep it holy. Exodus 20:8

There is the highest reason for us to prize the true Sabbath and stand in its defense, for it is the sign which distinguishes the people of God from the world. The commandment that the world makes void is the one to which, for this very reason, God's people will give greater honor. It is when the unbelieving cast contempt upon the Word of God that the faithful Calebs are called for. It is then that they will stand firm at the post of duty, without parade, and without swerving because of reproach. The unbelieving spies stood ready to destroy Caleb. He saw the stones in the hands of those who had brought a false report, but this did not deter him; he had a message, and he would bear it. The same spirit will be manifested today by those who are true to God.

The psalmist says, "They have made void thy law. Therefore I love thy commandments above gold; yea, above fine gold" (Psalm 119:126, 127). When men press close to the side of Jesus, when Christ is abiding in their hearts by faith, their love for the commandments of God grows stronger in proportion to the contempt which the world heaps upon His holy precepts. It is at this time that the true Sabbath must be brought before the people by both pen and voice. As the fourth commandment and those who observe it are ignored and despised, the faithful feel that it is the time not to hide their faith but to exalt the law of Jehovah by unfurling the banner on which is inscribed the message of the third angel, the commandments of God and the faith of Jesus.[33]

July 28

The Change of Law

[H]e shall ... think to change times and laws: ... Daniel 7:25

The great apostate had succeeded in exalting himself "above all that is called God, or that is worshiped." 2 Thessalonians 2:4. He had dared to change the only precept of the divine law that unmistakably points all mankind to the true and living God. ... Satan strives to turn men from their allegiance to God, and from rendering obedience to His law; therefore he directs his efforts especially against that commandment which points to God as the Creator.[34]

That institution which points to God as the Creator is a sign of his rightful authority over the beings he has made. The change of the Sabbath is the sign, or mark, of the authority of the Romish Church. ... The change in the fourth commandment is the change pointed out in the prophecy, and the keeping of the counterfeit Sabbath is the reception of the mark. But Christians of past generations observed the first day, supposing that they were keeping the Bible Sabbath, and there are in the churches of today many who honestly believe that Sunday is the Sabbath of divine appointment. None of these have received the mark of the beast. ... The test upon this question does not come until Sunday observance is enforced by law, and the world is enlightened concerning the obligation of the true Sabbath. Not until the issue is thus plainly set before the people, and they are brought to choose between the commandments of God and the commandments of men, will those who continue in transgression receive the mark of the beast.[35]

July 29

Repairing the Breach

... thou shalt raise up the foundations of many generations; and thou shalt be called, The repairer of the breach ... Isaiah 58:12

In the issue of the great contest ... One class "worship the beast and his image, and receive his mark," ... The other class ... "keep the commandments of God and the faith of Jesus." ... The work of Sabbath reform ... in the last days is clearly brought to view in the prophecy of Isaiah: "Thus saith the Lord, Keep ye judgment, and do justice; for my salvation is near to come, and my righteousness to be revealed. Blessed is the man that doeth this, and the son of man that layeth hold on it; that keepeth the Sabbath from polluting it, and keepeth his hand from doing any evil." "The sons of the stranger, that join themselves to the Lord, to serve him, and to love the name of the Lord, to be his servants, every one that keepeth the Sabbath from polluting it, and taketh hold of my covenant; even them will I bring to my holy mountain, and make them joyful in my house of prayer." [Isaiah 56:1, 2, 6, 7.]

These words apply in the Christian age, as is shown by the context: "The Lord God which gathereth the outcasts of Israel saith, Yet will I gather others to him, beside those that are gathered unto him." [Isaiah 56:8.] Here is foreshadowed the gathering in of the Gentiles by the gospel. ... Thus the obligation of the fourth commandment extends past the crucifixion, resurrection, and ascension of Christ, to the time when his servants should preach to all nations the message of glad tidings.[36]

July 30

The Seal of the Law

Bind up the testimony, seal the law among my disciples. Isaiah 8:16

The seal of God's law is found in the fourth commandment. This only, of all the ten, brings to view both the name and the title of the Lawgiver. It declares him to be the Creator of the heavens and the earth, and thus shows his claim to reverence and worship above all others. Aside from this precept, there is nothing in the decalogue to show by whose authority the law is given. When the Sabbath was changed by the papal power, the seal was taken from the law. The disciples of Jesus are called upon to restore it, by exalting the Sabbath of the fourth commandment to its rightful position as the Creator's memorial and the sign of his authority. ...

The prophet thus points out the ordinance which has been forsaken: "Thou shalt raise up the foundations of many generations; and thou shalt be called, The repairer of the breach, the restorer of paths to dwell in. If thou turn away thy foot from the Sabbath, from doing thy pleasure on my holy day; and call the Sabbath a delight, the holy of the Lord, honorable; and shalt honor him, not doing thine own ways, nor finding thine own pleasure, nor speaking thine own words; then shalt thou delight thyself in the Lord." [Isaiah 58:12, 13.] ... The breach was made in the law of God when the Sabbath was changed by the Romish power. But the time has come for that divine institution to be restored.[37]

July 31

To Fulfill the Law

For verily I say unto you, Till heaven and earth pass, one jot or one tittle shall in no wise pass from the law ... Matthew 5:18

The observance of the true Sabbath is to be the sign that distinguishes those who serve God from those who serve Him not. ... We are called to be holy, and we should carefully avoid giving the impression that it is of little consequence whether or not we retain the peculiar features of our faith. Upon us rests the solemn obligation of taking a more decided stand for truth and righteousness than we have taken in the past. ...[38]

While the worshipers of God will be especially distinguished by their regard for the fourth commandment, — since this is the sign of His creative power and the witness to His claim upon man's reverence and homage...

The claim so often put forth that Christ changed the Sabbath is disproved by His own words. In His Sermon on the Mount He said: "Think not that I am come to destroy the law, or the prophets: I am not come to destroy, but to fulfill. For verily I say unto you, Till heaven and earth pass, one jot or one tittle shall in no wise pass from the law, till all be fulfilled. Whosoever therefore shall break one of these least commandments, and shall teach men so, he shall be called the least in the kingdom of heaven: but whosoever shall do and teach them, the same shall be called great in the kingdom of heaven," Matthew 5:17-19.[39]

August 1

He Rested

And they returned, and prepared spices and ointments; and rested the sabbath day according to the commandment. Luke 23:56

At last Jesus was at rest. The long day of shame and torture was ended. As the last rays of the setting sun ushered in the Sabbath, the Son of God lay in quietude in Joseph's tomb. His work completed, His hands folded in peace, He rested through the sacred hours of the Sabbath day. …

In the beginning the Father and the Son had rested upon the Sabbath after Their work of creation. … Now Jesus rested from the work of redemption; and though there was grief among those who loved Him on earth, yet there was joy in heaven. Glorious to the eyes of heavenly beings was the promise of the future. A restored creation, a redeemed race, that having conquered sin could never fall, — this, the result to flow from Christ's completed work, God and angels saw. With this scene the day upon which Jesus rested is forever linked. For "His work is perfect;" and "whatsoever God doeth, it shall be forever." Deuteronomy 32:4; Ecclesiastes 3:14. When there shall be a "restitution of all things, which God hath spoken by the mouth of all His holy prophets since the world began" (Acts 3:21), the creation Sabbath, the day on which Jesus lay at rest in Joseph's tomb, will still be a day of rest and rejoicing. Heaven and earth will unite in praise, as "from one Sabbath to another" (Isaiah 66:23) the nations of the saved shall bow in joyful worship to God and the Lamb.[1]

August 2

Proclaiming the Sabbath

Therefore the Son of man is Lord also of the Sabbath. Mark 2:28

At the commencement of the time of trouble, we were filled with the Holy Ghost as we went forth and proclaimed the Sabbath more fully. This enraged the churches, and nominal Adventists, as they could not refute the Sabbath truth. And at this time God's chosen all saw clearly that we had the truth, and they came out and endured the persecution with us. And I saw the sword, famine, pestilence and great confusion in the land. The wicked thought that we had brought the judgments down on them. They rose up and took counsel to rid the earth of us, thinking that then the evil would be stayed.[2]

[P]redictions that religious intolerance would gain control in the United States, that church and state would unite to persecute those who keep the commandments of God, have been pronounced groundless and absurd. It has been confidently declared that this land could never become other than what it has been — the defender of religious freedom. But as the question of enforcing Sunday observance is widely agitated, the event so long doubted and disbelieved is seen to be approaching, and the ... message will produce an effect which it could not have had before. ...

[T]he Spirit of God came upon them as it came upon Elijah, moving him to rebuke the sins of a wicked king and an apostate people; they could not refrain from preaching the plain utterances of the Bible ...[3]

August 3

Persecution of Sabbath Keepers

I beheld, and the same horn made war with the saints, and prevailed against them; Daniel 7:21

When the people accept and exalt a spurious sabbath, and turn souls away from obedience and loyalty to God, they will reach the point that was reached by the people in the days of Christ.

Oh, if the world could only know this perilous fact, and turn away from the course which they are pursuing! How shortsighted is the policy that is being brought in by the rulers in the land to restore to the man of sin his lost ascendancy! They are manifesting wonderful zeal in taking this spurious sabbath under the care and protection of their legislatures; but they know not what they are doing. They are placing upon a false sabbath divine honors, and when this is fully done, persecution will break forth upon those who observe the Sabbath that God gave in Eden as a memorial of His creative power. Then the commandment of men will be clothed with sacred garments, and will be pronounced holy.[4]

Prophecy tells us that the man of sin, the papacy, was to change times and laws; and because we are not, with the whole world, accepting a spurious Sabbath for the genuine, persecution will be poured out upon us. And it is fast coming to that point when we shall see the power of the oppressive hand brought against our religious liberty, and have our right disputed to keep the day that God has blessed, and given to the world as a memorial of his creative work.[5]

August 4

A Powerful Message

The officers answered, Never man spake like this man. John 7:46

At the commencement of the time of trouble, we were filled with the Holy Ghost as we went forth and proclaimed the Sabbath more fully. This enraged the churches ... as they could not refute the Sabbath truth.[6]

The zeal and power with the people of God had aroused and enraged them. Confusion, confusion, was on every side.[7]

The power attending the message ... only madden[s] those who oppose it. The clergy will put forth almost superhuman efforts to shut away the light lest it should shine upon their flocks. By every means at their command they will endeavor to suppress the discussion of these vital questions. The church appeals to the strong arm of civil power, and, in this work, papists and Protestants unite. As the movement for Sunday enforcement becomes more bold and decided, the law will be invoked against commandment keepers. They will be threatened with fines and imprisonment, and some will be offered positions of influence, and other rewards and advantages, as inducements to renounce their faith. But their steadfast answer is: "Show us from the word of God our error" — the same plea that was made by Luther under similar circumstances. Those who are arraigned before the courts make a strong vindication of the truth, and some who hear them are led to take their stand to keep all the commandments of God.[8]

August 5

Having Done All to Stand

Put on the whole armour of God, that ye may be able to stand against the wiles of the devil. Ephesians 6:11

Go to God for yourselves, pray for divine enlightenment, that you may know that you do know what is truth, that when the wonderful miracle-working power of Satan shall be displayed, and the enemy shall come as an angel of light, you may distinguish between the genuine work of God and the imitative work of the powers of darkness. Ministers may do a great work for God if Jesus abides in the heart by faith. "Without me," says Christ, "ye can do nothing." ...

The law of God is made void, and even among those who advocate its binding claims, are some who break its sacred precepts. The Bible will be opened from house to house, and men and women will find access to these homes, and minds will be opened to receive the word of God; and when the crisis comes, many will be prepared to make right decisions even in the face of the formidable difficulties that will be brought about through the deceptive miracles of Satan. ... There will be an army of steadfast believers who will stand as firm as a rock through the last test. But where in that army are those who have been standard-bearers? Where are those whose voices have sounded in proclaiming the truth to the sinning? Some of them are not there. We look for them, but in the time of shaking they have been unable to stand, and have passed over to the enemy's ranks. [9]

August 6

Before Magistrates

And ye shall be brought before governors and kings for my sake, for a testimony against them and the Gentiles. Matthew 10:18

This worship of a false sabbath … had not a text of Scripture to sustain their false god, but yet a deception, hoary with age but still a deception, was commended to reverence, and exalted, while the Sabbath of the fourth commandment was trampled upon and God dishonored. The Bible was before them with a plain "Thus saith the Lord" and the penalty that is the part of the transgressor; …

Satan, who was expelled from heaven, is leading the world, blindfolded by his sophistry, in the same way that he led the angels who accepted his theology before a "Thus saith the Lord." … While they would rein up the faithful and loyal subjects of the kingdom of God, depriving them of their liberty of conscience, bringing them before magistrates and judges, and pronouncing sentence against them, delivering them into prison, putting them into the chain gang and even condemning them to death, they themselves before the universe are showing determined and obstinate contempt of the laws of the eternal Jehovah. …

To maintain principle at all hazard is the highest path one can travel, because by doing this we follow Jesus. That which has a "Thus saith the Lord" is right and expedient. God has said, "He that walketh uprightly walketh surely" [Proverbs 10:9]. If you suffer for the truth's sake, you are partakers with Christ in His suffering, and will be partakers with Him in His glory.[10]

August 7

A Great Light

For thou wilt light my candle: the LORD my God will enlighten my darkness.
Psalm 18:28

Disguised as an angel of light, he will walk the earth as a wonder-worker. … Christ will be personified, but on one point there will be a marked distinction. Satan will turn the people from the law of God. Notwithstanding this, so well will he counterfeit righteousness, that if it were possible, he would deceive the very elect. Crowned heads, presidents, rulers in high places, will bow to his false theories. …

Every mind should turn with reverent attention to the revealed word of God. … Great truths that have lain unheeded and unseen since the day of Pentecost, are to shine from God's word in their native purity. To those who truly love God the Holy Spirit will reveal truths that have faded from the mind, and will also reveal truths that are entirely new. Those who eat the flesh and drink the blood of the Son of God will bring from the books of Daniel and Revelation truth that is inspired by the Holy Spirit. They will start into action forces that cannot be repressed. The lips of children will be opened to proclaim the mysteries that have been hidden from the minds of men. The Lord has chosen the foolish things of this world to confound the wise, and the weak things of the world to confound the mighty.[11]

August 8

They Shall Deceive Many

... [T]he spirits of devils, working miracles ... go forth unto ... the whole world, to gather them to the battle of that great day of God Almighty. Revelation 16:14

"And many false prophets shall rise, and shall deceive many." False Christs did arise, deceiving the people, and leading great numbers into the desert. Magicians and sorcerers, claiming miraculous power, drew the people after them into the mountain solitudes. But this prophecy was also spoken for the last days. Companies inspired by Satan will be formed to deceive and delude. This will be a sign of the second advent.[12]

The coming of the Lord is to be preceded by "the working of Satan with all power and signs and lying wonders, and with all deceivableness of unrighteousness." 2 Thessalonians 2:9, 10. ... No mere impostures are here foretold. Men are deceived by the miracles which Satan's agents have power to do, not which they pretend to do.[13]

Evil angels come in the form of those loved ones, and relate incidents connected with their lives, and perform acts which they performed while living. In this way they lead persons to believe that their dead friends are angels, hovering over them, and communicating with them. These evil angels, who assume to be the deceased friends, are regarded with a certain idolatry, and with many their word has greater weight than the word of God. Thus men and women are led to reject the truth, and give "heed to seducing spirits."[14]

August 9

A Short Time

*And except those days should be shortened, there should no flesh be saved ...
Mathew 24:22*

Our precious Saviour invites us to join ourselves to Him, to unite our weakness to His strength, our ignorance to His wisdom, our unworthiness to His merits. ... It rests with us to co-operate with the agencies which Heaven employs in the work of conforming our characters to the divine model. None can neglect or defer this work but at the most fearful peril to their souls.

The apostle John in vision heard a loud voice in heaven exclaiming: "Woe to the inhabiters of the earth and of the sea! for the devil is come down unto you, having great wrath, because he knoweth that he hath but a short time." Revelation 12:12. Fearful are the scenes which call forth this exclamation from the heavenly voice. The wrath of Satan increases as his time grows short, and his work of deceit and destruction will reach its culmination in the time of trouble.

Fearful sights of a supernatural character will soon be revealed in the heavens, in token of the power of miracle-working demons. The spirits of devils will go forth to the kings of the earth and to the whole world, to fasten them in deception, and urge them on to unite with Satan in his last struggle against the government of heaven. ... Persons will arise pretending to be Christ Himself, and claiming the title and worship which belong to the world's Redeemer. They will perform wonderful miracles of healing and will profess to have revelations from heaven contradicting the testimony of the Scriptures.[15]

August 10

Wonderful Scenes

Search the scriptures; for ... they ... testify of me. John 5:39

While appearing to the children of men as a great physician who can heal all their maladies, he will bring disease and disaster, until populous cities are reduced to ruin and desolation. ... In accidents and calamities by sea and by land, in great conflagrations, in fierce tornadoes and terrific hailstorms, in tempests, floods, cyclones, tidal waves, and earthquakes ... Satan is exercising his power. ... These visitations are to become more and more frequent and disastrous.[16]

The enemy is preparing to deceive the whole world by his miracle-working power. He will assume to personate the angels of light, to personate Jesus Christ.[17]

Wonderful scenes, with which Satan will be closely connected, will soon take place. God's Word declares that Satan will work miracles. He will make people sick, and then will suddenly remove from them his satanic power. They will then be regarded as healed. These works of apparent healing will bring Seventh-day Adventists to the test. Many who have had great light will fail to walk in the light, because they have not become one with Christ. ...

Let us study the Word of God. Let us make it a part of our lives, bringing its teachings into the daily experience. Thus only can we gain the knowledge that will enable us, in these days of peril, to distinguish the true from the false.[18]

August 11

Against Spiritual Wickedness

For we wrestle not against flesh and blood, but against principalities, against powers, against the rulers of the darkness of this world, against spiritual wickedness in high places. Ephesians 6:12

I am instructed to say that in the future great watchfulness will be needed. ... Evil spirits are actively engaged in seeking to control the minds of human beings. ... Christians are to be sober and vigilant, steadfastly resisting their adversary the devil, who is going about as a roaring lion, seeking whom he may devour. Men under the influence of evil spirits will work miracles. They will make people sick by casting their spell upon them, and will then remove the spell, leading others to say that those who were sick have been miraculously healed. This Satan has done again and again.[19]

Evil angels are upon our track every moment. ... [W]hile our minds are unguarded against Satan's invisible agents, they will assume new ground, and will work marvels and miracles in our sight. Are we prepared to resist them by the word of God, the only weapon we can use successfully? Some will be tempted to receive these wonders as from God. The sick will be healed before us. Miracles will be performed in our sight. Are we prepared for the trial when the lying wonders of Satan shall be more fully exhibited? ... We must all now seek to arm ourselves for the contest in which we must soon engage. Faith in God's word, prayerfully studied and practically applied will be our shield from Satan's power...[20]

August 12

In the Form of Men

For such are false apostles, deceitful workers, transforming themselves into the apostles of Christ. 2 Corinthians 11:13

I have been shown that evil angels in the form of believers will work in our ranks to bring in a strong spirit of unbelief. Let not even this discourage you; but bring a true heart to the help of the Lord against the powers of satanic agencies.[21]

[E]vil angels in the form of men will talk with those who know the truth. They will misinterpret and misconstrue the statements of the messengers of God.[22]

Through the agency of spiritualism, miracles will be wrought, the sick will be healed, and many undeniable wonders will be performed. And as the spirits will profess faith in the Bible, and manifest respect for the institutions of the church, their work will be accepted as a manifestation of divine power. ...

Church members love what the world loves and are ready to join with them, and Satan determines to unite them in one body and thus strengthen his cause by sweeping all into the ranks of spiritualism. Papists, who boast of miracles as a certain sign of the true church, will be readily deceived by this wonder-working power; and Protestants, having cast away the shield of truth, will also be deluded. Papists, Protestants, and worldlings ... will see in this union a grand movement for the conversion of the world and the ushering in of the long-expected millennium.[23]

August 13

The Final Effort

... the spirits of devils, working miracles ... go forth unto the kings of the earth and of the whole world, to gather them to the battle of that great day of God Almighty. Revelation 16:14

Satan has long been preparing for his final effort to deceive the world. The foundation of his work was laid by the assurance given to Eve in Eden: "Ye shall not surely die." "In the day ye eat thereof, then your eyes shall be opened, and ye shall be as gods, knowing good and evil." Genesis 3:4, 5. ... He has not yet reached the full accomplishment of his designs; but it will be reached in the last remnant of time. ... Except those who are kept by the power of God, through faith in His word, the whole world will be swept into the ranks of this delusion.[24]

Through the two great errors, the immortality of the soul and Sunday sacredness, Satan will bring the people under his deceptions. While the former lays the foundation of spiritualism, the latter creates a bond of sympathy with Rome.[25]

A belief in spiritual manifestations opens the door to seducing spirits and doctrines of devils, and thus the influence of evil angels will be felt in the churches.[26]

[L]oved ones will appear in robes of light, as familiar to the sight as when they were upon the earth. They will teach them, and converse with them. And many will be deceived by this wonderful display of Satan's power.[27]

August 14

Perfect Counterfeits

Now the Spirit speaketh expressly, that in the latter times some shall depart from the faith, giving heed to seducing spirits, and doctrines of devils;
1 Timothy 4:1

It is not difficult for the evil angels to represent both saints and sinners who have died, and make these representations visible to human eyes. These manifestations will be more frequent, and developments of a more startling character will appear as we near the close of time.[28]

How can those who believe in man's consciousness in death reject what comes to them as divine light communicated by glorified spirits? ... The fallen angels who do his bidding appear as messengers from the spirit world. While professing to bring the living into communication with the dead, the prince of evil exercises his bewitching influence upon their minds.

He has power to bring before men the appearance of their departed friends. The counterfeit is perfect; the familiar look, the words, the tone, are reproduced with marvelous distinctness. Many are comforted with the assurance that their loved ones are enjoying the bliss of heaven, and without suspicion of danger, they give ear "to seducing spirits, and doctrines of devils."[29]

Many will be confronted by the spirits of devils personating beloved relatives or friends and declaring the most dangerous heresies. These visitants will appeal to our tenderest sympathies and will work miracles to sustain their pretensions.[30]

August 15

Strong Delusion

And for this cause God shall send them strong delusion, that they should believe a lie: That they all might be damned who believed not the truth, but had pleasure in unrighteousness. 2 Thessalonians 2:11, 12

It is Satan's most successful and fascinating delusion, — one calculated to take hold of the sympathies of those who have laid their loved ones in the grave. Evil angels come in the form of those loved ones, and relate incidents connected with their lives, and perform acts which they performed while living. In this way they lead persons to believe that their dead friends are angels, hovering over them, and communicating with them. These evil angels, who assume to be the deceased friends, are regarded with a certain idolatry, and with many their word has greater weight than the word of God. Thus men and women are led to reject the truth, and give "heed to seducing spirits."[31]

The miracle-working power manifested through spiritualism will exert its influence against those who choose to obey God rather than men. Communications from the spirits will declare that God has sent them to convince the rejecters of Sunday of their error, affirming that the laws of the land should be obeyed as the law of God. They will lament the great wickedness in the world and second the testimony of religious teachers that the degraded state of morals is caused by the desecration of Sunday. Great will be the indignation excited against all who refuse to accept their testimony.[32]

August 16

Coming Soon

Then if any man shall say unto you, Lo, here is Christ, or there; believe it not. For there shall arise false Christs, and false prophets, and shall shew great signs and wonders.... Behold, I have told you before. Wherefore if they shall say unto you, Behold, he is in the desert; go not forth: behold, he is in the secret chambers; believe it not. Matthew 24:23 - 26

The last great delusion is soon to open before us. Antichrist is to perform his marvelous works in our sight.[33]

The world is a theater. The actors, its inhabitants, are preparing to act their part in the last great drama. God is lost sight of. ... A power from beneath is working to bring about the last great scenes in the drama, — Satan coming as Christ, and working with all deceivableness of unrighteousness in those who are binding themselves together in secret societies.[34]

Satan is striving to gain every advantage. ... Disguised as an angel of light, he will walk the earth as a wonder-worker. In beautiful language he will present lofty sentiments. Good words will be spoken by him, and good deeds performed. Christ will be personified, but on one point there will be a marked distinction. Satan will turn the people from the law of God. Notwithstanding this, so well will he counterfeit righteousness, that if it were possible, he would deceive the very elect. Crowned heads, presidents, rulers in high places, will bow to his false theories.[35]

August 17

The Appearing

Let no man deceive you by any means: for that day shall not come, except there come a falling away first, and that man of sin be revealed ... Who opposeth and exalteth himself above all that is called God, or that is worshipped
2 Thessalonians 2:3, 4

If men are so easily misled now, how will they stand when Satan shall personate Christ, and work miracles? Who will be unmoved by his misrepresentations then — professing to be Christ when it is only Satan assuming the person of Christ, and apparently working the works of Christ? What will hold God's people from giving their allegiance to false christs? "Go not after them" (Luke 17:23).[36]

Satan ... makes one last desperate effort to overcome the faithful by deception. He does this in personating Christ. He clothes himself with the garments of royalty which have been accurately described in the vision of John. He has power to do this. He will appear to his deluded followers, the Christian world who received not the love of the truth but had pleasure in unrighteousness (transgression of the law), as Christ coming the second time.[37]

Christ will be personified, but ... there will be a marked distinction. Satan will turn the people from the law of God. Notwithstanding this, so well will he counterfeit righteousness, that if it were possible, he would deceive the very elect. Crowned heads, presidents, rulers in high places, will bow to his false theories.[38]

August 18

Surrounded by Glory

And then if any man shall say to you, Lo, here is Christ; or, lo, he is there; believe him not: Mark 13:21

He who could appear clothed with the brightness of the heavenly seraphs before Christ in the wilderness of temptation, comes to men in the most attractive manner as an angel of light. He ... will present his temptations to men in a manner to pervert the senses of all who are not shielded by divine power.[39]

As the crowning act in the great drama of deception, Satan himself will personate Christ. ... [T]he great deceiver ... make[s] it appear that Christ has come. ... Satan will manifest himself among men as a majestic being of dazzling brightness, resembling the description of the Son of God given by John in the Revelation. ... The glory that surrounds him is unsurpassed by anything that mortal eyes have yet beheld. The shout of triumph rings out upon the air: "Christ has come! Christ has come!" The people prostrate themselves in adoration before him, while he lifts up his hands and pronounces a blessing upon them, as Christ blessed His disciples when He was upon the earth. ... In gentle, compassionate tones he presents some of the same gracious, heavenly truths which the Saviour uttered; he heals the diseases of the people, and then, in his assumed character of Christ, he claims to have changed the Sabbath to Sunday, and commands all to hallow the day which he has blessed. He declares that those who persist in keeping holy the seventh day are blaspheming his name by refusing to listen to his angels sent to them with light and truth.[40]

August 19

All Shall Worship

And all that dwell upon the earth shall worship him, whose names are not written in the book of life of the Lamb slain from the foundation of the world.
Revelation 13:8

We must come to the sure word of prophecy for our authority. Unless we are intelligent in the Scriptures, may we not, when this mighty miracle-working power of Satan is manifested in our world, be deceived and call it the workings of God; for the word of God declares that, if it were possible, the very elect should be deceived. Unless we are rooted and grounded in the truth, we shall be swept away by Satan's delusive snares. We must cling to our Bibles. If Satan can make you believe that there are things in the word of God that are not inspired, he will then be prepared to ensnare your soul. We shall have no assurance, no certainty, at the very time we need to know what is truth. Our feet should be shod with the preparation of the gospel, and the truth of God should be our shield and buckler. We must know for ourselves that we have the truth of God. Therefore let no one entertain the question whether this or that portion of the word of God is inspired. Go to work; gird on the armor of Christ's righteousness. ...

He will come personating Jesus Christ, working mighty miracles; and men will fall down and worship him as Jesus Christ. We shall be commanded to worship this being, whom the world will glorify as Christ. What shall we do?[41]

August 20

In Garments of Royalty

... the voice of the bridegroom and of the bride shall be heard no more at all in thee: ... for by thy sorceries were all nations deceived. Revelation 18:23

He clothes himself with the garments of royalty which have been accurately described in the vision of John. He has power to do this. He will appear to his deluded followers, the Christian world who received not the love of the truth but had pleasure in unrighteousness (transgression of the law), as Christ coming the second time.

He proclaims himself Christ, and he is believed to be Christ, a beautiful, majestic being clothed with majesty and, with soft voice and pleasant words, with glory unsurpassed by anything their mortal eyes had yet beheld. Then his deceived, deluded followers set up a shout of victory, "Christ has come the second time! Christ has come! He has lifted up His hands just as He did when He was upon the earth, and blessed us."[42]

[A]ntichrist will appear as the true Christ, and then the law of God will be fully made void in the nations of our world. Rebellion against God's holy law will be fully ripe. ... Men will be deceived and will exalt him to the place of God, and deify him. But Omnipotence will interpose, and to the apostate churches that unite in the exaltation of Satan, the sentence will go forth, 'Therefore shall her plagues come in one day, death, and mourning, and famine; and she shall be utterly burned with fire: for strong is the Lord God who judgeth her.'"[43]

August 21

Abomination of Desolation

... they shall pollute the sanctuary of strength ... and they shall place the abomination that maketh desolate. Daniel 11:31

"When ye therefore shall see the abomination of desolation ... stand in the holy place ... then let them which be in Judea flee into the mountains ..." This warning was given to be heeded forty years after, at the destruction of Jerusalem. The Christians obeyed, and not one of them perished in the destruction of the city.

"But pray ye that your flight be not in the winter, neither on the Sabbath day." Christ, who made the Sabbath, did not abolish it, nailing it to His cross. The fourth commandment was not rendered null and void by His death. It was to be held sacred forty years after His death; even as long as the heavens and the earth remain, so long will it hold its claim upon the human family.

"Then if any man shall say unto you, Lo, here is Christ, or there; believe it not. For there shall arise false Christs, and false prophets, and shall show great signs and wonders; insomuch that, if it were possible, they shall deceive the very elect. Behold, I have told you before. Wherefore if they shall say unto you, Behold, He is in the desert; go not forth; behold, He is in the secret chambers; believe it not. For as the lightning cometh out of the east, and shineth even unto the west; so shall also the coming of the Son of man be." Here, again, the warning concerning Jerusalem is blended with the warning of the second advent.[44]

August 22

Drinking the Wine

And there followed another angel, saying, Babylon is fallen, is fallen, that great city, because she made all nations drink of the wine of the wrath of her fornication. Revelation 14:8

Not yet, however, can it be said that "Babylon is fallen ... because she made all nations drink of the wine of the wrath of her fornication." She has not yet made all nations do this. The spirit of world conforming and indifference to the testing truths for our time exists and has been gaining ground in churches of the Protestant faith in all the countries of Christendom; and these churches are included in the solemn and terrible denunciation of the second angel. But the work of apostasy has not yet reached its culmination.

The Bible declares that before the coming of the Lord, Satan will work "with all power and signs and lying wonders, and with all deceivableness of unrighteousness;" and they that "received not the love of the truth, that they might be saved," will be left to receive "strong delusion, that they should believe a lie." 2 Thessalonians 2:9-11. Not until this condition shall be reached, and the union of the church with the world shall be fully accomplished throughout Christendom, will the fall of Babylon be complete. The change is a progressive one, and the perfect fulfillment of Revelation 14:8 is yet future.[45]

August 23

Slay and Persecute

... I will send them prophets and apostles, and some of them they shall slay and persecute: Luke 11:49

In the twelfth chapter of Revelation is represented the last great conflict between the obedient and the disobedient. [Revelation 12:17; 13:11-17, quoted].

Satan will work the miracles to deceive those who dwell upon the earth. Spiritualism will do its work by causing the dead to be personated. Those religious bodies who refuse to hear God's messages of warning will be under strong deception, and will unite with the civil power to persecute the saints. ...

They profess to be meek and humble but they speak and legislate with the spirit of Satan, showing by their actions that they are the opposite of what they profess to be. This lamb-like power unites with the dragon in making war upon those who keep the commandments of God and have the testimony of Jesus Christ. And Satan unites with Protestants and papists, acting in consort with them as the god of this world, dictating to men as if they were the subjects of his kingdom, to be handled and governed and controlled as he pleases.

If men will not agree to trample under foot the commandments of God, the spirit of the dragon is revealed. They are imprisoned, brought before councils, and fined. "He causeth all, both small and great, rich and poor, free and bond, to receive a mark in their right hand, or in their foreheads" [Revelation 13:16]. ... Thus Satan usurps the prerogatives of Jehovah.[46]

August 24

Deeds of Their Father

Ye are of your father the devil, and the lusts of your father ye will do. ...
John 8:44

When this grand work is to take place in the battle, prior to the last closing conflict, many will be imprisoned, many will flee for their lives from cities and towns, and many will be martyrs for Christ's sake in standing in defense of the truth.[47]

When our nation ... shall enact laws ... enforcing Sunday observance ... the law of God will, to all intents and purposes, be made void in our land ...[48]

Protestantism will in this act join hands with the Papacy; it will be giving life to the tyranny which has long been eagerly watching its opportunity to spring again into active despotism.[49]

It is at the time of the national apostasy, when, acting on the policy of Satan, the rulers of the land will rank themselves on the side of the man of sin — it is then the measure of guilt is full; the national apostasy is the signal for national ruin.[50]

We need not marvel at any developments of horror. Those who trample under their unholy feet the law of God have the same spirit as had the men who insulted and betrayed Jesus. Without any compunction of conscience, they will do the deeds of their father, the devil.[51]

August 25

Babylon Is Fallen

And there followed another angel, saying, 'Babylon is fallen, is fallen, that great city, because she made all nations drink of the wine of the wrath of her fornication.' Revelation 14:8

What is that wine? — Her false doctrines. She has given to the world a false Sabbath instead of the Sabbath of the fourth commandment, and has repeated the falsehood that Satan first told to Eve in Eden, — the natural immortality of the soul. Many kindred errors she has spread far and wide, "teaching for doctrines the commandments of men."[52]

Not yet, however, can it be said that "Babylon is fallen ... because she made all nations drink of the wine of the wrath of her fornication." She has not yet made all nations do this ... the work of apostasy has not yet reached its culmination.

The Bible declares that before the coming of the Lord, Satan will work "with all power and signs and lying wonders, and with all deceivableness of unrighteousness;" and they that "received not the love of the truth, that they might be saved," will be left to receive "strong delusion, that they should believe a lie." 2 Thessalonians 2:9-11. Not until this condition shall be reached, and the union of the church with the world shall be fully accomplished throughout Christendom, will the fall of Babylon be complete. The change is a progressive one, and the perfect fulfillment of Revelation 14:8 is yet future.[53]

August 26

Come Out

For her sins have reached unto heaven ... Revelation 18:5

This scripture points forward to a time when the announcement of the fall of Babylon, as made by the second angel of Revelation 14, is to be repeated, with the additional mention of the corruptions which have been entering ... Babylon.... A terrible condition of the religious world is here described... In defiance of the warnings which God has given, they will continue to trample upon one of the precepts of the Decalogue, until they are led to persecute those who hold it sacred. ... A belief in spiritual manifestations opens the door to seducing spirits and doctrines of devils, and thus the influence of evil angels will be felt in the churches.[54]

She has filled up the measure of her guilt, and destruction is about to fall upon her. But God still has a people in Babylon; and before the visitation of His judgments these faithful ones must be called out, that they partake not of her sins and "receive not of her plagues."⁵⁵

The fearful results of enforcing the observances of the church by civil authority, the inroads of spiritualism, the stealthy but rapid progress of the papal power — all will be unmasked. ... But since many refuse to be satisfied with the mere authority of men and demand a plain "Thus saith the Lord," the popular ministry ... will denounce the message as of Satan and stir up the sin-loving multitudes to revile and persecute those who proclaim it.⁵⁶

August 27

Another Angel

... Babylon the great is fallen, is fallen, and is become the habitation of devils, and the hold of every foul spirit, and a cage of every unclean and hateful bird.
Revelation 18:2

When the land which the Lord provided as an asylum for his people, that they might worship him according to the dictates of their own consciences, the land over which for long years the shield of Omnipotence has been spread, the land which God has favored by making it the depository of the pure religion of Christ, — when that land shall, through its legislators, abjure the principles of Protestantism, and give countenance to Romish apostasy in tampering with God's law, — it is then that the final work of the man of sin will be revealed. Protestants will throw their whole influence and strength on the side of the Papacy; by a national act enforcing the false Sabbath, they will give life and vigor to the corrupt faith of Rome, reviving her tyranny and oppression of conscience. ...

The prophet says: "I saw another angel come down from heaven ... And he cried mightily with a strong voice, saying, Babylon the great is fallen, is fallen. ... Come out of her, my people, that ye be not partakers of her sins, and that ye receive not of her plagues. ..." When do her sins reach unto heaven? When the law of God is finally made void by legislation. ... As a Satanic power is stirring up the elements from beneath, God will send light and power to his people, that the message of truth may be proclaimed to all the world.⁵⁷

August 28

One Fierce Struggle

For all nations have drunk of the wine of the wrath of her fornication, and the kings of the earth have committed fornication with her, and the merchants of the earth are waxed rich through the abundance of her delicacies.
Revelation 18:3

Scenes of stupendous interest are right upon us, and these things will be sure indications of the presence of Him who has directed in every aggressive movement, [the One] who has accompanied the march of His cause through all the ages, and who has graciously pledged Himself to be with His people in all their conflicts to the end of the world. He will vindicate His truth. He will cause it to triumph. He is ready to supply His faithful ones with motives and power of purpose, inspiring them with hope and courage and valor in increased activity as the time is at hand.

Deceptions, delusions, impostures will increase. The cries will come in from every quarter, "Lo, here is Christ! Lo, there is Christ!" "But," said Christ, "Go ye not after them." There will be one fierce struggle before the man of sin shall be disclosed to this world, who he is and what has been his work. While the Protestant world is becoming very tender and affectionate toward the man of sin, shall God's people take their place as bold and valiant soldiers of Jesus Christ, to meet the issue which must come, their lives hid with Christ in God? Mystic Babylon has not been sparing in the blood of the saints, and shall we be wide-awake to catch the beams of light which have been shining from the light of the angel who is to brighten the earth with his glory?[58]

August 29

The Drunken Woman

And I saw the woman drunken with the blood of the saints, and with the blood of the martyrs of Jesus: and when I saw her, I wondered with great admiration.
Revelation 17:6

The term Babylon, derived from Babel, and signifying confusion, is applied in Scripture to the various forms of false or apostate religion. But the message announcing the fall of Babylon must apply to some religious body that was once pure, and has become corrupt. It cannot be the Romish Church which is here meant; for that church has been in a fallen condition for many centuries. But how appropriate the figure as applied to the Protestant churches, all professing to derive their doctrines from the Bible, yet divided into almost innumerable sects. The unity for which Christ prayed does not exist. Instead of one Lord, one faith, one baptism, there are numberless conflicting creeds and theories. Religious faith appears so confused and discordant that the world know not what to believe as truth. God is not in all this; it is the work of man, — the work of Satan. ...

Babylon is said to be a harlot; and the prophet beheld her drunken with the blood of saints and martyrs. The Babylon thus described represents Rome, that apostate church which has so cruelly persecuted the followers of Christ. But Babylon the harlot is the mother of daughters who follow her example of corruption. Thus are represented those churches that cling to the doctrines and traditions of Rome and follow her worldly practices, and whose fall is announced in the second angel's message.[59]

August 30

Fashionable Sins

And upon her forehead was a name written, MYSTERY, BABYLON THE GREAT, THE MOTHER OF HARLOTS AND ABOMINATIONS OF THE EARTH.
Revelation 17:5

But when ... she [Protestant churches] sought after vanity, and allowed the love of worldly things to separate her from God, she forfeited the privileges included in this peculiar and sacred [marriage] relation. By the apostle James those who assimilate to the world are addressed as "adulterers and adulteresses." [James 4:4.]

A profession of religion has become popular with the world. Rulers, politicians, lawyers, doctors, merchants, join the church as a means of securing the respect and confidence of society, and advancing their own worldly interests. ... The various religious bodies, re-enforced by the wealth and influence of these baptized worldlings, make a still higher bid for popularity and patronage. Splendid churches, embellished in the most extravagant manner, are erected on popular avenues. The worshipers array themselves in costly and fashionable attire. A high salary is paid for a talented minister to entertain and attract the people. His sermons must not touch popular sins, but be made smooth and pleasing for fashionable ears. Thus fashionable sinners are enrolled on the church-records, and fashionable sins are concealed under a pretense of godliness. God looks down upon these apostate bodies, and declares them daughters of a harlot. To secure the favor and support of the great men of earth, they have broken their solemn vows of allegiance and fidelity to the King of Heaven.[60]

August 31

The Wine of Babylon

... I will shew ... thee the ... great whore ... With whom the kings of the earth have committed fornication, and the inhabitants of the earth have been made drunk with the wine of her fornication. Revelation 17:1, 2

The great sin charged against Babylon is, that she "made all nations drink of the wine of the wrath of her fornication." This cup of intoxication which she presents to the world, represents the false doctrines which she has accepted as the result of her unlawful connection with the great ones of the earth. ...

The doctrine of the natural immortality of the soul has opened the way for the artful working of Satan through modern Spiritualism ...

And even more dangerous and more widely held ... are the assumptions that the law of God was abolished at the cross, and that the first day of the week is now a holy day, instead of the Sabbath of the fourth commandment.

When faithful teachers expound the word of God, there arise men of learning, ministers professing to understand the Scriptures, who denounce sound doctrine as heresy, and thus turn away inquirers after truth. Were it not that the world is hopelessly intoxicated with the wine of Babylon, multitudes would be convicted and converted by the plain, cutting truths of the word of God. The sin of the world's impenitence lies at the door of the church.[61]

September 1

All Nations Worship

... no man might buy or sell, save he that had the mark ... of the beast ...
Revelation 13:17

The adherents of truth are ... called upon to choose between disregarding a plain requirement of God's word or forfeiting their liberty. If we yield the word of God, and accept human customs and traditions, we may still be permitted to live among men, to buy and sell, and have our rights respected.[1]

Those who have step by step yielded to worldly demands and conformed to worldly customs will not find it a hard matter to yield to the powers that be, rather than subject themselves to derision, insult, threatened imprisonment, and death. The contest is between the commandments of God and the commandments of men. In this time the gold will be separated from the dross in the church.[2] Those who have had great light and precious privileges, but have not improved them, will, under one pretext or another, go out from us.[3]

The first day of the week, a common working day, possessing no sanctity whatever, will be set up as was the image at Babylon. All nations and tongues and peoples will be commanded to worship this spurious sabbath. This is Satan's plan to make of no account the day instituted by God, and given to the world as a memorial of creation.

The decree enforcing the worship of this day is to go forth to all the world.[4]

September 2

Students of the Word

[He] deceiveth them that dwell on the earth ... saying to them that dwell on the earth, that they should make an image to the beast ... Revelation 13:14

Only those who have been diligent students of the Scriptures and who have received the love of the truth will be shielded from the powerful delusion that takes the world captive. By the Bible testimony these will detect the deceiver in his disguise. To all the testing time will come. By the sifting of temptation the genuine Christian will be revealed. Are the people of God now so firmly established upon His word that they would not yield to the evidence of their senses? Would they, in such a crisis, cling to the Bible and the Bible only? Satan will, if possible, prevent them from obtaining a preparation to stand in that day. He will so arrange affairs as to hedge up their way, entangle them with earthly treasures, cause them to carry a heavy, wearisome burden, that their hearts may be overcharged with the cares of this life and the day of trial may come upon them as a thief.

As the decree issued by the various rulers of Christendom against commandment keepers shall withdraw the protection of government and abandon them to those who desire their destruction, the people of God will flee from the cities and villages and associate together in companies, dwelling in the most desolate and solitary places. Many will find refuge in the strongholds of the mountains. ... But many of all nations and of all classes, high and low, rich and poor, black and white, will be cast into the most unjust and cruel bondage.[5]

September 3

The Last Opportunity

... Write, Blessed are the dead which die in the Lord from henceforth: ...
Revelation 14:13

In seeking to cast contempt upon the divine statutes, Satan has perverted the doctrines of the Bible, and errors have thus become incorporated into the faith of thousands who profess to believe the Scriptures. The last great conflict between truth and error is but the final struggle of the long-standing controversy concerning the law of God. Upon this battle we are now entering — a battle between the laws of men and the precepts of Jehovah, between the religion of the Bible and the religion of fable and tradition.[6]

Through the apostles, God gave the Jewish people a last opportunity to repent. But they turned away from every entreaty. In the arrest, the trial, and the imprisonment of his witnesses, God manifested himself. He gave them words to speak, and a tongue and voice with which to vindicate the truth and acknowledge him as the Son of God. They were men of whom the world was not worthy, yet their judges pronounced on them the death sentence. They were not allowed to live and serve their God. By killing them, the Jews crucified afresh the Son of God.

So it will be again. But it is over the seventh-day Sabbath that the battle will be fought. The authorities of this world will rise up in their pride and power to make laws to restrict religious liberty. ... Then God will interpose in behalf of his loyal, commandment-keeping people.[7]

September 4

Prepare the Way of the Lord

The voice of one crying in the wilderness, Prepare ye the way of the Lord, make his paths straight. Mark 1:3

As John prepared the way for the first [advent], so we are to prepare the way for the second, advent of the Saviour. Our publishing institutions are to exalt the claims of God's downtrodden law. ...

Let it never be forgotten that these institutions are to co-operate with the ministry of the delegates of heaven. They are among the agencies represented by the angel flying "in the midst of heaven, having the everlasting gospel to preach unto them that dwell on the earth, and to every nation, and kindred, and tongue, and people, saying with a loud voice, Fear God, and give glory to Him; for the hour of His judgment is come." Revelation 14:6, 7. ...

And in a large degree through our publishing houses is to be accomplished the work of that other angel who comes down from heaven with great power and who lightens the earth with his glory. ...

Never did this message apply with greater force than it applies today. ... This earth has almost reached the place where God will permit the destroyer to work his will upon it. The substitution of the laws of men for the law of God, the exaltation, by merely human authority, of Sunday in place of the Bible Sabbath, is the last act in the drama. When this substitution becomes universal, God will reveal Himself. ...

The great conflict that Satan created in the heavenly courts is soon, very soon, to be forever decided.[8]

September 5

How Long O Lord?

And they cried with a loud voice, saying, How long, O Lord, holy and true,
dost thou not judge and avenge our blood on them that dwell on the earth?
Revelation 6:10

Laws enforcing the observance of Sunday as the Sabbath will bring about a national apostasy from the principles of republicanism upon which the government has been founded. The religion of the Papacy will be accepted by the rulers, and the law of God will be made void.

When the fifth seal was opened, John the Revelator in vision saw beneath the altar the company that were slain for the Word of God and the testimony of Jesus Christ. After this came the scenes described in the eighteenth of Revelation, when those who are faithful and true are called out from Babylon. [Revelation 18: 1-5, quoted.][9]

The world has converted the church. ... Roman Catholic principles will be taken under the care and protection of the state. This national apostasy will speedily be followed by national ruin. The protest of Bible truth will be no longer tolerated by those who have not made the law of God their rule of life. Then will the voice be heard from the graves of martyrs, represented by the souls that John saw slain for the word of God and the testimony of Jesus Christ which they held...[10]

September 6

History Repeated

And I saw in the right hand of him that sat on the throne a book written within and on the backside, sealed with seven seals. Revelation 5:1

There in His open hand lay the book, the roll of the history of God's providences, the prophetic history of nations and the church. Herein was contained the divine utterances, His authority, His commandments, His laws, the whole symbolic counsel of the Eternal, and the history of all ruling powers in the nations. In symbolic language was contained in that roll the influence of every nation, tongue, and people from the beginning of earth's history to its close.

This roll was written within and without. John says: [Revelation 5:4, 5, 8-14; 6:8-11; 8:1-4; quoted.]

The same spirit is seen today that is represented in Revelation 6:6-8. History is to be repeated. That which has been will be again.

Revelation is a sealed book, but it is also an opened book. It records marvelous events that are to take place in the last days of this earth's history. The teachings of this book are definite, not mystical and unintelligible. In it the same line of prophecy is taken up as in Daniel. Some prophecies God has repeated, thus showing that importance must be given to them. The Lord does not repeat things that are of no great consequence.[11]

September 7

Sitting in the Temple

... so that he as God sitteth in the temple of God, shewing himself that he is God.
2 Thessalonians 2:4

An idol sabbath has been set up, as the golden image was set up in the plains of Dura. And as Nebuchadnezzar, the king of Babylon, issued a decree that all who would not bow down and worship this image should be killed, so a proclamation will be made that all who will not reverence the Sunday institution will be punished with imprisonment and death. Thus the Sabbath of the Lord is trampled underfoot. But the Lord has declared, "Woe unto them that decree unrighteous decrees, and write grievousness which they have prescribed" [Isaiah 10:1]. [Zephaniah 1:14-18; 2:1-3, quoted.]

The Lord of heaven permits the world to choose whom they will have as ruler. Let all read carefully the thirteenth chapter of Revelation, for it concerns every human agent, great and small. Every human being must take sides, either for the true and living God, who has given to the world the memorial of creation in the seventh-day Sabbath, or for a false sabbath, instituted by men who have exalted themselves above all that is called God or that is worshiped, who have taken upon themselves the attributes of Satan in oppressing the loyal and true who keep the commandments of God. This persecuting power will compel the worship of the beast by insisting on the observance of the sabbath he has instituted. Thus he blasphemes God, "sitting in the temple of God, shewing himself that he is God."[12]

September 8

The Days of Wrath

... If any man worship the beast and his image ... The same shall drink of the wine of the wrath of God... Revelation 14:9, 10

John beheld a new power coming up to echo the dragon's voice ... the last that is to wage war against the church and the law of God, was symbolized by a beast with lamblike horns. ... Those who first found an asylum on the shores of America ... determined to establish a government upon the broad foundation of civil and religious liberty. ...

But the ... beast with lamblike horns speaks with the voice of a dragon, and "exerciseth all the power of the first beast before him." Prophecy declares that he will say to them that dwell on the earth that they should make an image to the beast, and that "he causeth all, ... to receive a mark in their right hand, or in their foreheads; and that no man might buy or sell, save he that had the mark, or the name of the beast, or the number of his name." ...

It is at this time that the third angel is seen flying in the midst of heaven, proclaiming: "If any man worship the beast and his image ... the same shall drink of the wine of the wrath of God, which is poured out without mixture into the cup of His indignation." ... In marked contrast to the world stands the little company who will not swerve from their allegiance to God. These are they of whom Isaiah speaks as repairing the breach which had been made in the law of God, they who are building the old waste places, raising up the foundation of many generations.[13]

September 9

Universal Execration

... they have no rest day nor night, who worship the beast and his image, and whosoever receiveth the mark of his name. Revelation 14:11

As the Sabbath has become the special point of controversy throughout Christendom, and religious and secular authorities have combined to enforce the observance of the Sunday, the persistent refusal of a small minority to yield to the popular demand will make them objects of universal execration. It will be urged that the few who stand in opposition to an institution of the church and a law of the state ought not to be tolerated; that it is better for them to suffer than for whole nations to be thrown into confusion and lawlessness. The same argument many centuries ago was brought against Christ by the "rulers of the people." "It is expedient for us," said the wily Caiaphas, "that one man should die for the people, and that the whole nation perish not." John 11:50. This argument will appear conclusive; and a decree will finally be issued against those who hallow the Sabbath of the fourth commandment, denouncing them as deserving of the severest punishment and giving the people liberty, after a certain time, to put them to death. Romanism in the Old World and apostate Protestantism in the New will pursue a similar course toward those who honor all the divine precepts.[14]

Then such laws will be made by the counsel and direction of Satan, that unless time should be very short, no flesh could be saved.[15]

September 10

Faith That Will Not Falter

By faith Enoch was translated that he should not see death; ... for before his translation ... he pleased God. Hebrews 11:5

Especially will the wrath of man be aroused against those who hallow the Sabbath of the fourth commandment; and at last a universal decree will denounce these as deserving of death.

The season of distress before God's people will call for a faith that will not falter. ... To the loyal heart the commands of sinful, finite men will sink into insignificance beside the word of the eternal God. Truth will be obeyed though the result be imprisonment or exile or death.[16]

I saw the leading men of the earth consulting together, and Satan and his angels busy around them. I saw a writing, copies of which were scattered in different parts of the land, giving orders that unless the saints should yield their peculiar faith, give up the Sabbath, and observe the first day of the week, the people were at liberty after a certain time to put them to death. But in this hour of trial the saints were calm and composed, trusting in God and leaning upon His promise that a way of escape would be made for them. ... Satan wished to have the privilege of destroying the saints of the Most High; but Jesus bade His angels watch over them. God would be honored by making a covenant with those who had kept His law, in the sight of the heathen round about them; and Jesus would be honored by translating, without their seeing death, the faithful, waiting ones who had so long expected Him.[17]

September 11

Keeping the Faith

Here is the patience of the saints: here are they that keep the commandments of God, and the faith of Jesus. Revelation 14:12

The decree shall go forth enforcing the counterfeit sabbath, and the loud cry of "the third angel" shall warn men against the worship of the beast and his image, the line will be clearly drawn between the false and the true. Then those who still continue in transgression will receive the mark of the beast. ...

The decree which is to go forth against the people of God in the near future is in some respects similar to that issued by Ahasuerus against the Jews in the time of Esther. ... Satan instigated this scheme in order to rid the earth of those who preserved a knowledge of the true God. But his plots were defeated by a counter-power that reigns among the children of men. Angels who excel in strength were commissioned to protect the people of God, and the plots of their adversaries returned upon their own heads.

History repeats itself. The same masterful mind that plotted against the faithful in ages past is now at work to gain control of the Protestant churches, that through them he may condemn and put to death all who will not worship the idol sabbath. ...

To every soul will come the searching test.... Who are prepared to stand firmly under the banner on which is inscribed, "The commandments of God and the faith of Jesus"?[18]

September 12

Lighting the Earth

God also bearing them witness, both with signs and wonders, and with divers miracles ... Hebrews 2:4

The first, second, and third angels' messages are to be repeated.[19]

The angel who unites in the proclamation of the third message is to lighten the whole earth with his glory. A work of world-wide extent and unwonted power is here brought to view. The Advent movement of 1840-44 was a glorious manifestation of the power of God; the first message was carried to every missionary station in the world, and in this country there was the greatest religious interest which has been witnessed in any land since the Reformation of the sixteenth century; but these are to be far exceeded by the mighty movement under the loud cry of the third message. The work will be similar to that of the day of

Pentecost. ... By thousands of voices, all over the earth, the message will be given. Miracles are wrought, the sick are healed, and signs and wonders follow the believers.[20]

We see before us a special work to be done in the time when the whole earth shall be filled with the light and the glory of the Lord, as the waters cover the sea. The prophecies in the eighteenth of Revelation will soon be fulfilled. ... The Spirit of the Lord will so graciously and universally bless consecrated human instrumentalities, that men, women, and children will open their lips in praise and testimony, filling the earth with the knowledge of God, and with his unsurpassed glory, as the waters cover the sea. [21]

September 13

A Loud Voice

And the third angel followed them, saying with a loud voice ... Revelation 14:9

These three angels represent the people who accept the light of God's messages, and go forth as His agents to sound the warning throughout the length and breadth of the earth. ...

In this day, God has called His church, as He called ancient Israel, to stand as a light in the earth. ... [T]he messages of the first, second, and third angels ... are a sacred trust to be communicated to the world.

Prophecy declares that the first angel would make his announcement to "every nation, and kindred, and tongue, and people." The warning of the third angel, which forms a part of the same threefold message, and is the message for this time, will be no less widespread. ... The power of the first and second messages is to be intensified in the third. It is represented in the prophecy as being proclaimed with a loud voice by an angel flying in the midst of heaven, and it will command the attention of the world.

The most fearful threatening ever addressed to mortals is contained in the third angel's message. ... [T]he warning against the worship of the beast and his image is to be given to the world before the visitation of God's judgments, that all may know why the judgments are inflicted, and may have opportunity to escape.[22]

September 14

To the Ends of the Earth

... I saw another angel ... having great power; and the earth was lightened with his glory. Revelation 18:1

The Lord God of heaven will not send upon the world His judgments for disobedience and transgression until He has sent His watchmen to give the warning. He will not close up the period of probation until the message shall be more distinctly proclaimed. The law of God is to be magnified; its claims must be presented in their true, sacred character, that the people may be brought to decide for or against the truth. Yet the work will be cut short in righteousness. The message of Christ's righteousness is to sound from one end of the earth to the other to prepare the way of the Lord. This is the glory of God, which closes the work of the third angel. ...

Mysteries into which angels desire to look, which prophets and kings and righteous men desired to understand, the remnant church will carry in messages from God to the world. The prophets prophesied of these things, and they longed to understand that which they foretold; but to them this privilege was not given. They longed to see what we see, and to hear what we hear; but they could not. ...

Through this message the character of God in Christ is to be manifested to the world. ...

Now, with John the Baptist, we are to point men to Jesus, saying: "Behold the Lamb of God, which taketh away the sin of the world." John 1:29. Now as never before is to be sounded the invitation: ...[23]

September 15

Purified and Tried

Many shall be purified, and made white, and tried; ... but the wise shall understand. Daniel 12:10

All power is given into His hands, that He may dispense rich gifts unto men, imparting the priceless gift of His own righteousness to the helpless human agent. This is ... the third angel's message, which is to be proclaimed with a loud voice, and attended with the outpouring of His Spirit in a large measure.

The uplifted Saviour is to appear in His efficacious work as the Lamb slain, sitting upon the throne, to dispense the priceless covenant blessings, the benefits He died to purchase for every soul who should believe on Him. ...

The efficacy of the blood of Christ was to be presented to the people with freshness and power, that their faith might lay hold upon its merits. ... [W]hile we confess our sins and plead the efficacy of Christ's atoning blood, our prayers are to ascend to heaven, fragrant with the merits of our Saviour's character. ... This faith is the life of the church.[24]

The Church and the world are united in trampling upon God's commandments, and those who obey these commandments they threaten with death. ...

God's requirements must be laid before those who are transgressing His law. ... God's remnant people are to fill the earth with the cry of the third angel.[25]

September 16

A Voice Like a Trumpet

Cry aloud, spare not, lift up thy voice like a trumpet, and shew my people their transgression ... Isaiah 58:1

The third angel's message is to be given to our world in clear, distinct lines. ... The Sabbath truth is the message to be proclaimed with a loud voice, as presented in the fifty-eighth chapter of Isaiah. And in the fourteenth chapter of Revelation we read, "The third angel followed them, saying with a loud voice, If any man worship the beast and his image, and receive his mark in his forehead or in his hand, the same shall drink of the wine of the wrath of God, which is poured out without mixture into the cup of His indignation; and he shall be tormented with fire and brimstone in the presence of the holy angels, and in the presence of the Lamb." [verses 9, 10]. This message embraces the two preceding messages. It is represented as being given with a loud voice, that is, with the power of the Holy Spirit. ...

The third angel's message is to be at this time regarded as of the highest importance. ...

The eighteenth chapter of Revelation reveals the importance of presenting the truth in no measured terms, but with boldness and power. There must be no toning down of the truth, no muffling of the message for this time. ...

Satan will so mingle his deceptions with truth that side issues will be created to turn the attention of the people from the great issue, the test to be brought upon the people of God in these last days.[26]

September 17

To Know Him

[T]he Son of God ... hath given us an understanding, that we may know him ...
1 John 5:20

We are to realize that the judgments of God are about to fall upon the earth, and we should most earnestly present before the people the warning that the Lord has commissioned us to give: "For then shall be great tribulation, such as was not since the beginning of the world to this time, no, nor ever shall be." "Men's hearts failing them for fear, and for looking after those things which are coming on the earth: for the powers of heaven shall be shaken. ..."

The time of test is just upon us, for the loud cry of the third angel has already begun in the revelation of the righteousness of Christ, the sin-pardoning Redeemer. This is the beginning of the light of the angel whose glory shall fill the whole earth. For it is the work of every one to whom the message of warning has come, to lift up Jesus, to present him to the world as revealed in types, as shadowed in symbols, as manifested in the revelations of the prophets, as unveiled in the lessons given to his disciples and in the wonderful miracles wrought for the sons of men. Search the Scriptures; for they are they that testify of him.

If you would stand through the time of trouble, you must know Christ, and appropriate the gift of his righteousness, which he imputes to the repentant sinner. ... Man is privileged to connect with Christ, and then the divine and the human combine; and in this union the hope of man must rest alone ...[27]

September 18

The Ark Was Seen

And the temple of God was opened in heaven, and there was seen in his temple the ark of his testament ... Revelation 11:19

The angel of Revelation 14 is represented as flying in the midst of heaven, saying with a loud voice, "Here are they that keep the commandments of God and the faith of Jesus." This angel presents a message that is to be proclaimed to the world just before Christ comes ... then, the attention of the people is to be called to the down-trodden law of God, which is contained in the ark of the testament.

The people of God are seeking for light; and as they examine his law ... they find in its bosom the fourth commandment as it was instituted in Eden, and proclaimed in awful grandeur from Sinai's mount: "Remember the Sabbath-day, to keep it holy. Six days shalt thou labor ... but the seventh day is the Sabbath ..."

They see that instead of observing the seventh day, the day that God sanctified, and commanded to be observed as the Sabbath, they are keeping the first day of the week. But they honestly desire to do God's will, and they begin to search the Scriptures to find the reason for the change. Failing to find any scriptural authority for the custom, the question arises, Shall we ... obey the commandments of God, or shall ... obey the commandments of men? With open Bibles they weep, and pray, and compare scripture with scripture, until, convinced of the truth, they conscientiously take their stand as keepers of the commandments of God.[28]

September 19

Until All Have Heard

And cried with a loud voice, saying, Salvation to our God which sitteth upon the throne, and unto the Lamb. Revelation 7:10

Very precious to God is his work in the earth. Christ and heavenly angels are watching in every moment. As we draw near to the coming of Christ, more and still more of missionary work will engage our efforts. The message of the renewing power of God's grace will belt the world. Those that will be sealed will be from every nation and kindred and tongue and people. From every country will be gathered men and women who will stand before the throne of God and before the Lamb in worship, crying, "Salvation to our God which sitteth upon the throne, and unto the Lamb." But before this work can be accomplished, we must experience right here in our own country the work of the Holy Spirit upon our hearts.

The truth will be proclaimed in clear, unmistakable language. As a people, we must prepare the way of the Lord, under the overruling guidance of the Holy Spirit. The gospel is to be given in its purity. … In all fields, nigh and afar off, men will be called from the plow and from the more common commercial business vocations that largely occupy the mind, and will be educated in connection with men of experience. … The message that means so much to the dwellers upon the earth, will be heard and understood. Men will know what is truth. Onward, and still onward the work will advance, until the whole earth shall have been warned. And then shall the end come.[29]

September 20

God in the Flesh

[Y]e are the temple of the living God; as God hath said, I will dwell in them, and walk in them; and I will be their God, and they shall be my people.
2 Corinthians 6:16

There is no excuse for sinning. A holy temper, a Christlike life, is accessible to every repenting, believing child of God.

The ideal of Christian character is Christlikeness. As the Son of man was perfect in His life, so His followers are to be perfect in their life. … He became flesh, even as we are. … He was God in the flesh. His character is to be ours. The Lord says of those who believe in Him, "I will dwell in them, and walk in them; and I will be their God, and they shall be My people." 2 Corinthians 6:16.[30]

The faith essential for salvation is not mere nominal faith, but an abiding principle, deriving vital power from Christ. It will lead the soul to feel the love of Christ to such a degree that the character will be refined, purified, ennobled. This faith in Christ is not merely an impulse, but a power that works by love and purifies the soul. It accomplishes something, bringing the soul under discipline, elevating it from defilement, and bringing it into connection with Christ, till it appropriates his virtue to the soul's need. This is saving faith. ...

Every temptation may be conquered through the strength of Christ. God desires us to have pure characters; purity is power, but sin is weakness and ruin.[31]

September 21

Partakers of His Nature

Whereby are given unto us exceeding great and precious promises: that by these ye might be partakers of the divine nature, having escaped the corruption that is in the world through lust. 2 Peter 1:4

This is a training process, a constant discipline of the mind and heart, that Christ shall work His great work in human hearts. Self, the old natural self, dies, and Christ's will is our will, His way is our way, and the human agent becomes, with heart, mind, and intellect, an instrument in the hands of God to work no more wickedness but the righteousness of Christ.[32]

Nothing less than perfect obedience can meet the standard of God's requirement. ... We are to point sinners to His ideal of character and to lead them to Christ, by whose grace only can this ideal be reached.

The Saviour took upon Himself the infirmities of humanity and lived a sinless life, that men might have no fear that because of the weakness of human nature they could not overcome. Christ came to make us "partakers of the divine nature," and His life declares that humanity, combined with divinity, does not commit sin.

The Saviour overcame to show man how he may overcome. All the temptations of Satan, Christ met with the word of God. By trusting in God's promises, He received power to obey God's commandments, and the tempter could gain no advantage. To every temptation His answer was, "It is written." So God has given us His word wherewith to resist evil.[33]

September 22

Merging the Will

It is the spirit that quickeneth ... the words that I speak unto you, they are spirit, and they are life. John 6:63

We are to study the Word of God in the way pointed out in the sixth chapter of John. "... the words that I speak unto you, they are spirit, and they are life." ...

The Word of God is to become a part of our very being. ... It is only when we serve God in the strictest integrity and in humility of mind, trusting in Jesus, that we are safe. Everything is to be shaken that can be shaken.[34]

Whatever his hereditary or cultivated tendencies may be, the Holy Spirit's moulding power on his mind and character leads him into more and still more decided co-operation with the upbuilding of the instrumentalities God has established. ... Those who will stand firm as a rock to principle will not become corrupted with the leaven of deception and disaffection.

The will of every human being should be under the discipline and control of God, for it is a dangerous element if exercised in selfish schemes. ... The will of man is safe only when united with the will of God. When merged into the will of God it is a will joined to conscience, rightly exercised in advancing the honour and glory of God. The Lord has purchased the will, the affections, the mind, the soul, and the strength. Thus He has taken the whole man. Under the supervision of the divine power the will is to be cultivated to become strong, prompt, firm. It is not to fail nor become discouraged.[35]

September 23

One With God

At that day ye shall know that I am in my Father, and ye in me, and I in you. John 14:20

In the work of redemption there is no compulsion. No external force is employed. Under the influence of the Spirit of God, man is left free to choose whom he will serve. ... The expulsion of sin is the act of the soul itself. ... [W]hen we desire to be set free from sin, and in our great need cry out for a power out of and above ourselves, the powers of the soul are imbued with the divine energy of the Holy Spirit, and they obey the dictates of the will in fulfilling the will of God.

The only condition upon which the freedom of man is possible is that of becoming one with Christ. "The truth shall make you free;" and Christ is the truth. ... Subjection to God is restoration to one's self, — to the true glory and dignity of man. The divine law, to which we are brought into subjection, is "the law of liberty." James 2:12.[36]

To bring humanity into Christ, to bring the fallen race into oneness with divinity, is the work of redemption. Christ took human nature that men might be one with Him as He is one with the Father, that God may love man as He loves His only-begotten Son, that men may be partakers of the divine nature, and be complete in Him.

The Holy Spirit ... binds the human agent, body, soul, and spirit, to the perfect, divine-human nature of Christ. ... Through faith human nature is assimilated with Christ's nature. We are made one with God in Christ.[37]

September 24

One in Christ

Sanctify them thru Thy truth; Thy word is truth. ... I ... [pray also] for them also which shall believe on Me thru their word; that they all may be one, as Thou, Father, art in Me and I in Thee, that they also may be one in us; that the world may believe that Thou hast sent Me. John 17:17-21

These words present the grand result of Christian unity. Christians are to be one in Christ. By their unity they are to bear witness to the world that Christ is the Sent of God. All true disciples will realize that this is the standard they must reach. They will strive continually to help one another.

"I pray for them; I pray not for the world, but for them which Thou hast given Me." They are on My side. They stand under My banner. By receiving Me as their personal Saviour, they have pledged themselves to keep My holy law, to reveal Me in all their transactions in the church and in the world. I have purchased them by My manifestation of love and power in their behalf. For them I have sanctified Myself to the work Thou hast appointed Me, that they also may be sanctified to the work Thou hast appointed them, that by their union with Me and with one another they may reveal to the world that Thou didst send Me to the earth to save sinners.[38]

Through the eternal ages He is linked with us. ... Christ is our brother. ... By love's self-sacrifice, the inhabitants of earth and heaven are bound to their Creator in bonds of indissoluble union.[39]

September 25

So Are We

Herein is our love made perfect, that we may have boldness in the day of judgment: because as he is, so are we in this world. 1 John 4:17

The angels of glory find their joy in giving, — giving love and tireless watch-care to souls that are fallen and unholy; heavenly beings woo the hearts of men; they bring to this dark world light from the courts above; by gentle, patient ministry they move upon the human spirit, to bring the lost into a fellowship with Christ that is even closer than they themselves can know.[40]

[T]o pray in Christ's name means much. It means that we are to accept his character, manifest his spirit, and work his works. The Saviour's promise is given on condition. "If ye love me," he says, "keep my commandments." He saves men, not in sin, but from sin; and those who love him will show their love by obedience.

All true obedience comes from the heart. It was heart-work with Christ. And if we consent, he will so identify himself with our thoughts and aims, so blend our hearts and minds into conformity to his will, that when obeying him we shall be but carrying out our own impulses. The will, refined and sanctified, will find its highest delight in doing his service. When we know God as it is our privilege to know him, our life will be a life of continual obedience. Through an appreciation of the character of Christ, through communion with God, sin will become hateful to us.[41]

September 26

Conformity to His Word

... being knit together in love, and unto all riches of the full assurance of understanding, to the acknowledgement of the mystery of God ... Colossians 2:2

If we come to him in faith, he will speak his mysteries to us personally. Our hearts will often burn within us as One draws nigh to commune with us as he did with Enoch.[42]

God's word sets forth the will that is to be carried into the recesses of the soul. If the human agent consents, God can and will so identify His will with all our thoughts and aims, so blend our hearts and minds into conformity to His word, that when obeying His will we are only carrying out the impulses of our minds. All such will not possess an unsanctified, selfish disposition, ready to carry out their own wills, but will have a jealous, earnest, determined zeal for the glory of God. They will not want to do anything in their own strength, and will guard strictly against the danger of promoting self.

All who would perfect a Christian character must wear the yoke of Christ. .... Christ pleased not Himself. ... He assumed human nature to demonstrate to the fallen world, to Satan and his synagogue, to the universe of heaven, to the worlds unfallen, that human nature, united with His divine nature, could become entirely obedient to the law of God. ... God places us under the guidance of the Holy Spirit, and it will lead us into all truth.[43]

September 27

Revelation of the Mystery

Now to him that is of power to stablish you ... according to the revelation of the mystery, which was kept secret since the world began, But now is made manifest ... Romans 16:25, 26

That Christ should take human nature, and by a life of humiliation elevate man in the scale of moral worth with God; that he should carry his adopted nature to the throne of God, and there present his children to the Father, to have conferred upon them an honor exceeding that bestowed upon the angels, — this is love that melts the sinner's heart. ... God, having gathered together all the riches of the universe, and laid open all the resources of his power, should place them in the hand of his Son, saying, All these I give to you for man. These are my gifts to him. Confer them upon him, that he may know that there is no love like mine, and that his eternal happiness consists in giving me his love in return. As the sinner contemplates this love, it broadens and deepens into infinitude, passing beyond his comprehension. ...

Christ calls upon us to be "instant in prayer." By this he means that the heart is constantly to go out after God, while we watch for opportunities to do good to the souls that are ready to die. ...

[T]he powers of darkness are determined to oppose the way of advance. But when we look to the cross of Christ for grace, we can not fail. The promise of the Redeemer is, "I will never leave thee nor forsake thee." "I am with you alway, even unto the end of the world."[44]

September 28

Finishing the Mystery

But in the days of the voice of the seventh angel, when he shall begin to sound, the mystery of God should be finished ... Revelation 10:7

It is indeed the mystery by which everlasting righteousness is brought to all who believe. ... Christ, at an infinite cost, by a painful process ... assumed humanity. Hiding His divinity, laying aside His glory, He was born a babe in Bethlehem. In human flesh He lived the law of God, that He might condemn sin in the flesh ...⁴⁵

[H]e descended from one humiliation to another, until he ... was uplifted on the cross, to draw all men to himself. ...

This is the mystery of godliness, the mystery that has inspired heavenly agencies so to minister through fallen humanity that in the world an intense interest will be aroused in the plan of salvation. This is the mystery that has stirred all heaven to unite with man in carrying out God's great plan. ...

To every one who offers himself to the Lord for service, withholding nothing, is given power for the attainment of measureless results.

The Lord God is bound by an eternal pledge to supply power and grace to every one who is sanctified through obedience to the truth. Christ, to whom is given all power in heaven and on earth, co-operates in sympathy with his instrumentalities ... The church on earth, united with the church in heaven, can accomplish all things.⁴⁶

September 29

Fully Developed

But the judgment shall sit, and they shall take away his dominion, to consume and to destroy it unto the end. Daniel 7:26

Satan declared that mercy destroyed justice, that the death of Christ abrogated the Father's law. ... [T]he very means by which Christ established the law Satan represented as destroying it. Here will come the last conflict of the great controversy between Christ and Satan.

That the law which was spoken by God's own voice is faulty, that some specification has been set aside, is the claim which Satan now puts forward. It is the last great deception that he will bring upon the world. ... This work is foretold in prophecy. Of the great apostate power which is the representative of Satan, it is declared, "He shall speak great words against the Most

High, and shall wear out the saints of the Most High, and think to change times and laws: and they shall be given into his hand." Daniel 7:25. ...

The warfare against God's law, which was begun in heaven, will be continued until the end of time. ... All will be called to choose between the law of God and the laws of men. Here the dividing line will be drawn. There will be but two classes. Every character will be fully developed; and all will show whether they have chosen the side of loyalty or that of rebellion.

Then the end will come. God will vindicate His law and deliver His people. ...[47]

September 30

The Furnace of Affliction

... our God whom we serve is able to deliver us from the burning fiery furnace ...
Daniel 3:17

The remnant people of God are to endure persecutions. ... The prophet says of ... the Papacy: "There was given unto him a mouth speaking great things and blasphemies; and power was given unto him to continue forty and two months. And he opened his mouth in blasphemy against God, to blaspheme his name, and his tabernacle, and them that dwell in heaven. And it was given unto him to make war with the saints, and to overcome them; and power was given him over all kindreds, and tongues, and nations. And all that dwell upon the earth shall worship him, whose names are not written in the book of life of the Lamb slain from the foundation of the world." The remnant church of God are to give the warning of the third angel to the world: "If any man worship the beast and his image, and receive his mark in his forehead, or in his hand, the same shall drink of the wine of the wrath of God, which is poured out without mixture into the cup of his indignation."

The church of God, despised and persecuted ... are educated and disciplined in the school of Christ. They ... are purified in the furnace of afflictions. ... They follow Christ through sore conflicts; they endure self-denial, and experience bitter disappointments; but their painful experience teaches them the guilt and woe of sin, and they look upon it with abhorrence. Being partakers of Christ's sufferings, they are destined to be partakers of his glory.[48]

October 1

In the Greatest Danger

The Lord is slow to anger, and great in power, and will not at all acquit the wicked ... Nahum 1:3

What is needed in this, our time of danger, is fervent prayer, mingled with earnest faith, a reliance upon God when Satan casts his shadow over God's people. Let everyone bear in mind that God delights to listen to the supplications of His people; for the prevailing iniquity calls for more earnest prayer, and God has promised that He will avenge His own elect, who cry day and night unto Him, though He bear long with them.

Men are prone to abuse the long-suffering of God, and to presume on His forbearance. But there is a point in human iniquity when it is time for God to interfere; and terrible are the issues. The long-suffering of God is wonderful, because He puts constraint on His own attributes; but punishment is nonetheless certain. Every century of profligacy has treasured up wrath against the day of wrath; and when the time comes, and the iniquity is full, then God will do His strange work. It will be found a terrible thing to have worn out the divine patience; for the wrath of God will fall so signally and strongly that it is presented as being unmixed with mercy; and the very earth will be desolated. ...

God has thrust His people into the gap, to make up the hedge, to raise up the foundation of many generations. ... When His people shall be in the greatest danger, seemingly unable to stand against the power of Satan, God will work in their behalf. Man's extremity is God's opportunity.[1]

October 2

A Dark Day

That day is a day of wrath, a day of trouble and distress, a day of wasteness and desolation ... Zephaniah 1:15

The third angel's message, following the first and second which have proclaimed the hour of God's judgment and the fall of mystic Babylon, is proclaimed in louder and more explicit tones, giving a warning to all co-workers in the great anti-Christian apostasy: [Revelation 18:1-5, quoted]. ...

The world is in co-partnership with the professed Christian churches in making void the law of Jehovah. God's law is set aside; it is trampled underfoot; and from all the loyal people of God the prayer will ascend to heaven, "It is time, O Lord, for Thee to work: for they have made void Thy law." Satan is making his last and most powerful effort for the mastery, his last conflict against the principles of God's law. A defiant infidelity abounds. ...

[T]he dwellers in Sodom ... awoke with all their plans and inventions of iniquity; but suddenly the shower of fire came from heaven and consumed the godless inhabitants. "Thus shall it be in the day when the Son of man is revealed" [Luke 17:30]. ...

When the scorner, the rejecter of truth has become presumptuous, when the routine of work in the various money-making lines is being carried on without regard to principle, when the student is fully engaged in ambitious aims to obtain knowledge of everything but the Bible, Christ comes as a thief.[2]

October 3

Given To Jesus

The seventh angel sounded; ... The kingdoms of this world are become the kingdoms of our Lord, and of his Christ; and he shall reign for ever and ever.
Revelation 11:15

I was pointed down to the time when the third angel's message was closing. The power of God had rested upon His people; they had accomplished their work and were prepared for the trying hour before them. They had received the latter rain, or refreshing from the presence of the Lord, and the living testimony had been revived. The last great warning had sounded everywhere, and it had stirred up and enraged the inhabitants of the earth who would not receive the message.

I saw angels hurrying to and fro in heaven. An angel with a writer's inkhorn by his side returned from the earth and reported to Jesus that his work was done, and the saints were numbered and sealed. Then I saw Jesus, who had been ministering before the ark containing the Ten Commandments, throw down the censer. He raised His hands, and with a loud voice said, "It is done." And all the angelic host laid off their crowns as Jesus made the solemn declaration, "He that is unjust, let him be unjust still: and he which is filthy, let him be filthy still: and he that is righteous, let him be righteous still: and he that is holy, let him be holy still." Rev. 22:11. ...

The subjects of the kingdom were made up. The marriage of the Lamb was consummated. And the kingdom, and the greatness of the kingdom under the whole heaven, was given to Jesus and the heirs of salvation, and Jesus was to reign as King of kings and Lord of lords.[3]

October 4

An Everlasting Dominion

I saw in the night visions, and, behold, one like the Son of man came with the clouds of heaven, and came to the Ancient of days, and they brought him near before him. And there was given him dominion, and glory, and a kingdom, that all people, nations, and languages, should serve him: his dominion is an everlasting dominion, which shall not pass away, and his kingdom that which shall not be destroyed. Daniel 7:13, 14

"I beheld," says the prophet Daniel, "till thrones were placed, and One that was Ancient of Days did sit: His raiment was white as snow, and the hair of His head like pure wool; His throne was fiery flames, and the wheels thereof burning fire. A fiery stream issued and came forth from before Him: thousand thousands ministered unto Him, and ten thousand times ten thousand stood before Him: the judgment was set, and the books were opened." Daniel 7:9, 10, R.V. ...

The coming of Christ here described is not His second coming to the earth. He comes to the Ancient of Days in heaven to receive dominion and glory and a kingdom, which will be given Him at the close of His work as a mediator. It is this coming, and not His second advent to the earth, that was foretold in prophecy to take place at the termination of the 2300 days in 1844. Attended by heavenly angels, our great High Priest enters the holy of holies and there appears in the presence of God to engage in the last acts of His ministration in behalf of man — to perform the work of investigative judgment and to make an atonement for all who are shown to be entitled to its benefits.[4]

October 5

Done

This is a rebellious people, lying children ... that will not hear the law of the LORD: Which say to the seers, See not; and to the prophets, Prophesy not unto us right things, speak unto us smooth things, prophesy deceits: Isaiah 30:9, 10

As Jesus moved out of the most holy place ... a cloud of darkness covered the inhabitants of the earth. There was then no mediator between guilty man and an offended God. While Jesus had been standing between God and guilty man, a restraint was upon the people; but when He stepped out from between man and the Father, the restraint was removed and Satan had entire control of the finally impenitent. It was impossible for the plagues to be poured out while Jesus officiated in the sanctuary; but as His work there is finished, and His intercession closes, there is nothing to stay the wrath of God, and it breaks with fury upon the shelterless head of the guilty sinner, who has slighted salvation and hated reproof. In that fearful time, after the close of Jesus' mediation, the saints were living in the sight of a holy God without an intercessor.[5]

When Jesus rises up in the most holy place, lays off His mediatorial robes, and clothes Himself with the garments of vengeance, the mandate will go forth: "He that is unjust, let him be unjust still: ... and he that is righteous, let him be righteous still: and he that is holy, let him be holy still. And, behold, I come quickly; and My reward is with Me, to give every man according as his work shall be." Revelation 22:11, 12.[6]

October 6

Without Mercy

And another angel came out of the temple, crying with a loud voice ... Thrust in thy sickle, and reap: for the time is come for thee to reap; for the harvest of the earth is ripe. Revelation 14:15

The righteous and the wicked will still be living upon the earth in their mortal state — men will be planting and building, eating and drinking, all unconscious that the final, irrevocable decision has been pronounced in the sanctuary above.[7]

All the judgments upon men, prior to the close of probation, have been mingled with mercy. The pleading blood of Christ has shielded the sinner from receiving the full measure of his guilt; but in the final judgment, wrath is poured out unmixed with mercy.[8]

Oh, who will describe to you the lamentations that will arise when at the boundary line which parts time and eternity the righteous Judge will lift up His voice and declare, "It is too late." Long have the wide gates of heaven stood open and the heavenly messengers have invited and entreated "Whosoever will, let him take the water of life freely" (Revelation 22:17). "To day if ye will hear his voice, harden not your heart." But at length the mandate goes forth, "He that is unjust, let him be unjust still: and he which is filthy, let him be filthy still: and he that is righteous, let him be righteous still: and he that is holy, let him be holy still" (Revelation 22:11).

The heavenly gate closes, the invitation of salvation ceases. In heaven it is said, "It is done."[9]

October 7

The Grand Consummation

And at that time shall Michael stand up ... and there shall be a time of trouble, such as never was since there was a nation even to that same time ... Daniel 12:1

When this time of trouble comes, every case is decided; there is no longer probation, no longer mercy for the impenitent. The seal of the living God is upon His people. ... The decree has been passed by the highest earthly authority that they shall worship the beast and receive his mark under pain of persecution and death.[10]

Grace and mercy will then descend from the throne, and justice will take their place. He for whom his people have looked will assume his right, — the office of Supreme Judge. "The Father ... hath committed all judgment unto the Son. ... And he hath given him authority to execute judgment also ..." It was he, says Peter, who was ordained to "judge the quick [the living] and the dead." "He hath appointed a day, in the which he will judge the world in righteousness by that man whom he hath ordained."

The faith and patience of those who have waited long, have been sorely tried. ... the cry has come up before God, "Lord, how long?" ... startling calamities by land and by sea, famine, pestilence, fearful storms, sweeping floods, and great conflagrations ... testify that we are approaching the grand consummation. The cry going up to God from the waiting ones, will not be in vain. The response will come, "It is done." "He which is filthy, let him be filthy still; ... he that is holy, let him be holy still."[11]

October 8

The Time of Trouble

Therefore shall her plagues come in one day, death, and mourning, and famine; and she shall be utterly burned with fire: for strong is the Lord God who judgeth her. Revelation 18:8

The "time of trouble, such as never was," is soon to open upon us; and we shall need an experience which we do not now possess and which many are too indolent to obtain. It is often the case that trouble is greater in anticipation than in reality; but this is not true of the crisis before us. The most vivid presentation cannot reach the magnitude of the ordeal.[12]

The substitution of the false for the true is the last act in the drama. When this substitution becomes universal, God will reveal himself. When the laws of men are exalted above the laws of God, when the powers of this earth try to force men to keep the first day of the week, know that the time has come for God to work. He will arise in His majesty, and will shake terribly the earth. He will come out of His place to punish the inhabitants of the world for their iniquity. The earth shall disclose her blood, and shall no more cover her slain.[13]

Men can not discern the sentinel angel restraining the four winds … but when God shall bid His angels loose the winds, there will be such a scene of strife as no pen can picture. …

Even before the last great destruction comes upon the world, the flattering monuments of man's greatness will be crumbled in the dust.[14]

October 9

The Hour of Power

… ten kings, which have received no kingdom as yet; but receive power as kings one hour with the beast. Revelation 17:12

All society is ranging into two great classes … [t]hose who keep God's commandments, those who live … by every word that proceedeth out of the mouth of God, [who] compose the church of the living God [, and those] who choose to follow Antichrist … break God's law, and lead others to break it. They endeavor so to frame the laws of nations that men shall show their loyalty to earthly governments by trampling upon the laws of God's kingdom. …

Men in authority will enact laws controlling the conscience, after the example of the Papacy. Babylon will make all nations drink of the wine of the wrath of her fornication. Every nation will be involved. Of this time John the Revelator declares: …

"These have one mind, and shall give their power and strength unto the beast. These shall make war with the Lamb, and the Lamb shall overcome them …" (Revelation 17:13, 14).

There will be a universal bond of union, one great harmony, a confederacy of Satan's forces. … Thus is manifested the same … power against … freedom to worship God according to the dictates of conscience, as was manifested by the Papacy, when in the past it persecuted those who dared to refuse to conform with the religious rites and ceremonies of Romanism.[15]

October 10

The Trying Hour

The kingdoms of this world are become the kingdoms of our Lord, and of his Christ; and he shall reign for ever and ever. And the four and twenty elders, which sat before God on their seats, fell upon their faces, and worshipped God, Saying, We give thee thanks, O Lord God Almighty, which art, and wast, and art to come; because thou hast taken to thee thy great power, and hast reigned. And the nations were angry, and thy wrath is come ... Revelation 11:15-18

The multitudes do not want Bible truth, because it interferes with the desires of the sinful, world-loving heart; and Satan supplies the deceptions which they love.[16]

[I]n the prophecies the future is opened before us as plainly as it was opened to the disciples by the words of Christ. The events connected with the close of probation and the work of preparation for the time of trouble, are clearly presented. But multitudes have no more understanding of these important truths than if they had never been revealed. Satan watches to catch away every impression that would make them wise unto salvation, and the time of trouble will find them unready.[17]

The people of God have accomplished their work. They have received "the latter rain," "the refreshing from the presence of the Lord," and they are prepared for the trying hour before them.[18]

October 11

Great Distress

But they mocked the messengers of God, and despised his words, and misused his prophets, until the wrath of the LORD arose against his people, till there was no remedy. 2 Chronicles 36:16

The time of trouble was upon us. I saw our people in great distress, weeping and praying, pleading the sure promises of God, while the wicked were all around us, mocking us and threatening to destroy us. They ridiculed our feebleness, they mocked at the smallness of our numbers, and taunted us with words calculated to cut deep. They charged us with taking an independent position from all the rest of the world. They had cut off our resources so that we could not buy or sell, and they referred to our abject poverty and stricken condition. They could not see how we could live without the world. ... If we were the only people in the world whom the Lord favored, the appearances were awfully against us.

They declared that they had the truth, that miracles were among them; that angels from heaven talked with them and walked with them, that great power and signs and wonders were performed among them, and that this was the temporal millennium they had been expecting so long. The whole world was converted and in harmony with the Sunday law ...

They declared, "The angels from heaven have spoken to us," referring to those whom Satan personated that had died and they claimed had gone to heaven. "You will bear the testimony of the heavenly messengers." They sneered, they mocked, they derided and abused the sorrowing ones.[19]

October 12

The Winepress

... he treadeth the winepress of the fierceness and wrath of Almighty God. And he hath on his vesture and on his thigh a name written, KING OF KINGS, AND LORD OF LORDS. Revelation 19:15, 16

When He leaves the sanctuary, darkness covers the inhabitants of the earth. ... The restraint which has been upon the wicked is removed, and Satan has entire control of the finally impenitent. God's long-suffering has ended. The world has rejected His mercy, despised His love, and trampled upon His law. The wicked have passed the boundary of their probation; the Spirit of God, persistently resisted, has been at last withdrawn. Unsheltered by divine grace, they have no protection from the wicked one. Satan will then plunge the inhabitants of the earth into one great, final trouble. As the angels of God cease to hold in check the fierce winds of human passion, all the elements of strife will be let loose. The whole world will be involved in ruin more terrible than that which came upon Jerusalem of old. ...

Those who honor the law of God have been accused of bringing judgments upon the world, and they will be regarded as the cause of the fearful convulsions of nature and the strife and bloodshed among men that are filling the earth with woe. The power attending the last warning has enraged the wicked; their anger is kindled against all who have received the message, and Satan will excite to still greater intensity the spirit of hatred and persecution.[20]

October 13

As Upon Jerusalem

... I send unto you prophets, and wise men, and scribes: and some of them ye shall kill and crucify; and some of them shall ye scourge in your synagogues, and persecute them ... : That upon you may come all the righteous blood shed upon the earth ... All these things shall come upon this generation. Matthew 23:34-36

The world is soon to be left by the angel of mercy, and the seven last plagues are to be poured out. ... The bolts of God's wrath are soon to fall, and when He shall begin to punish the transgressors, there will be no period of respite until the end.[21]

The Saviour's prophecy concerning the visitation of judgments upon Jerusalem is to have another fulfillment, of which that terrible desolation was but a faint shadow. In the fate of the chosen city we may behold the doom of a world that has rejected God's mercy and trampled upon His law. Dark are the records of human misery that earth has witnessed during its long centuries of crime. The heart sickens, and the mind grows faint in contemplation. Terrible have been the results of rejecting the authority of Heaven. But a scene yet darker is presented in the revelations of the future. The records of the past, — the long procession of tumults, conflicts, and revolutions, the ... — what are these, in contrast with the terrors of that day when the restraining Spirit of God shall be wholly withdrawn from the wicked, no longer to hold in check the outburst of human passion and satanic wrath! The world will then behold, as never before, the results of Satan's rule.[22]

October 14

As in Egypt

And the kings of the earth ... shall bewail her, and lament for her, when they shall see the smoke of her burning ... saying, Alas, alas, that great city Babylon, that mighty city! for in one hour is thy judgment come. Revelation 18:9, 10

The Lord expects His people to have faith in the living God who made all things. The chosen people of God will be proved and tried before they are pronounced good and faithful servants, worthy to inherit eternal life with its endowment of heavenly riches. ... The Lord brought Israel out of bondage, desolating the fertile land of Egypt to accomplish His purpose, to teach them the first and highest lesson — that God was their God, the only true and living God, and that in Him they must trust.

We are to have faith in the living God who made the world and all things that are therein, and who overrules all events to His own name's glory. ... We are to have faith in Christ, faith in His power to redeem the soul and keep it in perfect peace. ...

This faith must be the great element in the power which rules the characters of God's people. He displayed great signs and wonders in Egypt, showing His command over all the natural world and over the powers which the Egyptian oppressors worshiped. Once again the Lord God of Israel is to execute judgment upon the gods of this world, as upon the gods of Egypt. With fire and flood, plagues and earthquakes, He will spoil the whole land. Then His redeemed people will exalt His name and make it glorious in the earth.²³

October 15

Woe to the Earth

...Woe to the inhabiters of the earth and of the sea! for the devil is come down unto you, having great wrath, because he knoweth that he hath but a short time.
Revelation 12:12

John sees the elements of nature — earthquake, tempest, and political strife — represented as being held by four angels. These winds are under control until God gives the word to let them go.²⁴

[T]he four angels ... hold the four winds until Jesus' work was done in the Sanctuary, and then will come the seven last plagues.²⁵ He will say to the angels, "No longer combat Satan in his efforts to destroy. Let him work out his malignity upon the children of disobedience; for the cup of their iniquity is full. They have advanced from one degree of wickedness to another, adding daily to their lawlessness. I will no longer interfere to prevent the destroyer from doing his work."

Satan will do the evil deeds he has long wished to do. Storm and tempest, war and bloodshed, — in these things he delights, and thus he gathers in his harvest. And so completely will men be deceived by him that they will declare that these calamities are the result of the desecration of the first day of the week. From the pulpits of the popular churches will be heard the statement that the world is being punished because Sunday is not honored as it should be.²⁶

October 16

Two Full Cups

… her sins have reached unto heaven, and God hath remembered her iniquities. … double unto her double according to her works: in the cup which she hath filled fill to her double. Revelation 18:5, 6

God's retributive judgments will fall on those who in the face of great light have continued in sin. Costly buildings, supposed to be fire-proof, are erected. But as Sodom perished in the flames of God's vengeance, so will these proud structures become ashes. I have seen vessels which cost immense sums of money wrestling with the mighty ocean, seeking to breast the angry billows. But with all their treasures of gold and silver, and with all their human freight, they sank into a watery grave. Man's pride will be buried with the treasures he has accumulated by fraud. …

The words of Revelation 18 will be fulfilled. John writes: "I heard another voice from heaven, saying, Come out of her, My people, that ye be not partakers of her sins, and that ye receive not of her plagues. For her sins have reached unto heaven, and God hath remembered her iniquities. Reward her even as she rewarded you, and double unto her double according to her works: in the cup which she hath filled fill to her double. How much she hath glorified herself, and lived deliciously, so much torment and sorrow give her; for she saith in her heart, I sit a queen, and am no widow, and shall see no sorrow. Therefore shall her plagues come in one day, death, and mourning, and famine; and she shall be utterly burned with fire; for strong is the Lord God who judgeth her."[27]

October 17

Like the Plagues Upon Egypt

… Take … ashes of the furnace, and … sprinkle it toward the heaven in the sight of Pharaoh. And it shall become small dust in all the land of Egypt, and shall be a boil breaking forth with blains upon man, and upon beast, throughout all the land of Egypt. Exodus 9:8, 9

When Christ ceases His intercession in the sanctuary, the unmingled wrath threatened against those who worship the beast and his image and receive his mark (Revelation 14:9, 10), will be poured out. The plagues upon Egypt when God was about to deliver Israel were similar in character to those more terrible and extensive judgments which are to fall upon the world just before the final deliverance of God's people. Says the revelator, in describing those terrific scourges: "There fell a noisome and grievous sore upon the men which had the mark of the beast, and upon them which worshiped his image." The sea "became as the blood of a dead man: and every living soul died in the sea." And "the rivers and fountains of waters ... became blood." Terrible as these inflictions are, God's justice stands fully vindicated. The angel of God declares: "Thou art righteous, O Lord ... because Thou hast judged thus. For they have shed the blood of saints and prophets, and Thou hast given them blood to drink; for they are worthy." Revelation 16:2-6. By condemning the people of God to death, they have as truly incurred the guilt of their blood as if it had been shed by their hands. In like manner Christ declared the Jews of His time guilty ... for they possessed the same spirit and were seeking to do the same work with these murderers of the prophets.[28]

October 18

Blood

And the second angel poured out his vial upon the sea; and it became as the blood of a dead man: and every living soul died in the sea. Revelation 16:3

Satan hoped ... to shake the faith of Moses and Aaron in the divine origin of their mission.... He was unwilling that the children of Israel should be released from bondage to serve the living God. ...

He well knew that Moses, in breaking the yoke of bondage from off the children of Israel, pre-figured Christ, who was to break the reign of sin over the human family. ... By counterfeiting the work of God ... he hoped ... to exert an influence ... to destroy faith in the miracles of Christ. Satan is constantly seeking to counterfeit the work of Christ and to establish his own power and claims. ...

Moses and Aaron were directed to visit the riverside next morning, where the king was accustomed to repair. The overflowing of the Nile being the source of food and wealth for all Egypt, the river was worshiped as a god, and the monarch came thither daily to pay his devotions. Here the two brothers again repeated the message to him, and then they stretched out the rod and smote upon the water. The sacred stream ran blood, the fish died, and the river became offensive to the smell. The water in the houses, the supply preserved in cisterns, was likewise changed to blood.[29]

October 19

Suffering

When the poor and needy seek water ... and their tongue faileth for thirst, I the Lord will hear them, I the God of Israel will not forsake them. Isaiah 41:17

The people of God will not be free from suffering; but while persecuted and distressed, while they endure privation and suffer for want of food they will not be left to perish. That God who cared for Elijah will not pass by one of His self-sacrificing children. He who numbers the hairs of their head will care for them, and in time of famine they shall be satisfied. While the wicked are dying from hunger and pestilence, angels will shield the righteous and supply their wants. ...

"The Lord is thy keeper: the Lord is thy shade upon thy right hand. The sun shall not smite thee by day, nor the moon by night. The Lord shall preserve thee from all evil: He shall preserve thy soul." "He shall deliver thee from the snare of the fowler, and from the noisome pestilence. He shall cover thee with His feathers, and under His wings shalt thou trust: His truth shall be thy shield and buckler. Thou shalt not be afraid for the terror by night; nor for the arrow that flieth by day; nor for the pestilence that walketh in darkness; nor for the destruction that wasteth at noonday. A thousand shall fall at thy side, and ten thousand at thy right hand; but it shall not come nigh thee. Only with thine eyes shalt thou behold and see the reward of the wicked. Because thou hast made the Lord, which is my refuge, even the Most High, thy habitation; there shall no evil befall thee, neither shall any plague come nigh thy dwelling." Psalm 121:5-7; 91:3-10.[30]

October 20

The Day of the Sun

These have power to shut heaven, that it rain not in the days of their prophecy: and have power over waters to turn them to blood ... Revelation 11:6

By terrible things in righteousness He will vindicate the authority of His downtrodden law. The severity of the retribution awaiting the transgressor may be judged by the Lord's reluctance to execute justice. The nation with which He bears long, and which He will not smite until it has filled up the measure of its iniquity in God's account, will finally drink the cup of wrath unmixed with mercy.

[P]ower is given to the sun "to scorch men with fire. And men were scorched with great heat." Verses 8, 9. The prophets thus describe the condition of the earth at this fearful time:

"The land mourneth; ... because the harvest of the field is perished. ... All the trees of the field are withered...." "How do the beasts groan! the herds of cattle are perplexed, because they have no pasture. ... The rivers of water are dried up, and the fire hath devoured the pastures of the wilderness." "... in that day, saith the Lord God: there shall be many dead bodies in every place; they shall cast them forth with silence." Joel 1:10-12, 17-20; Amos 8:3.

"Although the fig tree shall not blossom, neither shall fruit be in the vines; the labor of the olive shall fail, and the fields shall yield no meat; the flock shall be cut off from the fold, and there shall be no herd in the stalls;" yet shall they that fear Him "rejoice in the Lord" and joy in the God of their salvation. Habakkuk 3:17, 18.[31]

October 21

A Voice of Trembling

...We have heard a voice of trembling, of fear, and not of peace. ... wherefore do I see every man with his hands on his loins, as a woman in travail, and all faces are turned into paleness? Alas! for that day is great, so that none is like it: it is even the time of Jacob' trouble; but he shall be saved out of it. Jeremiah 30:5-7

As Satan influenced Esau to march against Jacob, so he will stir up the wicked to destroy God's people in the time of trouble. ... He numbers the world as his subjects; but the little company who keep the commandments of God are resisting his supremacy. ... He sees that holy angels are guarding them, and he infers that their sins have been pardoned; ... He claims them as his prey and demands that they be given into his hands to destroy. ...

[T]he Lord permits him to try them to the uttermost. Their confidence in God, their faith and firmness, will be severely tested. As they review the past, their hopes sink; for in their whole lives they can see little good. They are fully conscious of their weakness and unworthiness. Satan endeavors to terrify them with the thought that their cases are hopeless, that the stain of their defilement will never be washed away. He hopes so to destroy their faith that they will yield to his temptations and turn from their allegiance to God.

Though God's people will be surrounded by enemies who are bent upon their destruction, yet the anguish which they suffer is not a dread of persecution for the truth's sake; they fear that every sin has not been repented of ...[32]

October 22

Though He Bear Long

And shall not God avenge his own elect, which cry day and night unto him, though he bear long with them? Luke 18:7

The whole universe is watching with inexpressible interest the closing scenes of the great controversy between good and evil. The people of God are nearing the borders of the eternal world …[33] Their faith does not fail because their prayers are not immediately answered. Though suffering the keenest anxiety, terror, and distress, they do not cease their intercessions.[34]

As they review the events of their past lives, their hopes will almost sink. But as they realize that it is a case of life or death, they will earnestly cry unto God, and appeal to him in regard to their past sorrow for, and humble repentance of, their many sins, and then will refer to his promise: "Let him take hold of my strength, that he may make peace with me, and he shall make peace with me." Thus will their earnest petitions be offered to God day and night. God would not have heard the prayer of Jacob, and mercifully saved his life, if he had not previously repented of his wrongs in obtaining the blessing by fraud. …

The righteous, like Jacob, will manifest unyielding faith and earnest determination, which will take no denial. They … feel their unworthiness, but will have no concealed wrongs to reveal.[35]

October 23

Except Thou Bless

… I will not let thee go, except thou bless me. Genesis 32:26

The righteous will not cease their earnest, agonizing cries for deliverance. They cannot bring to mind any particular sins; but in their whole life they can see little good. Their sins have gone before hand to judgment, and pardon has been written. Their sins have been borne away into the land of forgetfulness, and they can not bring them to remembrance. Certain destruction threatens them, and, like Jacob, they will not suffer their faith to grow weak because their prayers are not immediately answered. Though suffering the pangs of hunger, they will not cease their intercessions. They lay hold of the strength of God, as Jacob laid hold of the angel; and the language of their soul is, "I will not let thee go except thou bless me."

That season of distress and anguish will require an effort of earnestness and determined faith that can endure delay and hunger, and will not fail under weakness, though severely tried.

... Jacob prevailed because he was persevering and determined. All who desire the blessing of God, as did Jacob, and who will lay hold of the promises as he did, and be as earnest and persevering as he was, will succeed as he succeeded. The reason there is so little exercise of true faith, and so little of the weight of truth resting upon many professed believers, is they are indolent in spiritual things. They are unwilling to make exertions, to deny self, to agonize before God, to pray long and earnestly for the blessing, and therefore they do not obtain it. That faith which will live through the time of trouble must be developed now.[36]

October 24

About Them That Fear

The angel of the LORD encampeth round about them that fear him, and delivereth them. Psalm 34:7

It will appear that the people of God must soon seal their testimony with their blood as did the martyrs before them. ... The wicked exult, and the jeering cry is heard: "Where now is your faith? Why does not God deliver you out of our hands if you are indeed His people?" ... Like Jacob, all are wrestling with God. Their countenances express their internal struggle. ... Yet they cease not their earnest intercession. ...[37]

As Jesus poured out his soul in agony in the garden, they will earnestly cry and agonize with him day and night for deliverance. ... Satan's host, and wicked men, will surround them, and exult over them, because there will seem to be no way of escape for them.[38]

Could men see with heavenly vision, they would behold companies of angels that excel in strength stationed about [them]. With sympathizing tenderness, angels have witnessed their distress and have heard their prayers. They are waiting the word of their Commander to snatch them from their peril. ... The people of God must drink of the cup and be baptized with the baptism. ... As they endeavor to wait trustingly for the Lord to work they are led to exercise faith, hope, and patience, which have been too little exercised during their religious experience. Yet for the elect's sake the time of trouble will be shortened.[39]

October 25

Passing the Cup

... Behold, I have taken out of thine hand the cup of trembling, even the dregs of the cup of my fury; thou shalt no more drink it again: But I will put it into the hand of them that afflict thee... Isaiah 51:22, 23

The heavenly sentinels, faithful to their trust, continue their watch. Though a general decree has fixed the time when commandment keepers may be put to death, their enemies will in some cases anticipate the decree, and before the time specified, will endeavor to take their lives. But none can pass the mighty guardians stationed about every faithful soul. Some are assailed in their flight from the cities and villages; but the swords raised against them break and fall powerless as a straw. Others are defended by angels in the form of men of war.[40]

The eye of God, looking down the ages, was fixed upon the crisis which His people are to meet, when earthly powers shall be arrayed against them. Like the captive exile, they will be in fear of death by starvation or by violence. But the Holy One who divided the Red Sea before Israel, will manifest His mighty power and turn their captivity. … If the blood of Christ's faithful witnesses were shed at this time, it would not, like the blood of the martyrs, be as seed sown to yield a harvest for God. Their fidelity would not be a testimony to convince others of the truth; for the obdurate heart has beaten back the waves of mercy until they return no more. … Glorious will be the deliverance of those who have patiently waited for His coming and whose names are written in the book of life.[41]

October 26

Darkness and Deliverance

And the fifth angel poured out his vial upon the seat of the beast; and his kingdom was full of darkness … Revelation 16:10

As the time appointed in the decree draws near, the people will conspire to root out the hated sect. It will be determined to strike in one night a decisive blow, which shall utterly silence the voice of dissent and reproof.

The people of God — some in prison cells, some hidden in solitary retreats in the forests and the mountains — still plead for divine protection, while in every quarter companies of armed men, urged on by hosts of evil angels, are preparing for the work of death. It is now, in the hour of utmost extremity, that the God of Israel will interpose for the deliverance of His chosen. …

With shouts of triumph, jeering, and imprecation, throngs of evil men are about to rush upon their prey, when, lo, a dense blackness, deeper than the darkness of the night, falls upon the earth. Then a rainbow, shining with the glory from the throne of God, spans the heavens and seems to encircle each praying company. The angry multitudes are suddenly arrested. Their mocking cries die away. The objects of their murderous rage are forgotten. With fearful forebodings they gaze upon the symbol of God's covenant and long to be shielded from its overpowering brightness.

By the people of God a voice, clear and melodious, is heard, saying, "Look up," and lifting their eyes to the heavens, they behold the bow of promise.[42]

October 27

The Valley of Decision

Let the heathen ... come up to the valley of Jehoshaphat: for there will I sit to judge all the heathen round about. ... Multitudes, multitudes in the valley of decision: for the day of the LORD is near in the valley of decision. The sun and the moon shall be darkened, and the stars shall withdraw their shining.
Joel 3:12, 14, 15

The heavens have gathered blackness, and are only illuminated by the blazing light and terrible glory from heaven, as God utters His voice from His holy habitation.

The foundations of the earth shake; buildings totter and fall with a terrible crash. The sea boils like a pot, and the whole earth is in terrible commotion. The captivity of the righteous is turned, and with sweet and solemn whisperings they say to one another: "We are delivered. It is the voice of God." With solemn awe they listen to the words of the voice. The wicked hear, but understand not the words of the voice of God. They fear and tremble, while the saints rejoice. Satan and his angels, and wicked men, who had been exulting that the people of God were in their power, that they might destroy them from off the earth, witness the glory conferred upon those who have honored the holy law of God. They behold the faces of the righteous lighted up and reflecting the image of Jesus. Those who were so eager to destroy the saints cannot endure the glory resting upon the delivered ones, and they fall like dead men to the earth. Satan and evil angels flee from the presence of the saints glorified. Their power to annoy them is gone forever.[43]

October 28

Midnight

[T]he day of the LORD cometh, cruel both with wrath and fierce anger, to lay the land desolate: ... For the stars of heaven ... shall not give their light: the sun shall be darkened in his going forth, and the moon shall not cause her light to shine. And I will punish the world for their evil ... Isaiah 13:9-11

The black, angry clouds that covered the firmament are parted, and like Stephen they look up steadfastly into heaven and see the glory of God and the Son of man seated upon His throne. In His divine form they discern the marks of His humiliation; and from His lips they hear the request presented before His Father and the holy angels: "I will that they also, whom Thou hast given Me, be with Me where I am." John 17:24. Again a voice, musical and triumphant, is heard, saying: "They come! they come! holy, harmless, and undefiled. They have kept the word of My patience; they shall walk among the angels;" and the pale, quivering lips of those who have held fast their faith utter a shout of victory.

It is at midnight that God manifests His power for the deliverance of His people. The sun appears, shining in its strength. …The wicked look with terror and amazement upon the scene, while the righteous behold with solemn joy the tokens of their deliverance. Everything in nature seems turned out of its course. The streams cease to flow. Dark, heavy clouds come up and clash against each other. In the midst of the angry heavens is one clear space of indescribable glory, whence comes the voice of God like the sound of many waters, saying: "It is done." Revelation 16:17.[44]

October 29

The Last Cup

… there was a great earthquake; and the sun became black as sackcloth of hair … And the stars of heaven fell unto the earth … And the heaven departed as a scroll when it is rolled together… Revelation 6:12-14

There is a mighty earthquake … The firmament appears to open and shut. The glory from the throne of God seems flashing through. The mountains shake like a reed in the wind, and ragged rocks are scattered on every side. There is a roar as of a coming tempest. The sea is lashed into fury. There is heard the shriek of a hurricane like the voice of demons upon a mission of destruction. The whole earth heaves and swells like the waves of the sea. Its surface is breaking up. Its very foundations seem to be giving way. Mountain chains are sinking. Inhabited islands disappear. The seaports that have become like Sodom for wickedness are swallowed up by the angry waters. … Great hailstones, every one "about the weight of a talent," are doing their work of destruction. Verses 19, 21. The proudest cities of the earth are laid low. The lordly palaces, upon which the world's great men have lavished their wealth in order to glorify themselves, are crumbling to ruin before their eyes. Prison walls are rent asunder, and God's people, who have been held in bondage for their faith, are set free.[45]

The graves were opened, and those who had died in faith under the third angel's message, keeping the Sabbath, came forth from their dusty beds, glorified, to hear the covenant of peace that God was to make with those who had kept His law.[46]

October 30

The Awakening

... every ... man hid ... in the dens and in the rocks of the mountains; And said to the mountains and rocks, Fall on us, and hide us from the face of him that sitteth on the throne ... For the great day of his wrath is come...
Revelation 6:15-17

"They also which pierced Him" (Revelation 1:7), those that mocked and derided Christ's dying agonies, and the most violent opposers of His truth and His people, are raised to behold Him in His glory and to see the honor placed upon the loyal and obedient.

Thick clouds still cover the sky; yet the sun now and then breaks through, appearing like the avenging eye of Jehovah. Fierce lightnings leap from the heavens, enveloping the earth in a sheet of flame. Above the terrific roar of thunder, voices, mysterious and awful, declare the doom of the wicked. ... Those who a little before were so reckless, so boastful and defiant, so exultant in their cruelty to God's commandment-keeping people, are now overwhelmed with consternation and shuddering in fear. Their wails are heard above the sound of the elements. Demons acknowledge the deity of Christ and tremble before His power, while men are supplicating for mercy and groveling in abject terror.

Said the prophets of old, as they beheld in holy vision the day of God: ... "In that day a man shall ... go into the clefts of the rocks, and into the tops of the ragged rocks, for fear of the Lord, and for the glory of His majesty, when He ariseth to shake terribly the earth." Isaiah 2:20, 21, margin.[47]

October 31

The Song of Triumph

... I saw ... them that had gotten the victory over the beast, and over his image, and over his mark, and over the number of his name ... And they sing the song of Moses the servant of God, and the song of the Lamb ... Revelation 15:2, 3

Through a rift in the clouds there beams a star whose brilliancy is increased fourfold in contrast with the darkness. It speaks hope and joy to the faithful, but severity and wrath to the transgressors of God's law. Those who have sacrificed all for Christ are now secure, hidden as in the secret of the Lord's pavilion. They have been tested, and before the world and the despisers of truth they have evinced their fidelity to Him who died for them. A marvelous change has come over those who have held fast their integrity in the very face of death. They have been suddenly delivered from the dark and terrible tyranny of men transformed to demons. Their faces, so lately pale, anxious, and haggard, are now aglow with wonder, faith, and love. Their voices rise in triumphant song …

While these words of holy trust ascend to God, the clouds sweep back, and the starry heavens are seen, unspeakably glorious in contrast with the black and angry firmament on either side. The glory of the celestial city streams from the gates ajar. Then there appears against the sky a hand holding two tables of stone folded together. … That holy law, God's righteousness … is now revealed to men as the rule of judgment. The hand opens the tables, and there are seen the precepts of the Decalogue, traced as with a pen of fire.[48]

November 1

The Voice of God

... with the voice of the archangel, and with the trump of God: and the dead in Christ shall rise first: 1 Thessalonians 4:16

The voice of God is heard from heaven, declaring the day and hour of Jesus' coming, and delivering the everlasting covenant to His people. Like peals of loudest thunder His words roll through the earth.[1]

And as God spoke the day and the hour of Jesus' coming and delivered the everlasting covenant to His people, He spoke one sentence, and then paused, while the words were rolling through the earth. The Israel of God stood with their eyes fixed upward, listening to the words as they came from the mouth of Jehovah and rolled through the earth like peals of loudest thunder. It was awfully solemn. At the end of every sentence the saints shouted, "Glory! Hallelujah!" Their countenances were lighted up with the glory of God, and they shone with glory as did the face of Moses when he came down from Sinai. ... And when the never-ending blessing was pronounced on those who had honored God in keeping His Sabbath holy, there was a mighty shout of victory over the beast and over his image.[2]

The wicked hear, but understand not the words of the voice of God. They fear and tremble, while the saints rejoice. ... They behold the faces of the righteous lighted up, and reflecting the image of Jesus. Those who were so eager to destroy the saints could not endure the glory resting upon the delivered ones, and they fell like dead men to the earth.[3]

November 2

Woe to the Pastors

Woe be unto the pastors that destroy and scatter the sheep of my pasture! saith the LORD. Jeremiah 23:1

It is impossible to describe the horror and despair of those who have trampled upon God's holy requirements. The Lord gave them His law; they might have compared their characters with it and learned their defects while there was yet opportunity for repentance and reform; but in order to secure the favor of the world, they set aside its precepts and taught others to transgress. They have endeavored to compel God's people to profane His Sabbath. Now they are condemned by that law which they have despised. With awful distinctness they see that they are without excuse. They chose whom they would serve and worship. "Then shall ye return, and discern between the righteous and the wicked, between him that serveth God and him that serveth Him not." Malachi 3:18.

The enemies of God's law, from the ministers down to the least among them, have a new conception of truth and duty. Too late they see that the Sabbath of the fourth commandment is the seal of the living God. Too late they see the true nature of their spurious sabbath and the sandy foundation upon which they have been building. They find that they have been fighting against God. Religious teachers have led souls to perdition while professing to guide them to the gates of Paradise. Not until the day of final accounts will it be known how great is the responsibility of men in holy office and how terrible are the results of their unfaithfulness.[4]

November 3

No Escape

Howl, ye shepherds, and cry ... for the days of your slaughter ... are accomplished ... And the shepherds shall have no way to flee, nor the principal of the flock to escape. Jeremiah 25:34, 35

When the voice of God turns the captivity of His people, there is a terrible awakening of those who have lost all in the great conflict of life. While probation continued they were blinded by Satan's deceptions, and they justified their course of sin. ... Now they are stripped of all that made them great and are left destitute and defenseless. ...

The minister who has sacrificed truth to gain the favor of men now discerns the character and influence of his teachings. ... Every emotion of the soul, every line written, every word uttered, every act that led men to rest in a refuge of falsehood, has been scattering seed; and now, in the wretched, lost souls around him, he beholds the harvest.

The setting aside of the divine precepts gave rise to thousands of springs of evil, discord, hatred, iniquity, until the earth became one vast field of strife, one sink of corruption. ... No language can express the longing which the disobedient and disloyal feel for that which they have lost forever — eternal life. Men whom the world has worshiped for their talents and eloquence now see these things in their true light. They realize what they have forfeited by transgression, and they fall at the feet of those whose fidelity they have despised and derided, and confess that God has loved them.[5]

November 4

Strife and Bloodshed

[T]he ten horns which thou sawest upon the beast, these shall hate the whore, and shall make her desolate and naked, and shall eat her flesh, and burn her with fire. Revelation 17:16

It will not be sufficient for the false shepherds to be tormented with one or two of these plagues. God's hand at that time will be stretched out still in wrath and justice and will not be brought to Himself again until His purposes are fully accomplished, and the hireling priests are led to worship at the feet of the saints, and to acknowledge that God has loved them because they held fast the truth and kept God's commandments, and until all the unrighteous ones are destroyed from the earth.[6]

[U]pon those who have taken upon them the work of shepherds of the flock, will be visited the heaviest judgments, because they have presented to the people fables instead of truth. ... Church members, who have seen the light and been convicted, but who have trusted the salvation of their souls to the minister, will learn in the day of God that no other soul can pay the ransom for their transgression. A terrible cry will be raised, "I am lost, eternally lost." Men will feel as though they could rend in pieces the ministers who have preached falsehoods and condemned the truth.[7]

[A]ll unite in heaping their bitterest condemnation upon the ministers. ... The multitudes are filled with fury. ... The swords which were to slay God's people are now employed to destroy their enemies. Everywhere there is strife and bloodshed.[8]

November 5

The Gain of a Lifetime

For what is a man profited, if he shall gain the whole world, and lose his own soul? or what shall a man give in exchange for his soul? Matthew 16:26

"The merchants of the earth," that have "waxed rich through the abundance of her delicacies," "shall stand afar off for the fear of her torment, weeping and wailing ... For in one hour so great riches is come to nought." Revelation 18:11, 3, 15-17. ...

The rich prided themselves upon their superiority to those who were less favored; but they had obtained their riches by violation of the law of God. They had neglected to feed the hungry, to clothe the naked, to deal justly, and to love mercy. ... Now they are stripped of all that made them great and are left destitute and defenseless. They look with terror upon the destruction of the idols which they preferred before their Maker. They have sold their souls for earthly riches and enjoyments, and have not sought to become rich toward God. The result is their lives are a failure; their pleasures are now turned to gall, their treasures to corruption. The gain of a lifetime is swept away in a moment. The rich bemoan the destruction of their grand houses, the scattering of their gold and silver. But their lamentations are silenced by the fear that they themselves are to perish with their idols.

The wicked are filled with regret … They lament that the result is what it is; but they do not repent of their wickedness.[9]

November 6

The Great Cloud

And after these things I heard a great voice of much people in heaven, saying, Alleluia; Salvation, and glory, and honour, and power, unto the Lord our God
Revelation 19:1

Soon appeared the great white cloud. It looked more lovely than ever before. On it sat the Son of Man. At first we did not see Jesus on the cloud, but as it drew near the earth, we could behold his lovely person. This cloud when it first appeared was the Sign of the Son of Man in heaven.[10]

In solemn silence they gaze upon it as it draws nearer the earth, becoming lighter and more glorious, until it is a great white cloud, its base a glory like consuming fire, and above it the rainbow of the covenant. Jesus rides forth as a mighty conqueror. … He comes, victor in heaven and earth, to judge the living and the dead. "Faithful and True," "in righteousness He doth judge and make war." And "the armies which were in heaven" (Revelation 19:11, 14) follow Him. With anthems of celestial melody the holy angels, a vast, unnumbered throng, attend Him on His way. The firmament seems filled with radiant forms — "ten thousand times ten thousand, and thousands of thousands." … "His glory covered the heavens, and the earth was full of His praise. And His brightness was as the light." Habakkuk 3:3, 4. As the living cloud comes still nearer, every eye beholds the Prince of life. … His countenance outshines the dazzling brightness of the noonday sun. "And He hath on His vesture and on His thigh a name written, King of kings, and Lord of lords." Revelation 19:16.[11]

November 7

Wailing

Behold, he cometh with clouds; and every eye shall see him, and they also which pierced him: and all kindreds of the earth shall wail because of him.
Revelation 1:7

That voice which penetrates the ear of the dead, they know. How often have its plaintive, tender tones called them to repentance. ... That voice awakens memories which they would fain blot out — warnings despised, invitations refused, privileges slighted.

Those who derided His claim to be the Son of God are speechless now. There is the haughty Herod who jeered at His royal title and bade the mocking soldiers crown Him king. There are the very men who with impious hands placed upon His form the purple robe, upon His sacred brow the thorny crown, and in His unresisting hand the mimic scepter, and bowed before Him in blasphemous mockery. ... Those who drove the nails through His hands and feet, the soldier who pierced His side, behold these marks with terror and remorse.

With awful distinctness do priests and rulers recall the events of Calvary. ...

Louder than the shout, "Crucify Him, crucify Him," which rang through the streets of Jerusalem, swells the awful, despairing wail, "He is the Son of God! He is the true Messiah!" They seek to flee from the presence of the King of kings. In the deep caverns of the earth, rent asunder by the warring of the elements, they vainly attempt to hide.[12]

November 8

The Glorious Triumph

But if there be no resurrection of the dead, then is Christ not risen: And if Christ be not risen, then is our preaching vain, and your faith is also vain.
1 Corinthians 15:13, 14

The apostle carried the minds of the Corinthian brethren forward to the triumphs of the resurrection morn, when all the sleeping saints are to be raised, henceforth to live forever with their Lord. "Behold," the apostle declared, "I show you a mystery: We shall not all sleep, but we shall all be changed, in a moment, in the twinkling of an eye, at the last trump: for the trumpet shall sound, and the dead shall be raised incorruptible, and we shall be changed. For this corruptible must put on incorruption, and this mortal must put on immortality. So when this corruptible shall have put on incorruption, and this mortal shall have put on immortality, then shall be brought to pass the saying that is written, Death is swallowed up in victory. O death, where is thy sting? O grave, where is thy victory? … Thanks be to God, which giveth us the victory through our Lord Jesus Christ."

Glorious is the triumph awaiting the faithful. The apostle, realizing the possibilities before the Corinthian believers, sought to set before them that which uplifts from the selfish and the sensual, and glorifies life with the hope of immortality. Earnestly he exhorted them to be true to their high calling in Christ. "My beloved brethren," he pleaded, "be ye steadfast, unmovable, always abounding in the work of the Lord, forasmuch as ye know that your labor is not in vain in the Lord."[13]

November 9

Soon to Dawn

Marvel not at this: for the hour is coming, in the which all that are in the graves shall hear his voice, And shall come forth; they that have done good, unto the resurrection of life; and they that have done evil, unto the resurrection of damnation. John 5:28, 29

The doctrine of the coming of Jesus was to have a marked effect and influence upon the lives and characters of men, … This great event, — the advent of our Lord in all the glory of heaven, — must be brought to the attention of men, and all should live with reference to this, — the day of God that is soon to dawn upon us. The expectation of Christ's coming was to make men fear the Lord, and fear his judgments upon the transgressors of his law. It was to awaken them to a realization of the great sin of rejecting the offers of his mercy.

The hour will come; it is not far distant, and some of us who now believe will be alive upon the earth, and shall see the prediction verified, and hear the voice of the archangel, and the trump of God echo from mountain and plain and sea, to the uttermost parts of the earth. All creation will hear that voice, and those who have lived and died in Jesus, will respond to the call of the Prince of life. It will be heard in the dungeons of men, in the caverns of the deep, in the rocks and caves of the earth, only to be obeyed. … All those who have obeyed that voice when it said, "If any man will come after me, let him deny himself, and take up his cross, and follow me," will hear the "Well done, thou good and faithful servant, enter thou into the joy of thy Lord."[14]

November 10

The Wave Offering Promise

But now is Christ risen from the dead, and become the firstfruits of them that slept. 1 Corinthians 15:20

Those who came forth from the grave at Christ's resurrection were raised to everlasting life. They were the multitude of captives that ascended with him as trophies of his victory over death and the grave. ...

Those who were raised with Christ "appeared unto many," declaring, Christ has risen from the dead, and we are risen with him. They bore testimony in the city to the fulfillment of the scripture, "Thy dead men shall live, together with my dead body shall they arise. Awake and sing, ye that dwell in dust: ..."

Christ was the first-fruits of them that slept. It was to the glory of God that the Prince of life should be the first-fruits, the antitype of the wave-sheaf. ...

So those who had been raised were to be presented to the universe as a pledge of the resurrection of all who believe in Christ as their personal Saviour. The same power that raised Christ from the dead will raise his church, and glorify it with Christ, as his bride, above all principalities, above all powers, above every name that is named, not only in this world, but also in the heavenly courts, the world above. The victory of the sleeping saints will be glorious on the morning of the resurrection.[15]

November 11

Shine Like the Sun

The Son of man shall send forth his angels, and they shall gather out of his kingdom all things that offend, and them which do iniquity ... Then shall the righteous shine forth as the sun in the kingdom of their Father. ...
Matthew 13:41, 43

Christ claims all those as His who have believed in His name. The vitalizing power of the Spirit of Christ dwelling in the mortal body binds every believing soul to Jesus Christ. Those who believe in Jesus are sacred to His heart; for their life is hid with Christ in God. ...

The life-giver will call up His purchased possession in the first resurrection, and until that triumphant hour, when the last trump shall sound and the vast army shall come forth to eternal victory, every sleeping saint will be kept in safety and will be guarded as a precious jewel, who is known to God by name. By the power of the Saviour that dwelt in them while living and because they were partakers of the divine nature, they are brought forth from the dead. ...

Christ claimed to be the Only Begotten of the Father, but ... was charged with blasphemy, and was condemned to a cruel death, but He burst the fetters of the tomb, and rose from the dead triumphant, and over the rent sepulcher of Joseph He declared, "I am the resurrection, and the life" (John 11:25). All power in heaven and in earth was vested in Him, and the righteous will also come forth from the tomb free in Jesus. They shall be accounted worthy to obtain that world and the resurrection from the dead. "Then shall the righteous shine forth as the sun in the kingdom of their Father" (Matthew 13:43).[16]

November 12

Awake and Sing

I know that my Redeemer liveth, and that He shall stand at the latter day upon the earth: ... in my flesh shall I see God: whom I shall see for myself ...
Job 19:25-27

One of the most solemn and yet most glorious truths revealed in the Bible is that of Christ's second coming to complete the great work of redemption. To God's pilgrim people, so long left to sojourn in "the region and shadow of death," a precious, joy-inspiring hope is given in the promise of His appearing, who is "the resurrection and the life," to "bring home again His banished." ... "Behold ... the Lord cometh with ten thousands of His saints, to execute judgment upon all." Jude 14, 15 ...

The coming of Christ to usher in the reign of righteousness has inspired the most sublime and impassioned utterances of the sacred writers. ... "Let the heavens rejoice, and let the earth be glad ... before the Lord: for He cometh, for He cometh to judge the earth: He shall judge the world with righteousness ..." Psalm 96:11-13.

Said the prophet Isaiah: "Awake and sing, ye that dwell in dust: for thy dew is as the dew of herbs, and the earth shall cast out the dead." "Thy dead men shall live, together with my dead body shall they arise." "He will swallow up death in victory; and the Lord God will wipe away tears from off all faces; and the rebuke of His people shall He take away ... And it shall be said in that day, Lo, this is our God; we have waited for Him, and He will save us: this is the Lord; we have waited for Him, we will be glad and rejoice in His salvation." Isaiah 26:19; 25:8, 9.[17]

November 13

Awake, Awake!

For the Lord himself shall descend from heaven with a shout, with the voice of the archangel, and with the trump of God: and the dead in Christ shall rise first:
1 Thessalonians 1:16

This cloud, when it first appeared, was the Sign of the Son of Man in heaven. The voice of the Son of God called forth the sleeping saints, clothed with a glorious immortality.[18]

He looks upon the graves of the righteous, then, raising His hands to heaven, He cries: "Awake, awake, awake, ye that sleep in the dust, and arise!" … From the prison house of death they come, clothed with immortal glory, crying: "O death, where is thy sting? O grave, where is thy victory?" 1 Corinthians 15:55. And the living righteous and the risen saints unite their voices in a long, glad shout of victory.

All come forth from their graves the same in stature as when they entered the tomb. … The mortal, corruptible form, devoid of comeliness, once polluted with sin, becomes perfect, beautiful, and immortal. All blemishes and deformities are left in the grave. Restored to the tree of life in the long-lost Eden, the redeemed will "grow up" (Malachi 4:2) to the full stature of the race in its primeval glory. The last lingering traces of the curse of sin will be removed, and Christ's faithful ones will appear in "the beauty of the Lord our God," in mind and soul and body reflecting the perfect image of their Lord. Oh, wonderful redemption! long talked of, long hoped for, contemplated with eager anticipation, but never fully understood.[19]

November 14

Changed in a Moment

Behold, I shew you a mystery; We shall not all sleep, but we shall all be changed, In a moment, in the twinkling of an eye, at the last trump …
1 Corinthians 15:51, 52

Adam, who stands among the risen throng, is of lofty height and majestic form, in stature but little below the Son of God. He presents a marked contrast to the people of later generations; in this one respect is shown the great degeneracy of the race. … In the beginning, man was created in the likeness of God, not only in character, but in form and feature. Sin defaced and almost obliterated the divine image; but Christ came to restore that which had been lost. He will change our vile bodies and fashion them like unto His glorious body. …

The living righteous are changed "in a moment, in the twinkling of an eye." At the voice of God they were glorified; now they are made immortal and with the risen saints are caught up to meet their Lord in the air. Angels "gather together His elect from the four winds, from one end of heaven to the other." Little children are borne by holy angels to their mothers' arms. Friends long separated by death are united, nevermore to part, and with songs of gladness ascend together to the City of God.

On each side of the cloudy chariot are wings, and beneath it are living wheels; and as the chariot rolls upward, the wheels cry, "Holy," and the wings, as they move, cry, "Holy," and the retinue of angels cry, "Holy, holy, holy, Lord God Almighty." And the redeemed shout, "Alleluia!" as the chariot moves onward toward the New Jerusalem.[20]

November 15

In the Light of Eternity

Thus saith the LORD of hosts; If thou wilt walk in my ways, and if thou wilt keep my charge, then thou shalt also judge my house, and shalt also keep my courts, and I will give thee places to walk among these that stand by. Zechariah 3:7

Those who have made a full surrender are reconciled to God, and he will be their defense. He promises that they shall have places to walk among these that stand by. Who are these that stand by? — They are the angels of God that are sent to minister to those who shall be heirs of salvation. We shall never know what dangers, seen and unseen, we have been delivered from through the interposition of the angels, until we shall see in the light of eternity the providences of God. Then we shall better understand what God has done for us all the days of our life. We shall know then that the whole heavenly family watched to see our course of action from day to day. You should remember when trials come, that you are a spectacle to angels and to men, and that every time you fail to bear the proving of the Lord, you are lessening your spiritual strength. You should hold your peace from complaining, and take your burden to Jesus, and lay your whole soul open before him. … Say, "I will not gratify the enemy by murmuring. I will lay my care at the feet of Jesus. I will tell it to him in faith." If you do this, you will receive help from above; you will realize the fulfillment of the promise, "He is on my right hand that I should not be moved." "Lo, I am with you alway, even unto the end of the world." "If ye abide in me, and my words abide in you, ye shall ask what ye will, and it shall be done unto you."[21]

November 16

A Grand, Victorious Purpose

Be not forgetful to entertain strangers: for thereby some have entertained angels unawares. Hebrews 13:2

The history of the inception of sin; of fatal falsehood in its crooked working; of truth that, swerving not from its own straight lines, has met and conquered error — all will be made manifest. ...

Not until the providences of God are seen in the light of eternity shall we understand what we owe to the care and interposition of His angels. Celestial beings ... have come as men, in the garb of wayfarers. They have accepted the hospitalities of human homes; they have acted as guides to benighted travelers. They have thwarted the spoiler's purpose and turned aside the stroke of the destroyer. ...

Every redeemed one will understand the ministry of angels in his own life. The angel who was his guardian from his earliest moment; the angel who watched his steps, and covered his head in the day of peril; ... who marked his resting place, who was the first to greet him in the resurrection morning — what will it be to hold converse with him, and to learn the history of divine interposition in the individual life, of heavenly co-operation in every work for humanity!

All the perplexities of life's experience will then be made plain. Where to us have appeared only confusion and disappointment, broken purposes and thwarted plans, will be seen a grand, overruling, victorious purpose, a divine harmony.[22]

November 17

Joy in the Harvest

... sow thy seed, and ... withhold not thine hand: for thou knowest not whether shall prosper, either this or that, or whether they both shall be alike good. Ecclesiastes 11:6

There all who have wrought with unselfish spirit will behold the fruit of their labors. ...

How many toil unselfishly and unweariedly for those who pass beyond their reach and knowledge! Parents and teachers lie down in their last sleep, their lifework seeming to have been wrought in vain; they know not that their faithfulness has unsealed springs of blessing that can never cease to flow; only by faith they see the children they have trained become a benediction and an inspiration to their fellow men, and the influence repeat itself a thousandfold. Many a worker sends out into the world messages of strength and hope and courage, words that carry blessing to hearts in every land; but of the results he, toiling in loneliness and obscurity, knows little. ... Men sow the seed from which, above their graves, others reap blessed harvests. They plant trees, that others may eat the fruit. They are content here to know that they have set in motion agencies for good. In the hereafter the action and reaction of all these will be seen.

Of every gift that God has bestowed, leading men to unselfish effort, a record is kept in heaven. To trace this in its wide-spreading lines, to look upon those who by our efforts have been uplifted and ennobled, to behold in their history the outworking of true principles — this will be one of the studies and rewards of the heavenly school.[23]

November 18

The Exceeding Riches of Grace

That in the ages to come he might shew the exceeding riches of his grace in his kindness toward us through Christ Jesus. Ephesians 2:7

"Ye are My witnesses, saith the Lord, that I am God." Isaiah 43:12. This also we shall be in eternity.

For what was the great controversy permitted to continue throughout the ages? Why was it that Satan's existence was not cut short at the outset of his rebellion? It was that the universe might be convinced of God's justice in His dealing with evil; that sin might receive eternal condemnation. In the plan of redemption there are heights and depths that eternity itself can never exhaust, marvels into which the angels desire to look. The redeemed only, of all created beings, have in their own experience known the actual conflict with sin; they have wrought with Christ, and, as even the angels could not do, have entered into the fellowship of His sufferings ...

He "hath raised us up together, and made us sit together in heavenly places: ... that in the ages to come He might show the exceeding riches of His grace in His kindness toward us through Christ Jesus." Ephesians 3:10, R.V.; 2:6, 7. ...

And in the future state ... it is in service that our greatest joy and our highest education will be found — witnessing, and ever as we witness learning anew "the riches of the glory of this mystery;" "which is Christ in you, the hope of glory." Colossians 1:27[24]

November 19

Think on These Things

Finally, brethren, whatsoever things are true, whatsoever things are honest, whatsoever things are just, whatsoever things are pure, whatsoever things are lovely, whatsoever things are of good report; if there be any virtue, and if there be any praise, think on these things. Philippians 4:8

By dwelling upon the love of God and our Saviour, by contemplating the perfection of the divine character and claiming the righteousness of Christ as ours by faith, we are to be transformed into the same image. ...

And "while we look not at the things which are seen, but at the things which are not seen," we shall prove it true that "our light affliction, which is but for a moment, worketh for us a far more exceeding and eternal weight of glory."

In heaven God is all in all. There holiness reigns supreme; there is nothing to mar the perfect harmony with God. If we are indeed journeying thither, the spirit of heaven will dwell in our hearts here. But if we find no pleasure now in the contemplation of heavenly things; if we have no interest in seeking the knowledge of God, no delight in beholding the character of Christ; if holiness has no attractions for us — then we may be sure that our hope of heaven is vain. Perfect conformity to the will of God is the high aim to be constantly before the Christian. He will love to talk of God, of Jesus, of the home of bliss and purity which Christ has prepared for them that love Him. The contemplation of these themes, when the soul feasts upon the blessed assurances of God, the apostle represents as tasting "the powers of the world to come."[25]

November 20

A Vision of the Future

After this I beheld, and, lo, a great multitude, which no man could number, of all nations, and kindreds, and people, and tongues, stood before the throne, and before the Lamb, clothed with white robes, and palms in their hands;
Revelation 7:9

The day is coming when the battle will have been fought, the victory won. ... All will be a happy, united family, clothed with the garments of praise and thanksgiving, — the robe of Christ's righteousness. ...

There are revealed in these last days visions of future glory, scenes pictured by the hand of God, and these should be dear to his church. What sustained the Son of God in his betrayal and trial? He saw of the travail of his soul, and was satisfied. He caught a view of the expanse of eternity, and saw the happiness of those who through his humiliation should receive pardon and everlasting life. …

We must have a vision of the future on the blessedness of heaven. Stand on the threshold of eternity, and hear the gracious welcome given to those who in this life have co-operated with Christ, regarding it as a privilege and an honor to suffer for his sake. As they unite with the angels, they cast their crowns at the feet of the Redeemer, exclaiming, "Worthy is the Lamb that was slain to receive power, and riches, and wisdom, and strength, and honor, and glory, and blessing. … Honor, and glory, and power, be unto him that sitteth upon the throne, and unto the Lamb forever and ever."[26]

November 21

Songs of Victory

Therefore are they before the throne of God, and serve him day and night in his temple: and he that sitteth on the throne shall dwell among them. Revelation 7:15

At last the victory was gained. The army following the banner with the inscription, "The commandments of God, and the faith of Jesus," were gloriously triumphant. The soldiers of Christ were close beside the gates of the city of God, and with joy the city received her King. …

There the redeemed ones greet those who directed them to the uplifted Saviour. They unite in praising him who died that human beings might have the life that measures with the life of God. The conflict is over. All tribulation and strife are at an end. Songs of victory fill all heaven as the redeemed stand around the throne of God. All take up the joyful strain, "Worthy, worthy is the Lamb that was slain, and lives again, a triumphant conqueror." …

"These are they which came out of great tribulation, and have washed their robes, and made them White in the blood of the Lamb. Therefore are they before the throne of God, and serve him day and night in his temple: and he that sitteth on the throne shall dwell among them. They shall hunger no more, neither thirst any more; neither shall the sun light on them, nor any heat. For the Lamb which is in the midst of the throne shall feed them, and shall lead them unto living fountains of waters: and God shall wipe away all tears from their eyes."[27]

November 22

A Crown for Every Saint

Fear none of those things which thou shalt suffer ... be thou faithful unto death, and I will give thee a crown of life. Revelation 2:10

Before entering the City of God, the Saviour bestows upon His followers the emblems of victory and invests them with the insignia of their royal state.[28]

Then I saw a very great number of angels bring from the city glorious crowns — a crown for every saint, with his name written thereon. As Jesus called for the crowns, angels presented them to Him, and with His own right hand, the lovely Jesus placed the crowns on the heads of the saints. In the same manner the angels brought the harps, and Jesus presented them also to the saints.[29]

There stand the host of the redeemed, the palm branch of victory in their hand, the crown upon their head. These are the ones who by faithful, earnest labor, have obtained a fitness for Heaven. The life-work performed on earth is acknowledged in the heavenly courts as a work well done.

With joy unutterable, parents see the crown, the robe, the harp, given to their children. The days of hope and fear are ended. The seed sown with tears and prayers may have seemed to be sown in vain, but their harvest is reaped with joy at last. Their children have been redeemed. Fathers, mothers, shall the voices of your children swell the song of gladness in that day?[30]

November 23

Singing Unto Him That Loved Us

Now unto him that is able to keep you from falling, and to present you faultless before the presence of his glory with exceeding joy, To ... God our Saviour, be glory and majesty, dominion and power, both now and ever. Amen. Jude 24, 25

The commanding angels first struck the note, and then every voice was raised in grateful, happy praise, and every hand skillfully swept over the strings of the harp, sending forth melodious music in rich and perfect strains.[31]

Rapture unutterable thrills every heart, and each voice is raised in grateful praise: "Unto Him that loved us, and washed us from our sins in His own blood, and hath made us kings and priests unto God and His Father; to Him be glory and dominion for ever and ever." Revelation 1:5, 6.[32]

Then I saw Jesus lead the redeemed company to the gate of the city. He laid hold of the gate and swung it back on its glittering hinges and bade the nations that had kept the truth enter in. Within the city there was everything to feast the eye. Rich glory they beheld everywhere. Then Jesus looked upon His redeemed saints; their countenances were radiant with glory; and as He fixed His loving eyes upon them, He said, with His rich, musical voice, "I behold the travail of My soul, and am satisfied. This rich glory is yours to enjoy eternally. Your sorrows are ended. There shall be no more death, neither sorrow nor crying, neither shall there be any more pain."[33]

November 24

Adam, Jesus and the Tree

Blessed are they that do his commandments, that they may have right to the tree of life, and may enter in through the gates into the city. Revelation 22:14

The Son of God is standing with outstretched arms to receive the father of our race — the being whom He created, who sinned against his Maker, and for whose sin the marks of the crucifixion are borne upon the Saviour's form. As Adam discerns the prints of the cruel nails, he does not fall upon the bosom of his Lord, but in humiliation casts himself at His feet, crying: "Worthy, worthy is the Lamb that was slain!" Tenderly the Saviour lifts him up and bids him look once more upon the Eden home from which he has so long been exiled. …

After his expulsion from Eden … he repent[ed] of his sin and trust[ed] in the merits of the promised Saviour, and he died in the hope of a resurrection. …

His mind grasps the reality of the scene; he comprehends that this is indeed Eden restored, more lovely now than when he was banished from it. The Saviour leads him to the tree of life and plucks the glorious fruit and bids him eat. He looks about him and beholds a multitude of his family redeemed, standing in the Paradise of God. Then he casts his glittering crown at the feet of Jesus and, falling upon His breast, embraces the Redeemer. He touches the golden harp, and the vaults of heaven echo the triumphant song: "Worthy, worthy, worthy is the Lamb that was slain, and lives again!" The family of Adam take up the strain and cast their crowns at the Saviour's feet as they bow before Him in adoration.[34]

November 25

The Song of Moses and the Lamb

And they sing the song of Moses the servant of God, and the song of the Lamb, saying, Great and marvellous are thy works, Lord God Almighty; just and true are thy ways, thou King of saints. Revelation 15:3

Upon the crystal sea before the throne ... are gathered the company that have "gotten the victory over the beast, and over his image, and over his mark, and over the number of his name." ... And they sing "a new song" before the throne ... None but the hundred and forty-four thousand can learn that song; for it is the song of their experience — an experience such as no other company have ever had. ... These, having been translated from the earth, from among the living, are counted as "the first fruits unto God and to the Lamb." Revelation 15:2, 3; 14:1-5. "These are they which came out of great tribulation;" they have passed through the time of trouble such as never was since there was a nation; they have endured the anguish of the time of Jacob's trouble; they have stood without an intercessor through the final outpouring of God's judgments. But they have been delivered, for they have "washed their robes, and made them white in the blood of the Lamb." ... They have seen the earth wasted with famine and pestilence, the sun having power to scorch men with great heat, and they themselves have endured suffering, hunger, and thirst. But "they shall hunger no more, neither thirst any more; neither shall the sun light on them, nor any heat. For the Lamb which is in the midst of the throne shall feed them, and shall lead them unto living fountains of waters: and God shall wipe away all tears from their eyes." Revelation 7:14-17.³⁵

November 26

The Song of the Great Multitude

... I beheld, and, lo, a great multitude ... of all nations ... stood before the throne ... And cried with a loud voice, saying, Salvation to our God which sitteth upon the throne, and unto the Lamb. Revelation 7:9, 10

In all ages the Saviour's chosen have been educated and disciplined in the school of trial. They walked in narrow paths on earth; they were purified in the furnace of affliction. For Jesus' sake they endured opposition, hatred, calumny. ... By their own painful experience they learned the evil of sin, its power, its guilt, its woe; and they look upon it with abhorrence. A sense of the infinite sacrifice made for its cure humbles them in their own sight and fills their hearts with gratitude and praise which those who have never fallen cannot appreciate. They love much because they have been forgiven much. Having been partakers of Christ's sufferings, they are fitted to be partakers with Him of His glory. ...

Millions went down to the grave loaded with infamy because they steadfastly refused to yield to the deceptive claims of Satan. ... Now the decisions of earth are reversed. ... They are no longer feeble, afflicted, scattered, and oppressed. Henceforth they are to be ever with the Lord. They stand before the throne clad in richer robes than the most honored of the earth have ever worn. They are crowned with diadems more glorious than were ever placed upon the brow of earthly monarchs. The days of pain and weeping are forever ended. The King of glory has wiped the tears from all faces; every cause of grief has been removed.[36]

November 27

Surprise and Joy

For when the Gentiles ... do by nature the things contained in the law ... [they] shew the work of the law written in their hearts ... Romans 2:14, 15

In that day Christ ... presents the faithful work they have done for Him. ... But those whom Christ commends know not that they have been ministering unto Him. ...

Those whom Christ commends in the judgment may have known little of theology, but they have cherished His principles. Through the influence of the divine Spirit they have been a blessing to those about them. Even among the heathen are those who have cherished the spirit of kindness; before the words of life had fallen upon their ears, they have befriended the missionaries, even ministering to them at the peril of their own lives. Among the heathen are those who worship God ignorantly, those to whom the light is never brought by human instrumentality, yet they will not perish. Though ignorant of the written law of God, they have heard His voice speaking to them in nature, and have done the things that the law required. ...

How surprised and gladdened will be the lowly among the nations, and among the heathen, to hear from the lips of the Saviour, "Inasmuch as ye have done it unto one of the least of these My brethren, ye have done it unto Me"! How glad will be the heart of Infinite Love as His followers look up with surprise and joy at His words of approval![37]

November 28

The Faithful Workers

Blessed and holy is he that hath part in the first resurrection: on such the second death hath no power, but they shall be priests of God and of Christ, and shall reign with him a thousand years. Revelation 20:6

In order to determine how important are the interests involved in the conversion of the soul from error to truth, we must appreciate the value of immortality; we must realize how terrible are the pains of the second death; we must comprehend the honor and glory awaiting the ransomed, and understand what it is to live in the presence of Him who died that He might elevate and ennoble man, and give to the overcomer a royal diadem.

The worth of a soul cannot be fully estimated by finite minds. How gratefully will the ransomed and glorified ones remember those who were instrumental in their salvation! No one will then regret his self-denying efforts and persevering labors, his patience, forbearance, and earnest heart yearnings for souls that might have been lost had he neglected his duty or become weary in well-doing. …

The faithful worker and the soul saved through his labor are greeted by the Lamb in the midst of the throne, and are led to the tree of life and to the fountain of living waters. With what joy does the servant of Christ behold these redeemed ones, who are made to share the glory of the Redeemer! How much more precious is heaven to those who have been faithful in the work of saving souls![38]

November 29

Cheap Enough

In the midst of the street of it, and on either side of the river, was there the tree of life, which bare twelve manner of fruits, and yielded her fruit every month: …
Revelation 22:2

On the sea of glass the 144,000 stood in a perfect square. … And they were all clothed with a glorious white mantle from their shoulders to their feet. Angels were all about us as we marched over the sea of glass to the gate of the city. …

Here we saw the tree of life and the throne of God. Out of the throne came a pure river of water, and on either side of the river was the tree of life. On one side of the river was a trunk of a tree, and a trunk on the other side of the river, both of pure, transparent gold. At first I thought I saw two trees. I looked again, and saw that they were united at the top in one tree. So it was the tree of life on either side of the river of life. Its branches bowed to the place where we stood, and the fruit was glorious; it looked like gold mixed with silver.

We all went under the tree and sat down to look at the glory of the place, when Brethren …, who had preached the gospel of the kingdom, and whom God had laid in the grave to save them, came up to us and asked us what we had passed through while they were sleeping. We tried to call up our greatest trials, but they looked so small compared with the far more exceeding and eternal weight of glory that surrounded us that we could not speak them out, and we all cried out, "Alleluia, heaven is cheap enough!" and we touched our glorious harps and made heaven's arches ring.[39]

November 30

Emptied and Spoiled

Behold, the LORD maketh the earth empty, and maketh it waste, and turneth it upside down, and scattereth abroad the inhabitants thereof. … The land shall be utterly emptied, and utterly spoiled: for the LORD hath spoken this word.
Isaiah 24:1, 3

Behold, the day cometh, that shall burn as an oven; and all the proud, yea, and all that do wickedly, shall be stubble; and the day that cometh shall burn them up, saith the Lord of hosts, that it shall leave them neither root nor branch.

"But unto you that fear my name shall the Sun of Righteousness arise with healing in his wings … And ye shall tread down the wicked; for they shall be ashes under the soles of your feet in the day that I shall do this, saith the Lord of hosts." …

At the coming of Christ the wicked are blotted from the face of the whole earth, — consumed with the spirit of his mouth, and destroyed by the brightness of his glory. Christ takes his people to the city of God, and the earth is emptied of its inhabitants. …

For a thousand years, Satan will wander to and fro in the desolate earth, to behold the results of his rebellion against the law of God. The Revelator, after presenting the scenes of the Lord's second coming and the destruction of the wicked, prophesies of Satan's imprisonment, and declares that "he should deceive the nations no more, till the thousand years should be fulfilled; and after that he must be loosed a little season." [40]

December 1

Dumb Dogs

His watchmen are blind: they are all ignorant, they are all dumb dogs, they cannot bark; sleeping, lying down, loving to slumber. Isaiah 56:10

I saw that some of the people of God were stupid and dormant; and were but half awake, and did not realize the time we were now living in … The angel said, "Destruction is coming like a mighty whirlwind." I begged of the angel to pity and to save those who loved this world, and were attached to their possessions …

Then the suffering Jesus, his sacrifice and love so deep, as to give his life for them, was again held up before me; and then the lives of those who professed to be his followers, who had this world's goods, and considered it so great a thing to help the cause of salvation. The angel said, "Can such enter heaven?" Another angel answered, "No, never, never, never. Those who are not interested in the cause of God on earth, can never sing the song of redeeming love above."

I saw that … swift messengers must speed on their way to search out the scattered flock. …

I saw that the saints will rest in the Holy City, and reign as kings and priests one thousand years; then Jesus will descend with the saints upon the mount of Olives, and the mount will part asunder, and become a mighty plain or the Paradise of God to rest upon.[1]

December 2

Void and Without Form

I beheld the earth, and, lo, it was without form, and void; … I beheld, and, lo, there was no man, and all the birds of the heavens were fled. I beheld, and, lo, the fruitful place was a wilderness, and all the cities thereof were broken down at the presence of the LORD, and by his fierce anger. … The whole land shall be desolate … Jeremiah 4:23, 25-27

My attention was again directed to the earth. The wicked had been destroyed, and their dead bodies were lying upon its surface. The wrath of God in the seven last plagues had been visited upon the inhabitants of the earth, causing them to gnaw their tongues from pain and to curse God. The false shepherds had been the signal objects of Jehovah's wrath. Their eyes had consumed away in their holes, and their tongues in their mouths, while they stood upon their feet. After the saints had been delivered by the voice of God, the wicked multitude turned their rage upon one another. The earth seemed to be deluged with blood, and dead bodies were from one end of it to the other.

The earth looked like a desolate wilderness. Cities and villages, shaken down by the earthquake, lay in heaps. Mountains had been moved out of their places, leaving large caverns. Ragged rocks, thrown out by the sea, or torn out of the earth itself, were scattered all over its surface. Large trees had been uprooted and were strewn over the land. Here is to be the home of Satan with his evil angels for a thousand years. Here he will be confined, to wander up and down over the broken surface of the earth and see the effects of his rebellion against God's law.²

December 3

Time to Reflect

And he laid hold on the dragon, that old serpent, which is the Devil, and Satan, and bound him a thousand years, Revelation 20:2

Now the event takes place foreshadowed in the last solemn service of the Day of Atonement. When the ministration in the holy of holies had been completed, and the sins of Israel had been removed from the sanctuary by virtue of the blood of the sin offering, then the scapegoat was presented alive before the Lord; and in the presence of the congregation the high priest confessed over him "all the iniquities of the children of Israel, and all their transgressions in all their sins, putting them upon the head of the goat." Leviticus 16:21. ... And as the scapegoat was sent away into a land not inhabited, so Satan will be banished to the desolate earth, an uninhabited and dreary wilderness.

The revelator foretells the banishment of Satan and the condition of chaos and desolation to which the earth is to be reduced, and he declares that this condition will exist for a thousand years.³

During this time, Satan suffers extremely. Since his fall his evil traits have been in constant exercise. But he is then to be deprived of his power, and left to reflect upon the part which he has acted since his fall, and to look forward with trembling and terror to the dreadful future, when he must suffer for all the evil that he has done and be punished for all the sins that he has caused to be committed.⁴

December 4

Into A Land Not Inhabited

And cast him into the bottomless pit, and shut him up, and set a seal upon him, that he should deceive the nations no more, till the thousand years should be fulfilled ... Revelation 20:3

On the Day of Atonement two kids of the goats were brought to the door of the tabernacle, and lots were cast upon them, "one lot for the Lord, and the other lot for the scapegoat." …

"And Aaron shall lay both his hands upon the head of the live goat, and confess over him all the iniquities of the children of Israel, and all their transgressions in all their sins, putting them upon the head of the goat, and shall send him away by the hand of a fit man into the wilderness: and the goat shall bear upon him all their iniquities into a land not inhabited."[5]

Then while the plagues are falling, the Scape Goat is being led away. He makes a mighty struggle to escape, but he is held fast by the hand that leads him.[6]

[T]he scapegoat typified Satan, the author of sin, upon whom the sins of the truly penitent will finally be placed. … When Christ, by virtue of His own blood, removes the sins of His people from the heavenly sanctuary at the close of His ministration, He will place them upon Satan, who, in the execution of the judgment, must bear the final penalty. … So will Satan be forever banished from the presence of God and His people, and he will be blotted from existence in the final destruction of sin and sinners.[7]

December 5

When the Land Should Rest

To fulfil the word of the LORD by the mouth of Jeremiah, until the land had enjoyed her sabbaths: for as long as she lay desolate she kept Sabbath …
2 Chronicles 36:21

The sky opened and shut and was in commotion. The mountains shook like a reed in the wind and cast out ragged rocks all around. The sea boiled like a pot and cast out stones upon the land. And as God spoke the day and the hour of Jesus' coming and delivered the everlasting covenant to His people … The Israel of God stood with their eyes fixed upward … Their countenances were lighted up with the glory of God, and they shone with glory as did the face of Moses when he came down from Sinai. The wicked could not look upon them for the glory. …[8] Then commenced the jubilee, when the land should rest.[9]

For six thousand years [Satan] has wrought his will, filling the earth with woe and causing grief throughout the universe.[10] Here is to be the home of Satan with his evil angels for a thousand years. … During this time, Satan suffers extremely. Since his fall his evil traits have been in constant exercise. But he is then to be deprived of his power, and left to reflect upon the part which he has acted since his fall, and to look forward with trembling and terror to the dreadful future, when he must suffer for all the evil that he has done and be punished for all the sins that he has caused to be committed.[11]

December 6

The Great Feast

And it shall come to pass, that every one that is left of all the nations which came against Jerusalem shall even go up from year to year to worship the King, the LORD of hosts, and to keep the feast of tabernacles. Zechariah 14:16

The Feast of Tabernacles was not only commemorative but typical. It not only pointed back to the wilderness sojourn, but, as the feast of harvest, it celebrated the ingathering of the fruits of the earth, and pointed forward to the great day of final ingathering, when the Lord of the harvest shall send forth His reapers to gather the tares together in bundles for the fire, and to gather the wheat into His garner. At that time the wicked will all be destroyed. They will become "as though they had not been." Obadiah 16. And every voice in the whole universe will unite in joyful praise to God. …

The people of Israel praised God at the Feast of Tabernacles, as they called to mind His mercy in their deliverance from the bondage of Egypt and His tender care for them during their pilgrim life in the wilderness. They rejoiced also in the consciousness of pardon and acceptance, through the service of the day of atonement, just ended. But when the ransomed of the Lord shall have been safely gathered into the heavenly Canaan, forever delivered from the bondage of the curse, under which "the whole creation groaneth and travaileth in pain together until now" (Romans 8:22), they will rejoice with joy unspeakable and full of glory. Christ's great work of atonement for men will then have been completed, and their sins will have been forever blotted out.[12]

December 7

The Judgment of the Wicked

And I saw thrones, and they sat upon them, and judgment was given unto them: and I saw the souls of them that were beheaded for the witness of Jesus, and for the word of God, and which had not worshipped the beast … and they lived and reigned with Christ a thousand years. Revelation 20:4

I heard shouts of triumph from the angels and from the redeemed saints, which sounded like ten thousand musical instruments, because they were to be no more annoyed and tempted by Satan and because the inhabitants of other worlds were delivered from his presence and his temptations.

Then I saw thrones, and Jesus and the redeemed saints sat upon them; and the saints reigned as kings and priests unto God. Christ, in union with His people, judged the wicked dead, comparing their acts with the statute book, the Word of God, and deciding every case according to the deeds done in the body. Then they meted out to the wicked the portion which they must suffer, according to their works; and it was written against their names in the book of death. Satan also and his angels were judged by Jesus and the saints. ...

After the judgment of the wicked dead had been finished, at the end of the one thousand years, Jesus left the city, and the saints and a train of the angelic host followed Him. Jesus descended upon a great mountain, which as soon as His feet touched it, parted asunder and became a mighty plain.[13]

December 8

The Saints and the Judgment

Do ye not know that the saints shall judge the world? ... 1 Corinthians 6:2

During the thousand years ... the judgment of the wicked takes place. The apostle Paul points to this judgment as an event that follows the second advent. "Judge nothing before the time, until the Lord come, who both will bring to light the hidden things of darkness, and will make manifest the counsels of the hearts." 1 Corinthians 4:5. Daniel declares that when the Ancient of Days came, "judgment was given to the saints of the Most High." Daniel 7:22. At this time the righteous reign as kings and priests unto God. John in the Revelation says: "I saw thrones, and they sat upon them, and judgment was given unto them." "They shall be priests of God and of Christ, and shall reign with Him a thousand years." Revelation 20:4, 6. It is at this time that, as foretold by Paul, "the saints shall judge the world." 1 Corinthians 6:2. In union with Christ they judge the wicked, comparing their acts with the statute book, the Bible, and deciding every case according to the deeds done in the body. Then the portion which the wicked must suffer is meted out, according to their works; and it is recorded against their names in the book of death.

Satan also and evil angels are judged by Christ and His people. Says Paul: "Know ye not that we shall judge angels?" Verse 3. And Jude declares that "the angels which kept not their first estate, but left their own habitation, He hath reserved in everlasting chains under darkness unto the judgment of the great day." Jude 6.[14]

December 9

The Books

I saw the dead ... stand before God; and the books were opened: ... and the dead were judged out of those things which were written in the books ...
Revelation 20:12

The execution of the judgment will be at the close of the 1000 years. After the saints are changed to immortality, and are caught up together, with Jesus, receive their harps, crowns, etc., and enter the City, Jesus and the saints sit in judgment. The books are opened, the book of life and the book of death; the book of life contains the good deeds of the saints, and the book of death contains the evil deeds of the wicked. These books were compared with the Statute book, the Bible, and according to that they were judged. The saints in unison with Jesus pass their judgment upon the wicked dead. Behold ye! said the angel, the saints sit in judgment, in unison with Jesus, and mete out to each of the wicked, according to the deeds done in the body, and it is set off against their names, what they must receive at the execution of the judgment. This, I saw, was the work of the saints with Jesus, in the Holy City before it descends to the earth, through the 1000 years. Then at the close of the 1000 years, Jesus, and the angels, and all the saints with him, leaves the Holy City, and while he is descending to the earth with them, the wicked dead are raised ... It is at the close of the 1000 years that Jesus stands upon the Mount of Olives, and the Mount parts asunder, and it becomes a mighty plain, and those who flee at that time are the wicked, that have just been raised. Then the Holy City comes down and settles on the plain.[15]

December 10

Weighed

TEKEL; Thou art weighed in the balances, and art found wanting. Daniel 5:27

The Lord ... [in] his Word ... is represented as weighing men, their development of character and all their motives, whether they be good or evil. ... Isaiah said, "Thou, most upright, dost weigh the path of the just." Solomon wrote, "All the ways of a man are clean in his own eyes; but the Lord weigheth the spirits."

It is for the eternal interest of every one to search his own heart, and to improve every God-given faculty. ... The motives of each one are weighed as carefully as if the destiny of the human agent depended upon this one result. ... Men may plan out crooked actions for the future, thinking that God does not understand; but in that great day when the books are opened, and every man is judged by the things written in the books, those actions will appear as they are. ...

There are many who need now to consider the words, "Tekel; Thou art weighed in the balances, and art found wanting." God's holy, everlasting, immutable law is the standard by which man is to be tried. This law defines what we shall do and what we shall not do ... The law is summed up in the two great principles, "Thou shalt love the Lord thy God with all thy heart, and with all thy soul, and with all thy strength, and with all thy mind; and thy neighbor as thyself." ...

O how few will be prepared to meet the law of God in the great day of judgment![16]

December 11

Books of Record

Therefore whatsoever ye have spoken in darkness shall be heard in the light; and that which ye have spoken in the ear in closets shall be proclaimed upon the housetops. Luke 12:3

The judgment of the wicked is a distinct and separate work, and takes place at a later period. ...

The books of record in heaven, in which the names and the deeds of men are registered, are to determine the decisions of the judgment. ... "Another book was opened, which is the book of life: and the dead were judged out of those things which were written in the books, according to their works." Revelation 20:12.

The book of life contains the names of all who have ever entered the service of God. ... Paul speaks of his faithful fellow workers, "whose names are in the book of life." Philippians 4:3. ...

"A book of remembrance" is written before God, in which are recorded the good deeds of "them that feared the Lord, and that thought upon His name." Malachi 3:16. Their words of faith, their acts of love, are registered in heaven. Nehemiah refers to this when he says: "Remember me, O my God ... and wipe not out my good deeds that I have done for the house of my God." Nehemiah 13:14. In the book of God's remembrance every deed of righteousness is immortalized. There every temptation resisted, every evil overcome, every word of tender pity expressed, is faithfully chronicled. And every act of sacrifice, every suffering and sorrow endured for Christ's sake, is recorded.[17]

December 12

Every Word

For there is nothing covered, that shall not be revealed; neither hid, that shall not be known. Luke 12:2

There is a record also of the sins of men. "For God shall bring every work into judgment, with every secret thing, whether it be good, or whether it be evil." "Every idle word that men shall speak, they shall give account thereof in the day of judgment." Says the Saviour: "By thy words thou shalt be justified, and by thy words thou shalt be condemned." Ecclesiastes 12:14; Matthew 12:36, 37. The secret purposes and motives appear in the unerring register; for God "will bring to light the hidden things of darkness, and will make manifest the counsels of the hearts." 1 Corinthians 4:5. "Behold, it is written before Me … your iniquities, and the iniquities of your fathers together, saith the Lord." Isaiah 65:6, 7. …

Opposite each name in the books of heaven is entered with terrible exactness every wrong word, every selfish act, every unfulfilled duty, and every secret sin, with every artful dissembling. Heaven-sent warnings or reproofs neglected, wasted moments, unimproved opportunities, the influence exerted for good or for evil, with its far-reaching results, all are chronicled by the recording angel. …

"Fear God, and keep His commandments: for this is the whole duty of man. For God shall bring every work into judgment." Ecclesiastes 12:13, 14. The apostle James admonishes his brethren: "So speak ye, and so do, as they that shall be judged by the law of liberty." James 2:12[18]

December 13

Family Portrait

Husbands, love your wives, even as Christ also loved the church, and gave himself for it; Ephesians 5:25

The home is a place where we are to prepare for the home above. If there are such temperaments in the family that they cannot live in harmony here, they would not, unless converted, be in harmony in the heavenly family. There is altogether too much careless talking, censuring, faultfinding, in families that profess to love and serve God. The unkind words, the irreverence and disrespect in many families, make angels weep. What a record is made upon the books of heaven of unkind looks and words that sting and bite like an adder, and it is not the record of one day only in the year, but of day after day.

Oh, that these families would consider that angels of God are taking a [photograph] of the character just as accurate as the artist takes the likeness of the human features; and it is by our deeds that we will be judged, whether they be good or whether they be evil. ... We should be kind and forbearing, that we may keep love warm in our hearts and thus develop qualities that Heaven shall approve. ... Marriage, in the place of being the end of love, will then be the very beginning of love.

We have but one life to live, and nothing should be considered of sufficient value to lead to unhappy words or deeds. We must come into close relationship and be partakers of the divine nature in this life, if we would be a member of the holy family in heaven above.[19]

December 14

Words Once Spoken

So speak ye, and so do, as they that shall be judged by the law of liberty. James 2:12

Sins that have not been repented of and forsaken will not be pardoned and blotted out of the books of record, but will stand to witness against the sinner in the day of God. He may have committed his evil deeds in the light of day or in the darkness of night; but they were open and manifest before Him with whom we have to do. Angels of God witnessed each sin and registered it in the unerring records. Sin may be concealed, denied, covered up from father, mother, wife, children, and associates; no one but the guilty actors may cherish the least suspicion of the wrong; but it is laid bare before the intelligences of heaven. The darkness of the darkest night, the secrecy of all deceptive arts, is not sufficient to veil one thought from the knowledge of the Eternal. God has an exact record of every unjust account and every unfair dealing. He is not deceived by appearances of piety. He makes no mistakes in His estimation of character. ...

How solemn is the thought! Day after day, passing into eternity, bears its burden of records for the books of heaven. Words once spoken, deeds once done, can never be recalled. Angels have registered both the good and the evil. The mightiest conqueror upon the earth cannot call back the record of even a single day. Our acts, our words, even our most secret motives, all have their weight in deciding our destiny for weal or woe. Though they may be forgotten by us, they will bear their testimony to justify or condemn.[20]

December 15

I Know Thy Works

... I know thy works, that thou hast a name that thou livest, and art dead.
Revelation 3:1

All sin unrepented of and unconfessed, will remain upon the books of record. It will not be blotted out, it will not go beforehand to Judgment, to be canceled by the atoning blood of Jesus. The accumulated sins of every individual will be written with absolute accuracy, and the penetrating light of God's law will try every secret of darkness. ...

The day of final settlements is just before us. In that solemn and awful hour the unfaithfulness of the husband will be opened to the wife, and the unfaithfulness of the wife, to the husband. Parents will then learn, for the first time, what was the real character of their children, and children will see the errors and mistakes that marked the lives of their parents. The man who robbed his neighbor through false representations, is not to escape with his ill-gotten gains. God has an exact record in his books, of every unjust account and every unfair dealing. The secret doings of the licentious man are all known to God. God is not deceived by appearances of piety. He makes no mistake in his estimation of character. ... There is nothing gained by a life of sin but hopeless despair. ...

We have the instructions and admonitions, the invitations and promises, of the word of God, and shall we imperil our souls by departing one jot or tittle from the divine law? God says to each one of us, "I know thy works."[21]

December 16

Ministering Angels

Then Manoah knew that he was an angel of the LORD. Judges 13:21

In this speck of a world, the heavenly universe manifests the greatest interest: for Jesus paid an infinite price for the souls of its inhabitants. ...

All heaven is intensely interested in the human beings who are so full of activity, and yet have no thought for the unseen, whose thoughts are not upon the word of God and its instruction. ... Sometimes the heavenly intelligences draw aside the curtain that hides the unseen world, that our minds may be withdrawn from the hurry and rush, and consider that there are witnesses to all we do and say, when engaged in business, or when we think ourselves alone.

The Lord would have us understand that these mighty ones who visit our world have borne an active part in the work which we have called our own. These heavenly beings are ministering angels, and they frequently disguise themselves in the form of human beings, and as strangers converse with those who are engaged in the work of God. ... Many, under different circumstances, have listened to the voices of the inhabitants of other worlds. ...

We need to understand better than we do the work of these angel visitants. It would be well for us, as children of God, to consider that heavenly beings hear our words, and behold our works.[22]

December 17

Books of Blessings

[H]e that reapeth receiveth wages, and gathereth fruit unto life eternal: that both he that soweth and he that reapeth may rejoice together. John 4:36

To the students in the heavenly school ... [t]he outworking of every right principle and noble deed will be seen. Something of this we see here. But how little of the result of the world's noblest work is in this life manifest to the doer! How many toil unselfishly and unweariedly for those who pass beyond their reach and knowledge! Parents and teachers lie down in their last sleep, their lifework seeming to have been wrought in vain; they know not that their faithfulness has unsealed springs of blessing that can never cease to flow; only by faith they see the children they have trained become a benediction and an inspiration to their fellow men, and the influence repeat itself a thousandfold. Many a worker sends out into the world messages of strength and hope and courage, words that carry blessing to hearts in every land; but of the results he, toiling in loneliness and obscurity, knows little. ... In the hereafter the action and reaction of all these will be seen.

Of every gift that God has bestowed, leading men to unselfish effort, a record is kept in heaven. To trace this in its wide-spreading lines, to look upon those who by our efforts have been uplifted and ennobled, to behold in their history the outworking of true principles — this will be one of the studies and rewards of the heavenly school.[23]

December 18

Resurrection

And his feet shall stand in that day upon the mount of Olives, which is before Jerusalem on the east, and the mount of Olives shall cleave in the midst thereof ...
Zechariah 14:4

At the close of the thousand years, Christ again returns to the earth. He is accompanied by the host of the redeemed and attended by a retinue of angels. As He descends in terrific majesty He bids the wicked dead arise to receive their doom. They come forth, a mighty host, numberless as the sands of the sea. What a contrast to those who were raised at the first resurrection! The righteous were clothed with immortal youth and beauty. The wicked bear the traces of disease and death.

Every eye in that vast multitude is turned to behold the glory of the Son of God. With one voice the wicked hosts exclaim: "Blessed is He that cometh in the name of the Lord!" It is not love to Jesus that inspires this utterance. The force of truth urges the words from unwilling lips. As the wicked went into their graves, so they come forth with the same enmity to Christ and the same spirit of rebellion. ...

Christ descends upon the Mount of Olives, whence, after His resurrection, He ascended, and where angels repeated the promise of His return. Says the prophet: "The Lord my God shall come, and all the saints with Thee." "And His feet shall stand in that day upon the Mount of Olives, which is before Jerusalem on the east, and the Mount of Olives shall cleave in the midst thereof ... and there shall be a very great valley." Zechariah 14:4, 5.[24]

December 19

New Jerusalem on Earth

I John saw the holy city, new Jerusalem, coming down from God out of heaven, prepared as a bride adorned for her husband. Revelation 21:2

After the judgment of the wicked dead had been finished, at the end of the one thousand years, Jesus left the city, and the saints and a train of the angelic host followed Him. Jesus descended upon a great mountain, which as soon as His feet touched it, parted asunder and became a mighty plain. Then we looked up and saw the great and beautiful city, with twelve foundations, and twelve gates, three on each side, and an angel at each gate. ... And it came down in all its splendor and dazzling glory and settled in the mighty plain which Jesus had prepared for it. ...

The angels surrounded their Commander and escorted Him on His way, and the train of redeemed saints followed. Then, in terrible, fearful majesty, Jesus called forth the wicked dead; and they came up with the same feeble, sickly bodies that went into the grave. What a spectacle! what a scene! ... All behold the Son of man; ... And then there arises one long protracted wail of agony, as they flee to hide from the presence of the King of kings and Lord of lords.

All are seeking to hide in the rocks, to shield themselves from the terrible glory of Him whom they once despised. And, overwhelmed and pained with His majesty and exceeding glory, they with one accord raise their voices, and with terrible distinctness exclaim, "Blessed is He that cometh in the name of the Lord!"[25]

December 20

Battle Preparation

[Satan] shall go out to deceive the nations which are in the four quarters of the earth, Gog and Magog, to gather them together to battle: the number of whom is as the sand of the sea. Revelation 20:8

Now Satan prepares for a last mighty struggle for the supremacy. While deprived of his power and cut off from his work of deception, the prince of evil was miserable and dejected; but as the wicked dead are raised and he sees the vast multitudes upon his side, his hopes revive, and he determines not to yield the great controversy. He will marshal all the armies of the lost under his banner and through them endeavor to execute his plans. ... They are ready to receive his suggestions and to do his bidding. Yet, true to his early cunning, he does not acknowledge himself to be Satan. He claims to be the prince who is the rightful owner of the world and whose inheritance has been unlawfully wrested from him. He represents himself to his deluded subjects as a redeemer, assuring them that his power has brought them forth from their graves and that he is about to rescue them from the most cruel tyranny. The presence of Christ having been removed, Satan works wonders to support his claims. He makes the weak strong and inspires all with his own spirit and energy. He proposes to lead them against the camp of the saints and to take possession of the City of God. With fiendish exultation he points to the unnumbered millions who have been raised from the dead and declares that as their leader he is well able to overthrow the city and regain his throne and his kingdom.[26]

December 21

A Vast Army

And all the inhabitants of the earth are reputed as nothing: and he doeth according to his will in the army of heaven ... Daniel 4:35

In that vast throng are multitudes of the long-lived race that existed before the Flood; men of lofty stature and giant intellect, who, yielding to the control of fallen angels, devoted all their skill and knowledge to the exaltation of themselves; men whose wonderful works of art led the world to idolize their genius, but whose cruelty and evil inventions, defiling the earth and defacing the image of God, caused Him to blot them from the face of His creation.[27]

Satan ... passed around among his subjects, and made the weak and feeble strong, and told them that he and his angels were powerful. He pointed to the countless millions who had been raised. There were mighty warriors and kings who were well skilled in battle and who had conquered kingdoms. And there were mighty giants and valiant men who had never lost a battle. ... There stood men of lofty stature and dignified bearing, who had fallen in battle while thirsting to conquer. As they come forth from their graves, they resume the current of their thoughts where it ceased in death. They possess the same desire to conquer which ruled when they fell. Satan consults with his angels, and then with those kings and conquerors and mighty men. Then he looks over the vast army, and tells them that the company in the city is small and feeble, and that they can go up and take it, and cast out its inhabitants, and possess its riches and glory themselves.[28]

December 22

They Compassed the City

And they went up on the breadth of the earth, and compassed the camp of the saints about, and the beloved city: Revelation 20:9

Satan succeeds in deceiving them, and all immediately begin to prepare themselves for battle. There are many skillful men in that vast army, and they construct all kinds of implements of war.[29]

At last the order to advance is given, and the countless host moves on — an army such as was never summoned by earthly conquerors, such as the combined forces of all ages since war began on earth could never equal. Satan, the mightiest of warriors, leads the van, and his angels unite their forces for this final struggle. Kings and warriors are in his train, and the multitudes follow in vast companies.[30]

Each company has its leader, and order is observed as they march over the broken surface of the earth to the Holy City.[31] With military precision the serried ranks advance ... to the City of God.[32]

Jesus closes the gates of the city, and this vast army surround it, and place themselves in battle array, expecting a fierce conflict.[33]

December 23

High and Lifted Up

... I saw also the Lord sitting upon a throne, high and lifted up, and his train filled the temple. Isaiah 6:1

Jesus and all the angelic host and all the saints, with the glittering crowns upon their heads, ascend to the top of the wall of the city. Jesus speaks with majesty, saying, "Behold, ye sinners, the reward of the just! And behold, My redeemed, the reward of the wicked!" The vast multitude behold the glorious company on the walls of the city. And as they witness the splendor of their glittering crowns and see their faces radiant with glory, reflecting the image of Jesus, and then behold the unsurpassed glory and majesty of the King of kings and Lord of lords, their courage fails. A sense of the treasure and glory which they have lost rushes upon them, and they realize that the wages of sin is death. They see the holy, happy company whom they have despised, clothed with glory, honor, immortality, and eternal life, while they are outside the city with every mean and abominable thing.[34]

Far above the city, upon a foundation of burnished gold, is a throne, high and lifted up. Upon this throne sits the Son of God.... The power and majesty of Christ no language can describe, no pen portray. The glory of the Eternal Father is enshrouding His Son. The brightness of His presence fills the City of God, and flows out beyond the gates, flooding the whole earth with its radiance.[35]

December 24

Salvation to Our God

... he appointed singers unto the LORD, ... that should praise the beauty of holiness, as they went out before the army, and to say, Praise the LORD ...
2 Chronicles 20:17

The redeemed raise a song of praise that echoes and re-echoes through the vaults of heaven: "Salvation to our God which sitteth upon the throne, and unto the Lamb." ... As the redeemed have beheld the power and malignity of Satan, they have seen, as never before, that no power but that of Christ could have made them conquerors. In all that shining throng there are none to ascribe salvation to themselves, as if they had prevailed by their own power and goodness. Nothing is said of what they have done or suffered; but the burden of every song, the keynote of every anthem, is: Salvation to our God and unto the Lamb.

In the presence of the assembled inhabitants of earth and heaven the final coronation of the Son of God takes place. And now, invested with supreme majesty and power, the King of kings pronounces sentence upon the rebels against His government and executes justice upon those who have transgressed His law and oppressed His people. Says the prophet of God: "I saw a great white throne, and Him that sat on it, from whose face the earth and the heaven fled away; and there was found no place for them. And I saw the dead, small and great, stand before God; and the books were opened: and another book was opened, which is the book of life: and the dead were judged out of those things which were written in the books, according to their works." Revelation 20:11, 12.[36]

December 25

Seeing Clearly

For the Father judgeth no man, but hath committed all judgment unto the Son:
John 5:22

The final judgment is a most solemn event, which must take place before the assembled universe. When God honors His commandment-keeping people, not one of the enemies of truth and righteousness will be absent. And when transgressors receive their condemnation, all the righteous will see the result of sin. God will be honored, and His government vindicated; and that in the presence of the inhabitants of the universe. Oh, what a change will then take place in the minds of men! All will then see the value of eternal life.

To His Son the Father has committed all judgment. Christ will declare the reward of loyalty. "The Father judgeth no man, but hath committed all judgment unto the Son … and hath given Him authority to execute judgment also, because He is the Son of man." Christ accepted humanity, and lived on this earth a pure, sanctified life. For this reason He has received the appointment of judge. He who occupies the position of judge is God manifest in the flesh. …

When sinners are compelled to look upon Him who clothed His divinity with humanity, and who still wears this garb, their confusion is indescribable. The scales fall from their eyes, and they see that which before they would not see. They realize what they might have been had they received Christ, and improved the opportunities granted them.[37]

December 26

High Treason

The wicked are overthrown, and are not: but the house of the righteous shall
stand. Proverbs 12:7

As soon as the books of record are opened, and the eye of Jesus looks upon the wicked, they are conscious of every sin which they have ever committed. They see just where their feet diverged from the path of purity and holiness, just how far pride and rebellion have carried them in the violation of the law of God. The seductive temptations which they encouraged by indulgence in sin, the blessings perverted, the messengers of God despised, the warnings rejected, the waves of mercy beaten back by the stubborn, unrepentant heart — all appear as if written in letters of fire.

The whole wicked world stand arraigned at the bar of God on the charge of high treason against the government of heaven. They have none to plead their cause; they are without excuse; and the sentence of eternal death is pronounced against them.

It is now evident to all that the wages of sin is not noble independence and eternal life, but slavery, ruin, and death. The wicked see what they have forfeited by their life of rebellion. The far more exceeding and eternal weight of glory was despised when offered them; but how desirable it now appears. "All this," cries the lost soul, "I might have had; but I chose to put these things far from me. ..." All see that their exclusion from heaven is just. By their lives they have declared: "We will not have this Man [Jesus] to reign over us."[38]

December 27

The Sentence

Yet thou shalt be brought down to hell, to the sides of the pit. Isaiah 14:15

Satan seems paralyzed as he beholds the glory and majesty of Christ. He who was once a covering cherub remembers whence he has fallen. ... He has seen the crown placed upon the head of Christ by an angel of lofty stature and majestic presence, and he knows that the exalted position of this angel might have been his. ...

He reviews his work among men and its results — the enmity of man toward his fellow man, the terrible destruction of life, the rise and fall of kingdoms, the overturning of thrones, the long succession of tumults, conflicts, and revolutions. ... He sees that his hellish plots have been powerless to destroy those who have put their trust in Jesus. As Satan looks upon his kingdom, the fruit of his toil, he sees only failure and ruin. ...

For thousands of years this chief of conspiracy has palmed off falsehood for truth. But the time has now come when the rebellion is to be finally defeated and the history and character of Satan disclosed. ... Those who have united with him see the total failure of his cause. ... He is the object of universal abhorrence.

Satan sees that his voluntary rebellion has unfitted him for heaven. ... His accusations against the mercy and justice of God are now silenced. ... And now Satan bows down and confesses the justice of his sentence.[39]

December 28

Fire

... This is the second death. And whosoever was not found written in the book of life was cast into the lake of fire. Revelation 20:14, 15

"Upon the wicked he shall rain quick burning coals, fire and brimstone, and a horrible tempest: this shall be the portion of their cup." Fire comes down from God out of heaven. The earth is broken up. The weapons concealed in its depths are drawn forth. Devouring flames burst from every yawning chasm. The very rocks are on fire. ... The elements melt with fervent heat, the earth also, and the works that are therein are burned up. The wicked "shall be stubble; and the day that cometh shall burn them up, saith the Lord of hosts." All are punished "according to their deeds."

In the cleansing flames the wicked are at last destroyed, root and branch, — Satan the root, his followers the branches. The full penalty of the law has been visited; the demands of justice have been met; and Heaven and earth, beholding, declare the righteousness of Jehovah.[40]

Satan's work of ruin is forever ended. For six thousand years he has wrought his will, filling the earth with woe and causing grief throughout the universe. The whole creation has groaned and travailed together in pain. Now God's creatures are forever delivered from his presence and temptations. "The whole earth is at rest, and is quiet: they [the righteous] break forth into singing." Isaiah 14:7. And a shout of praise and triumph ascends from the whole loyal universe.[41]

December 29

For Them That Love Him

But as it is written, Eye hath not seen, nor ear heard, neither have entered into the heart of man, the things which God hath prepared for them that love him.
1 Corinthians 2:9

Every power will be developed, every capability increased. The grandest enterprises will be carried forward, the loftiest aspirations will be reached, the highest ambitions realized. And still there will arise new heights to surmount, new wonders to admire, new truths to comprehend, fresh objects to call forth the powers of body and mind and soul.

All the treasures of the universe will be open to the study of God's children. With unutterable delight we shall enter into the joy and the wisdom of unfallen beings. We shall share the treasures gained through ages upon ages spent in contemplation of God's handiwork. And the years of eternity, as they roll, will continue to bring more glorious revelations. "Exceeding abundantly above all that we ask or think" (Ephesians 3:20) will be, forever and forever, the impartation of the gifts of God. ...

In our life here, earthly, sin-restricted though it is, the greatest joy and the highest education are in service. And in the future state, untrammeled by the limitations of sinful humanity, it is in service that our greatest joy and our highest education will be found — witnessing, and ever as we witness learning anew "the riches of the glory of this mystery;" "which is Christ in you, the hope of glory." Colossians 1:27. [42]

December 30

To Know Him

And this is life eternal, that they might know thee the only true God, and Jesus Christ, whom thou hast sent. John 17:3

In this life we can only begin to understand the wonderful theme of redemption. With our finite comprehension we may consider most earnestly the shame and the glory, the life and the death, the justice and the mercy, that meet in the cross; yet with the utmost stretch of our mental powers we fail to grasp its full significance. ... The plan of redemption will not be fully understood, even when the ransomed see as they are seen and know as they are known; but through the eternal ages new truth will continually unfold to the wondering and delighted mind. Though the griefs and pains and temptations of earth are ended and the cause removed, the people of God will ever have a distinct, intelligent knowledge of what their salvation has cost.

The cross of Christ will be the science and the song of the redeemed through all eternity. ... Never will it be forgotten that He whose power created and upheld the unnumbered worlds through the vast realms of space, the Beloved of God, the Majesty of heaven, He whom cherub and shining seraph delighted to adore — humbled Himself to uplift fallen man; that He bore the guilt and shame of sin, and the hiding of His Father's face, till the woes of a lost world broke His heart and crushed out His life on Calvary's cross. That the Maker of all worlds, the Arbiter of all destinies, should lay aside His glory and humiliate Himself from love to man will ever excite the wonder and adoration of the universe.[43]

December 31

Blessed Are They

Blessed are they that do his commandments, that they may have right to the tree of life, and may enter in through the gates into the city. Revelation 22:14

Unfettered by mortality, they wing their tireless flight to worlds afar — worlds that thrilled with sorrow at the spectacle of human woe and rang with songs of gladness at the tidings of a ransomed soul. ... With undimmed vision they gaze upon the glory of creation — suns and stars and systems, all in their appointed order circling the throne of Deity. Upon all things, from the least to the greatest, the Creator's name is written, and in all are the riches of His power displayed. ...

The more men learn of God, the greater will be their admiration of His character. As Jesus opens before them the riches of redemption and the amazing achievements in the great controversy with Satan, the hearts of the ransomed thrill with more fervent devotion ...

The great controversy is ended. Sin and sinners are no more. The entire universe is clean. One pulse of harmony and gladness beats through the vast creation.[44]

I urge you to prepare for the coming of Christ in the clouds of heaven. Day by day cast the love of the world out of your hearts. Understand by experience what it means to have fellowship with Christ. Prepare for the judgment, that when Christ shall come, to be admired in all them that believe, you may be among those who will meet him in peace.[45]

Notes

Introduction
1. Maranatha, p. 71

January
1. Education, p. 15
2. Testimonies for the Church, vol. 8, p. 264
3. Steps to Christ, p. 17
4. Review and Herald, June 18, 1895
5. The Desire of Ages, p. 664
6. Testimonies for the Church Containing Messages of Warning and Instruction to Seventh-day Adventists, pp. 44, 45
7. The Desire of Ages, p. 25
8. Education, pp. 14, 15
9. The Desire of Ages, pp. 19 - 21
10. Atlantic Union Conference Record, June 1, 1900
11. The Desire of Ages, pp. 179 - 181
12. Manuscript Releases, vol 18, pp. 77 - 78
13. Review and Herald, July 15, 1909
14. Review and Herald, April 1, 1890
15. Selected Messages, vol. 1, p. 359
16. Christian Education, p. 96
17. Review and Herald, March 31, 1910
18. Review and Herald, March 31, 1910
19. Review and Herald, February 9, 1897
20. Manuscript Releases, vol 18, p. 178
21. Manuscript Releases, vol 18, pp. 14, 15
22. Manuscript Releases, vol 11, p. 207
23. Manuscript Releases, vol 18, pp. 23, 24
24. Christ's Object Lessons, p. 133
25. The Great Controversy, p. 488
26. The Great Controversy, pp. 488, 489
27. Manuscript Release No. 760, p. 27
28. Review and Herald, February 4, 1890
29. Manuscript Releases, vol 18, p. 24
30. Manuscript Releases, vol 15, p. 94
31. Christ's Object Lessons, p. 408
32. Christ's Object Lessons, p. 411
33. Testimonies for the Church, vol. 1, pp. 161, 162
34. Testimonies for the Church, vol. 1, pp. 188, 189
35. Review and Herald, November 18, 1909
36. Testimonies for the Church, vol. 1, p. 496
37. The Youth's Instructor, June 29, 1893
38. Spiritual Gifts, vol. 2, pp. 223 - 225
39. Review and Herald, November 18, 1909
40. Review and Herald, September 16, 1873

February
1. Review and Herald, June 28, 1887
2. Testimonies for the Church, vol. 1, pp. 143, 144
3. The Desire of Ages, p. 203
4. Signs of the Times, January 20, 1904
5. Testimonies for the Church, vol. 1, p. 88
6. Signs of the Times, July 1, 1889
7. Review and Herald, November 23, 1897
8. Testimonies for the Church, vol. 1, p. 707
9. Manuscript Releases, vol 13, pp. 153 - 155
10. The Bible Echo, December 1, 1892
11. The Desire of Ages, p. 83
12. Christ's Object Lessons, pp. 309, 310
13. Christ's Object Lessons, pp. 203 – 206
14. Review and Herald, April 5, 1898
15. Selected Messages, vol. 1, p. 124
16. The Ministry of Healing, p. 228
17. Battle Creek Letters, pp. 77, 78
18. Testimonies for the Church, vol. 8, p. 286
19. The Desire of Ages, p. 25
20. Steps to Christ, p. 26
21. Christ's Object Lessons, p. 118
22. The Youth's Instructor, November 23, 1893
23. The Ellen G. White 1888 Materials, pp. 71, 72
24. Christian Temperance and Bible Hygiene, p. 148
25. Selected Messages, vol. 1, p. 86
26. Thoughts from the Mount of Blessing, p. 114
27. Christ's Object Lessons, pp. 332, 333
28. Manuscript Releases, vol 14, p. 276
29. Review and Herald, June 25, 1889
30. Selected Messages, vol. 1, pp. 366 - 368
31. Signs of the Times, March 10, 1890
32. That I May Know Him, p. 55
33. The Desire of Ages, p. 466
34. Review and Herald, March 2, 1897
35. Early Writings, p. 71
36. Review and Herald, June 3, 1890
37. Review and Herald, February 18, 1904
38. Signs of the Times, August 1, 1878
39. Special Testimonies to Ministers and Workers, no. 9, p. 76

March
1. Thoughts from the Mount of Blessings, pp. 76, 77
2. Signs of the Times, June 17, 1897
3. Signs of the Times, June 21, 1905
4. The Desire of Ages, pp. 234, 235
5. Steps to Christ, pp. 88, 89
6. Review and Herald, November 23, 1905
7. Review and Herald, March 31, 1910
8. Review and Herald, February 18, 1904
9. Review and Herald, June 24, 1915
10. Signs of the Times, August 1, 1878
11. Review and Herald, July 21, 1896
12. Signs of the Times, February 24, 1909

13. Signs of the Times, March 11, 1889
14. The Desire of Ages, p. 753
15. Signs of the Times, January 28, 1903
16. The Youth's Instructor, February 10, 1898
17. The Desire of Ages, p. 300
18. Signs of the Times, January 28, 1903
19. Education, p. 263
20. Christ's Object Lessons, pp. 310, 311
21. Review and Herald, January 17, 1893
22. Christ's Object Lessons, p. 311
23. The Youth's Instructor, August 11, 1886
24. Review and Herald, March 22, 1887
25. The Acts of the Apostles, pp. 21 - 23
26. Review and Herald, February 11, 1890
27. The Great Controversy, p. 488
28. The Great Controversy, pp. 488, 489
29. The Great Controversy, pp. 489 - 491
30. Patriarchs and Prophets, p. 310
31. Patriarchs and Prophets, p. 533
32. The Youth's Instructor, November 8, 1900
33. Review and Herald, May 13, 1884
34. Testimonies for the Church, vol. 5, p. 520
35. Testimonies for the Church, vol. 5, p. 466
36. Lake Union Herald, November 11, 1908
37. The Great Controversy, pp. 483 - 485
38. Fundamentals of Christian Education, p 239

April
1. The Great Controversy, p. 622
2. Patriarchs and Prophets, p. 248
3. Review and Herald, November 28, 1893
4. Review and Herald, March 14, 1893
5. The Desire of Ages, p. 161
6. Signs of the Times, February 1, 1899
7. Christ's Object Lessons, pp. 330 - 332
8. Patriarchs and Prophets, p. 202, 203
9. Testimonies for the Church, vol. 1, pp. 618, 619
10. Signs of the Times, July 31, 1901
11. Letter 22, 1901
12. Review and Herald, November 23, 1897
13. The Ellen G. White 1888 Materials, pp. 27, 30
14. Letter 37, 1887
15. The Spirit of Prophecy, vol. 4, p. 186
16. Manuscript Releases, vol. 5, p. 76
17. Education, pp. 257, 258
18. Testimonies for the Church, vol. 5, p. 435
19. Testimonies for the Church, vol. 2, p. 511
20. Selected Messages, vol. 3, p. 427
21. Steps to Christ, p. 26
22. Review and Herald, March 8, 1881
23. The Great Controversy, p. 519
24. Testimonies to Ministers and Gospel Workers, p. 236
25. Review and Herald, September 3, 1889
26. Review and Herald, July 24, 1888
27. Manuscript Releases, vol. 6, p. 12
28. Review and Herald, October 27, 1896
29. Spalding and Magan Collection, p. 260
30. Review and Herald, July 24, 1888
31. Testimonies for the Church, vol. 5, pp. 208, 209
32. Review and Herald, November 23, 1905
33. Testimonies for the Church, vol. 9, p. 11
34. Manuscript Releases, vol. 18, pp. 29, 30
35. Selected Messages, vol. 3, p. 114
36. Review and Herald, July 16, 1908
37. Manuscript Releases, vol. 8, p. 399
38. Supplement to the Christian Experience and Views of Ellen G. White, pp. 5, 6
39. The Great Controversy, p. 589
40. The Great Controversy, pp. 585, 586
41. Education, p. 228
42. Testimonies for the Church, vol. 9, pp. 11, 13
43. The Bible Echo, October 8, 1894
44. Broadside 2 January 31, 1849
45. The Great Controversy, pp. 586, 587

May
1. The Spirit of Prophecy, vol. 4, pp. 337, 338
2. Testimonies for the Church, vol. 6, pp. 20, 21
3. Review and Herald, January 11, 1887
4. Review and Herald, November 20, 1913
5. Review and Herald, November 24, 1904
6. The Youth's Instructor, June 29, 1899
7. Review and Herald, November 22, 1906
8. Manuscript Releases, vol. 4, pp. 90, 91
9. Review and Herald, April 14, 1896
10. Manuscript Releases, vol. 10, p. 239
11. Manuscript Releases, vol. 13, p. 394
12. Prophets and Kings, pp. 183, 184
13. The Great Controversy, p. 581
14. The Great Controversy, p. 590
15. Testimonies for the Church, vol. 8, p. 49
16. Manuscript Releases, vol. 4, p. 445
17. Review and Herald, September 30, 1909
18. Manuscript Releases, vol. 15, p. 15
19. Review and Herald, December 11, 1888
20. The Great Controversy, p. 443
21. Testimonies for the Church, vol. 5, p. 451
22. Last Day Events, p. 144
23. The Great Controversy, p. 592
24. Review and Herald, June 15, 1897
25. Review and Herald, July 16, 1901
26. The Great Controversy, pp. 586, 587
27. The Great Controversy, p. 592
28. Testimonies for the Church, vol. 9, p. 28
29. Review and Herald, September 10, 1903
30. Evangelism, p. 29
31. Manuscript Releases, vol. 21, p. 91
32. Testimonies for the Church, vol. 7 p. 83
33. Testimonies for the Church, vol. 9, pp. 12, 13
34. Review and Herald, July 5, 1906
35. Broadside3, April 7, 1847
36. Testimonies for the Church, vol. 1, p. 268
37. The Desire of Ages, p. 121
38. Review and Herald, November 22, 1906
39. Signs of the Times, November 1, 1899
40. Maranatha, p. 211
41. Review and Herald, May 28, 1889
42. Review and Herald, December 22, 1885
43. Christ's Object Lessons, pp. 205 - 207
44. Christ's Object Lessons, pp. 310, 311
45. The Desire of Ages, pp. 667, 668

46. The Youth's Instructor, July 26, 1894
47. Manuscript Releases, vol. 18, pp. 27, 28

June
1. Review and Herald, January 11, 1887
2. Review and Herald, February 6, 1908
3. The Youth's Instructor, August 18, 1886
4. Signs of the Times, January 2, 1907
5. The Great Controversy, p. 484
6. Testimonies for the Church, vol. 1, p. 187
7. Australasian Union Conference Record, January 1, 1901
8. Manuscript Releases, vol. 1, p. 249
9. The Great Controversy, pp. 622, 623
10. Review and Herald, December 31, 1857
11. Signs of the Times, September 3, 1902
12. Signs of the Times, November 1, 1899
13. Review and Herald, May 21, 1895
14. Testimonies for the Church, vol. 5, p. 213, 214
15. Testimonies to Ministers and Gospel Workers, p. 445
16. Testimonies to Ministers and Gospel Workers, pp. 445, 446
17. Review and Herald, April 23, 1901
18. Signs of the Times, November 1, 1899
19. Christ's Object Lessons, p. 384
20. Review and Herald, November 17, 1891
21. Signs of the Times, September 3, 1896
22. Christ's Object Lessons, pp. 415, 419, 420
23. Christ's Object Lessons, pp. 66 - 69
24. Review and Herald, March 2, 1897
25. Manuscript Releases, vol. 1, p. 178
26. Review and Herald, February 25, 1902
27. The Acts of the Apostles, pp. 36, 37
28. Review and Herald, April 30, 1908
29. Review and Herald, August 25, 1896
30. Testimonies for the Church, vol. 8, p. 21
31. Review and Herald, March 2, 1897
32. Manuscript Releases, vol. 3, pp. 414, 415
33. Review and Herald, March 22, 1892
34. The Spirit of Prophecy, vol. 3, p. 272
35. Review and Herald, March 22, 1887
36. The Great Controversy, p. 464
37. Testimonies for the Church, vol. 5, pp. 214, 215
38. Testimonies for the Church, vol. 5, p. 475
39. Early Writings, p. 85
40. Early Writings, pp. 270, 271
41. Review and Herald, May 27, 1862
42. Review and Herald, March 31, 1910

July
1. Spiritual Gifts, vol. 1, pp. 271, 272
2. Review and Herald, December 5, 1912
3. Patriarchs and Prophets, p. 67
4. Signs of the Times, October 28, 1903
5. Review and Herald, November 23, 1905
6. Manuscript Releases, vol. 2, p. 20
7. Testimonies for the Church, vol. 6, pp. 126 - 128
8. Review and Herald, October 20, 1904
9. Review and Herald, March 31, 1910
10. Testimonies for the Church, vol. 6, pp. 23, 24
11. Southern Watchman, January 10, 1905
12. Testimonies for the Church, vol. 6, p. 22
13. Christ's Object Lessons, p. 235
14. Christ's Object Lessons, pp. 234 - 237
15. Christ's Object Lessons, pp. 228, 229
16. Christ's Object Lessons, pp. 229 - 231
17. Christ's Object Lessons, pp. 232 - 233
18. The Great Controversy, pp. 611, 612
19. Gospel Workers, pp. 27, 28
20. Christ's Object Lessons, pp. 415 - 417
21. The Ministry of Healing, pp. 89, 90
22. Signs of the Times, October 22, 1896
23. Christ's Object Lessons, pp. 188, 191, 192
24. Manuscript Releases, vol. 5, pp. 88, 89
25. Christ's Object Lessons, p. 227
26. The Great Controversy, p. 435
27. Prophets and Kings, p. 716
28. Manuscript Releases, vol. 18, p. 15
29. Selected Messages, vol. 2, pp. 105, 106
30. Testimonies for the Church, vol. 6, pp. 17 - 19
31. Southern Watchman, March 21, 1905
32. Manuscript Releases, vol. 19, p. 243
33. Selected Messages, vol. 2, p. 369
34. The Great Controversy, p. 53
35. Spirit of Prophesy, vol. 4, p. 281
36. Spirit of Prophesy, vol. 4, pp. 282, 283
37. Spirit of Prophesy, vol. 4, pp. 284, 285
38. Testimonies for the Church, vol. 7, p. 108
39. The Great Controversy, pp. 446, 447

August
1. The Desire of Ages, p. 769
2. Review and Herald, July 21, 1851
3. The Great Controversy, pp. 605, 606
4. Manuscript Releases, vol. 5, p. 78
5. Review and Herald, December 18, 1888
6. Review and Herald, July 21, 1851
7. Review and Herald, December 31, 1857
8. The Great Controversy, p. 607
9. Review and Herald, December 24, 1889
10. Manuscript Releases, vol. 14, p. 92, 94
11. Review and Herald, August 17, 1897
12. Review and Herald, December 20, 1898
13. The Great Controversy, p. 553
14. Signs of the Times, August 26, 1889
15. The Great Controversy, pp. 623, 624
16. The Great Controversy, p. 589
17. Selected Messages, vol. 2, p. 21
18. Manuscript Releases, vol. 19, p. 358
19. Selected Messages, vol. 2, p. 53
20. Review and Herald, February 18, 1862
21. Review and Herald, May 6, 1909
22. Review and Herald, August 11, 1903
23. The Great Controversy, p. 588
24. The Great Controversy, p. 561
25. The Great Controversy, p. 588
26. The Great Controversy, p. 603
27. Signs of the Times, April 12, 1883
28. Signs of the Times, April 12, 1883

29. The Great Controversy, pp. 551, 552
30. The Great Controversy, p. 560
31. Signs of the Times, August 26, 1889
32. The Great Controversy, p. 590
33. Review and Herald, June 7, 1906
34. Review and Herald, September 10, 1903
35. Review and Herald, August 17, 1897
36. Selected Messages, vol. 2, p. 394
37. Last Day Events, p. 164
38. Review and Herald, August 17, 1897
39. The Great Controversy, p. 553
40. The Great Controversy, p. 624
41. Review and Herald, December 18, 1888
42. Last Day Events, p. 164
43. Review and Herald, September 12, 1893
44. Signs of the Times, February 20, 1901
45. The Great Controversy, p. 389
46. Manuscript Releases, vol. 14, pp. 161, 162
47. Selected Messages, vol. 3, p. 397
48. Review and Herald, December 18, 1888
49. Signs of the Times, November 28, 1900
50. Selected Messages, vol. 2, p. 372
51. Review and Herald, January 30, 1900
52. Review and Herald, December 6, 1892
53. The Great Controversy, p. 389
54. The Great Controversy, p. 603
55. The Great Controversy, p. 604
56. The Great Controversy, p. 606
57. Signs of the Times, June 12, 1893
58. Manuscript Releases, vol. 14, p. 287
59. The Spirit of Prophecy, vol. 4, pp. 232, 233
60. The Spirit of Prophecy, vol. 4, pp. 233, 234
61. The Spirit of Prophecy, vol. 4, pp. 234, 235

September

1. The Home Missionary, November 1, 1893
2. Testimonies for the Church, vol. 5, p. 81
3. Testimonies for the Church, vol. 6, p. 400
4. Signs of the Times, May 6, 1897
5. The Great Controversy, pp. 625, 626
6. The Great Controversy, p. 582
7. Review and Herald, December 20, 1898
8. Testimonies for the Church, vol. 7, p. 139 - 141
9. Manuscript Releases, vol. 20, p. 14
10. Review and Herald, June 15, 1897
11. Manuscript Releases, vol. 9, p. 7
12. Manuscript Releases, vol. 14, p. 91
13. Signs of the Times, November 1, 1899
14. The Great Controversy, p. 615
15. Testimonies for the Church, vol. 1, p. 203
16. Prophets and Kings, p. 512
17. Early Writings, p. 282
18. Signs of the Times, November 8, 1899
19. Review and Herald, November 22, 1906
20. The Spirit of Prophecy, vol. 4, p. 429
21. Review and Herald, October 20, 1904
22. Signs of the Times, January 25, 1910
23. Testimonies for the Church, vol. 6, p. 19, 20
24. Testimonies to Ministers and Gospel Workers, pp. 91, 92
25. Review and Herald, July 16, 1901
26. Manuscript Releases, vol. 14, pp. 158 - 160
27. Review and Herald, November 22, 1892
28. Signs of the Times, May 5, 1887
29. Review and Herald, July 5, 1906
30. The Desire of Ages, p. 311
31. Review and Herald, August 18, 1891
32. That I May Know Him, p. 55
33. Ministry of Healing, pp. 180, 181
34. Battle Creek Letters, p. 58
35. The Bible Echo, July 20, 1896
36. The Desire of Ages, p. 466
37. Selected Messages, vol. 1, pp. 250, 251
38. Signs of the Times, June 19, 1901
39. Review and Herald, February 25, 1915
40. Signs of the Times, January 22, 1902
41. Review and Herald, July 14, 1910
42. Review and Herald, July 14, 1910
43. The Bible Echo, July 20, 1896
44. The Youth's Instructor, November 9, 1899
45. Seventh-Day Adventist Bible Commentary, vol. 7, p. 915
46. Review and Herald, January 13, 1903
47. The Desire of Ages, pp. 762, 763
48. Signs of the Times, June 18, 1894

October

1. Selected Messages, vol. 2, pp. 372, 373
2. Manuscript Releases, vol. 14, pp. 95 - 97
3. The Story of Redemption, p. 402
4. The Great Controversy, p. 479
5. Early Writings, p. 280
6. Testimonies for the Church, vol. 8, p. 315
7. The Great Controversy, p. 491
8. The Great Controversy, p. 628
9. In Heavenly Places, p. 362
10. Testimonies for the Church, vol. 5, p. 212
11. Review and Herald, January 1, 1889
12. The Great Controversy, p. 622
13. Review and Herald, April 23, 1901
14. Signs of the Times, October 9, 1901
15. Manuscript Releases, vol. 1, pp. 296, 297
16. The Great Controversy, p. 594
17. Review and Herald, June 7, 1906
18. The Great Controversy, p. 613
19. Manuscript Releases, vol. 2, pp. 207, 208
20. The Great Controversy, p. 614
21. Testimonies to Ministers and Gospel Workers, p. 182
22. The Great Controversy, p. 36
23. Manuscript Releases, vol. 10, pp. 239, 230
24. Testimonies to Ministers and Gospel Workers, p. 444
25. Broadside 2, January 31, 1849
26. Review and Herald, September 17, 1901
27. Signs of the Times, October 9, 1901
28. The Great Controversy, p. 627
29. Patriarchs and Prophets, pp. 264, 265
30. The Great Controversy, pp. 629, 630
31. The Great Controversy, pp. 627 - 629
32. The Great Controversy, pp. 618, 619
33. Review and Herald, September 18, 1913

34. The Spirit of Prophecy, vol. 4, p. 437
35. Signs of the Times, November 27, 1879
36. Signs of the Times, November 27, 1879
37. The Great Controversy, p. 630
38. Review and Herald, May 27, 1862
39. The Great Controversy, p. 630
40. The Great Controversy, p. 631
41. The Great Controversy, p. 634
42. The Great Controversy, pp. 635, 636
43. Testimonies for the Church, vol. 1, pp. 353, 354
44. The Great Controversy, p. 636
45. The Great Controversy, p. 636
46. Early Writings, p. 285
47. The Great Controversy, pp. 637, 638
48. The Great Controversy, pp. 638, 639

November
1. The Great Controversy, p. 640
2. Early Writings, p. 285
3. Review and Herald, May 27, 1862
4. The Great Controversy, pp. 639, 640
5. The Great Controversy, pp. 654, 655
6. Early Writings, p. 124
7. Manuscript Releases, vol. 19, p. 265
8. The Great Controversy, p. 655
9. The Great Controversy, pp. 653, 654
10. Broadside 3, April 7, 1847
11. The Great Controversy, p. 640
12. The Great Controversy, pp. 642, 643
13. The Acts of the Apostles, p. 320, 321
14. Review and Herald, July 31, 1888
15. The Youth's Instructor, August 11, 1898
16. Selected Messages, vol. 2, p. 271
17. The Great Controversy, pp. 299, 300
18. Review and Herald, July 21, 1851
19. The Great Controversy, p. 644
20. The Great Controversy, pp. 644, 645
21. Review and Herald, August 6, 1889
22. Education, pp. 304, 305
23. Education, pp. 305, 306
24. Education, pp. 308, 309
25. Testimonies for the Church, vol. 5, pp. 744, 745
26. Review and Herald, November 26, 1903
27. Review and Herald, November 26, 1903
28. The Great Controversy, p. 645
29. Early Writings, p. 288
30. Signs of the Times, July 1, 1886
31. Early Writings, p. 288
32. The Great Controversy, p. 645
33. Early Writings, p. 288
34. The Great Controversy, pp. 647, 648
35. The Great Controversy, p. 648
36. The Great Controversy, pp. 649, 650

37. The Desire of Ages, pp. 637, 638
38. Testimonies for the Church, vol. 5, pp. 620, 621
39. Early Writings, pp. 16, 17
40. Southern Watchman, March 14, 1905

December
1. Review and Herald, April 1, 1850
2. Early Writings, pp. 289, 290
3. The Great Controversy, p. 658
4. Early Writings, p. 290
5. Patriarchs and Prophets, p. 355
6. Spalding and Magan Collection, p. 2
7. The Great Controversy, p. 422
8. The Story of Redemption, p. 409
9. Review and Herald, July 21, 1851
10. The Great Controversy, p. 673
11. Early Writings, p. 290
12. Patriarchs and Prophets, pp. 541, 542
13. Early Writings, pp. 290, 291
14. The Great Controversy, pp. 660, 661
15. A Sketch of the Christian Experience and Views of Ellen G. White, p. 33
16. Review and Herald, March 8, 1906
17. The Great Controversy, pp. 480, 481
18. The Great Controversy, pp. 481, 482
19. Manuscript Releases, vol. 18, pp. 319, 320
20. The Great Controversy, p. 486
21. Review and Herald, March 27, 1888
22. Review and Herald, November 22, 1898
23. Education, pp. 305, 306
24. The Great Controversy, p. 662
25. Early Writings, pp. 291, 292
26. The Great Controversy, p. 663
27. The Great Controversy, p. 664
28. Early Writings, p. 293
29. Early Writings, p. 293
30. The Great Controversy, p. 664
31. Early Writings, p. 293
32. The Great Controversy, p. 664
33. Early Writings, p. 293
34. Early Writings, p. 293
35. The Great Controversy, p. 665
36. The Great Controversy, pp. 665, 666
37. Review and Herald, June 18, 1901
38. The Great Controversy, pp. 666, 668
39. The Great Controversy, pp. 669, 670
40. Southern Watchman, March 14, 1905
41. The Great Controversy, p. 673
42. Education, pp. 307, 309
43. The Great Controversy, p. 651
44. The Great Controversy, pp. 677, 678
45. Review and Herald, November 23, 1905

We invite you to view the complete
selection of titles we publish at:

www.TEACHServices.com

Scan with your mobile
device to go directly
to our website.

Please write or email us your praises, reactions, or
thoughts about this or any other book we publish at:

P.O. Box 954
Ringgold, GA 30736

info@TEACHServices.com

TEACH Services, Inc., titles may be purchased in bulk for
educational, business, fund-raising, or sales promotional use.
For information, please e-mail:

BulkSales@TEACHServices.com

Finally, if you are interested in seeing
your own book in print, please contact us at

publishing@TEACHServices.com

We would be happy to review your manuscript for free.